Foundations of Medical Anthropology

Anatomy, Physiology, Biochemistry, Pathology in Cultural Context

Michael R. Zimmerman, M.D., Ph.D.
University of Michigan
Ann Arbor, Michigan

and

Wayne County General Hospital
Westland, Michigan

1980
W. B. Saunders Company   Philadelphia • London • Toronto

W. B. Saunders Company: West Washington Square
                          Philadelphia, PA   19105

                          1 St. Anne's Road
                          Eastbourne, East Sussex BN21 3UN, England

                          1 Goldthorne Avenue
                          Toronto, Ontario M8Z 5T9, Canada

Cover illustration: *After* C. Schuessele: MEDICINE MAN CURING A PATIENT
                      Philadelphia Museum of Art; Smith, Kline & French
                      Laboratories Collection.

Foundations of Medical Anthropology   ISBN   0-7216-9712-7

Last digit is the print number: 9   8   7   6   5   4   3   2   1

Preface

Many students of physical anthropology take a medical school anatomy course—but usually too late in the graduate program for this knowledge to be applicable to other courses, although of considerable use in field work and thesis preparation. I had the advantage of having completed medical school and specialty training in pathology before entering a graduate program in anthropology. My knowledge of the basic medical sciences (including anatomy, physiology, biochemistry and pathology) proved invaluable in courses in genetics and anthropology, physiologic adaptation and medical anthropology, as well as in various ethnologically and archeologically oriented courses. In the courses more directly related to medicine, the initial lectures often were devoted to brief reviews of the biomedical sciences, and in teaching courses in paleopathology I have found it necessary to devote the beginning sessions to teaching a summary version of the preclinical years of medical school.

The difficulty of compressing this vast amount of material into a few hours of lecture time led to the conception of this book. The basic fund of knowledge presented to the medically oriented social scientist in the following pages is intended to provide either background material for courses integrating the medical and social sciences, a text for specific courses in biomedical basics for the advanced undergraduate or graduate student in a medically oriented social science program, or information for the social scientist working in a medical setting.

The book is organized into three sections. The first, Biomedical Principles, covers the general concepts of anatomy, physiology, biochemistry and pathology. The discussion of each field begins with a historical review, stressing the development of the thread of understanding from antiquity to the twentieth century. Paleopathologic evidence is also used to gain historical perspective, and many examples of cultural/medical interaction are given. Section Two, Organ Systems in Health, Disease and Cultural Context, considers the anatomy, physiology, biochemistry and pathology of the specific organ systems. Il-

iii

lustrations of disease processes taken from the anthropologic, medical and paleopathologic literature are given throughout. A note of caution must be interjected here, for many of the interpretations offered are speculative. A complete list of references is included, and, in cases of doubt, the reader is encouraged to refer to the original article or book. The final section, the Appendix, considers the role of the laboratory in the diagnosis of disease and is intended to serve as a guide to the tests and procedures available for the study of individuals and populations. The Glossary defines terms in general use. Specific diseases are defined within the text.

I am indebted to my many colleagues at the University of Michigan, Wayne County General Hospital and the University of Pennsylvania who have encouraged and aided me in the preparation of this book and in my career, particularly Dr. Baruch S. Blumberg and Dr. Russell Maulitz. Dr. T. A. Reyman and Dr. Gerald Hart have contributed illustrations. Dr. Gerald Rigg and Mrs. Constance Toomey supplied materials for illustrations and the manuscript was typed by Judy Horning. The artistic skills of Emet Schneiderman and the encouragement given me by the editorial staff of the W. B. Saunders Company are also greatly appreciated.

Contents

v

Section One
BIOMEDICAL PRINCIPLES

one

Anatomy

THE HISTORY OF ANATOMIC CONCEPTS

The word autopsy derives from the Greek *autopsia*, meaning to see with one's own eyes. It is ironic that most of the 5,000-year history of anatomy as a recognized scientific discipline was characterized by failure to observe anatomic facts unbiased by preconception of function. Anatomy cannot be said to have entered its modern era until 400 years ago when Vesalius performed the first objective human dissections.

The earlier teleologic approach was fostered, for the most part, by simple lack of exposure to anatomy. The embalmers of ancient Egypt acquired some anatomic knowledge, but apparently kept it to themselves. Surgeons did learn some anatomy. The Edwin Smith papyrus, a 5,000-year-old treatise on the care of wounds, contains some discussion of the anatomy of the head and brain (Breasted, 1930).

The Egyptians did not distinguish between blood vessels, nerves, muscles and tendons, referring to these structures by the hieroglyphic word *mtw*. It was felt that these were all vessels that had a main center in the heart. A secondary center around the anus was posited, this arrangement allowing for medication by suppository. The "vessels" carried blood, air, urine, tears or feces, depending on where they emptied.

The ancient Greeks cremated their dead, and most of their anatomy was surface anatomy based on the observation of athletes. Some writings on external anatomy have been credited to Hippocrates (c. 460–374 B.C.), but it is not likely that he ever performed dissections.

Aristotle (384–322 B.C.) did dissect animals, and he is considered the founder of comparative anatomy. He neither practiced medicine nor dissected humans, and his contributions to human anatomy were theoretical and often erroneous. Like Hippocrates, Aristotle considered the heart to be the seat of the intellect. Other views included a belief in the spontaneous generation of the lower forms of life, and that the veins, held in place by the organs (**viscera**), carried the blood from the heart, an inexhaustible fountain, to the rest of the body, with no return system. The aorta was believed to contain air. This belief was not uncommon or unnatural, as postmortem contraction of the arterial circulation drives blood into the venous side, leaving the arteries empty. Nerves, confused with ligaments and tendons, were thought to come from the heart, and the function of the diaphragm was to prevent the heart from being contaminated by the intestines. The brain was thought to be an insensate and bloodless mass of earth and water functioning to balance the heat of the heart.

The first anatomic treatise was published c. 350 B.C. by Diocles of Carystus, who was a member of the Hippocratic school and based his text on animal dissections.

The first attempts at true human dissection were performed in Egypt by the physicians of the school at Alexandria, which was the Greek-influenced center of medical training from 300 B.C. to 130 A.D. Anatomic investigations were done here with impunity. The Egyptian tradition of mummification, which involved evisceration and embalming, removed the fear of the dead, and the Ptolemaic rulers of Egypt, in the Greek tradition of natural philosophy, were active supporters of scientific investigation.

The two major figures of the Alexandrian school were Herophilus and Erisastratus. Herophilus was the first to understand the function of the brain as the central organ of the nervous system and seat of intelligence, and to study the anatomy of the brain and spinal cord. He distinguished the cerebrum and cerebellum, the connections between the central and peripheral nervous systems, and the motor and sensory nerves, probably by animal vivisection and experimentation.

Herophilus' book *On Anatomy* is lost, but is known to have described these findings, as well as others, such as the presence of blood in the aorta and arteries. His description of the lacteals, the lymphatics of the intestinal tract, was not duplicated until that of Aselli, an Italian anatomist of the 17th century.

Erisastratus, Herophilus' contemporary, shares the credit for much of this work, but claimed that the arteries and heart contained only air or some vital spirit. His idea of the body as a network of tubes, mostly too fine to see, has been interpreted as a premonition of the concept of capillaries and the circulation of blood.

With the demise of the Alexandrian school, medical leadership moved to Rome, in the person of Greek immigrant physicians. Anatomy was little studied and autopsies forbidden. There was observation of wounds suffered in gladiatorial combat, and Rufus of Ephesus, a surgeon c. 100 A.D., wrote a short text on the anatomy of the eye. The dominant figure of this age, and indeed of the next 1,300 years, was Galen of Pergamon, an Asiatic Greek of the 2nd century, and a prolific writer of books on anatomy and medical practice, many of which are preserved.

Galen made a number of accurate observations, including the presence of blood in the arteries and the elaboration of urine by the kidneys, but the influence of his work and that of his followers on medicine in general and anatomy in particular was a pernicious one, colored by the basic flaws in his approach. His anatomy was based on the dissection of animals, mostly apes and swine, rather than humans. Accurate description was subordinated to speculation on function, as anatomic structure was felt to have been determined by deities who had made the organs perfect for their roles.

Galen's theoretical approach to anatomy was a curious hodge-podge of fact and speculation. Blood was formed in the liver and flowed through the veins to the left ventricle of the heart. Arteries arose from the heart and distributed blood throughout the body. A cosmic life force, or **pneuma,** was taken in with the breath and distributed throughout the body by the vessels and nerves, along with spirits present in the liver, heart and brain. A tidal flow was proposed, requiring pores between the right and left ventricle. Galen was unable to demonstrate these pores and concluded that they were invisible.

Galen's teleologic dogma suited the purposes of the medieval Church, and became established and authoritative to the point that no questions were tolerated and anatomic research forbidden. Autopsies for the following 13 centuries were confined to public dissections, usually of executed criminals. The presiding physician would read from Galen while a barber-surgeon dissected, and an assistant would attempt to verify the readings from the cadaver, even though the text was erroneously based on animal anatomy.

In the early Christian era a few autopsies were performed by Talmudic scholars, but they confined their efforts mainly to animal studies (Sussman, 1967). The increasing practice of surgery in medieval Europe led to a demand for better anatomic knowledge, as speed was of the essence in the preanesthetic era. Dissections became more common, and Italy became a center for anatomy. Special buildings were constructed for anatomy, and dissections were attended by doctors, surgeons and students. However, the Galenic approach prevailed, even after the publication of a brief and unillustrated autopsy manual by Mundinus of Bologna in 1316.

Leonardo da Vinci (1452–1519) was the first to produce accurate drawings of anatomic structures. After beginning with surface anatomy, he performed some 30 autopsies, until he was expressly forbidden to continue by Pope Leo X. His anatomic notebooks show many structures that were rediscovered by anatomists of later centuries. Although his work was not published until the 18th century, in a sense Leonardo paved the way for Vesalius, the first true anatomist, the first to "see with his own eyes."

Andreas Vesalius (1514–1564) began his medical training in Paris under Jacques Dubois of Amiens, also known as Sylvius, the most popular teacher of his day. Sylvius was a Galenist, and his anatomy was confined to animal dissections. Vesalius, dissatisfied with this approach, dissected human bodies removed from cemeteries and the gallows. The subsequent confrontation between Vesalius' facts and Galenist fancies led to Vesalius leaving Paris and finishing his medical training in Padua in 1537. In 1543 he published *De Fabrica Humani Corporis*, the result of five years of intensive dissection. Thrown out were the errors of Galen's animal-based anatomy, such as the five-lobed liver, the seven-segment sternum, the double bile duct, the bicornuate uterus, etc. As might be expected, Vesalius' findings caused enormous controversy, which he successfully challenged by holding public dissections and inviting detractors to demonstrate his errors, which of course they could not do.

Finally, embittered by the opposition he encountered, Vesalius gave up anatomy to practice clinical medicine, but his book has survived to become the first real anatomic text and part of the foundation of modern medicine.

Vesalius established an anatomic tradition at Padua, being succeeded by a series of great anatomists. Fallopius, Eustachius, Fabricus and others of the Italian Renaissance led the 16th century parade of discovery of many structures, such as the fallopian tube, the pulmonary circulation, the anatomy of the eye, etc.

The dominant figure of the 17th century was the Englishman William Harvey (1578–1657), who discovered the circulation of the blood. Harvey's scientific orientation was physiologic, and, based on consideration of the cardiac output, he proposed a continuous cyclic flow of blood propelled by the heart acting as a pump. After publishing his discovery, Harvey spent the rest of his life searching for the capillaries, but they were not demonstrated until four years after his death. Malpighi transilluminated a portion of frog lung, and, with a magnifying glass, saw blood flowing in the capillaries.

After Harvey there was continuing discovery of the finer anatomic structures, a trend that has continued to the present day. The development of the microscope by Leeuwenhoek in the late 17th century was particularly important, extending the range of anatomy beyond the naked eye.

The educational structure of anatomy saw the development of anatomic schools such as those of the Hunters of England and the Munros in Edinburgh, and the eventual evolution of the modern medical school courses, facilitated by the development of antiseptics and fixatives, which eliminated the danger of infection from cadavers and preserved form and structure for long periods.

Darwin's formulation of the relatedness of species has also proved important for anatomy. In a sense we have come full cycle, as animal studies are again relevant to problems in human anatomy. Experimental studies are no longer limited to human cadavers but, with recognition of existing differences, can be extended to lower organisms.

Anatomy is now a well circumscribed science, and less and less time is devoted to its study in the typical medical school curriculum. An anatomic background remains necessary, but the emphasis has shifted to the study of function and dysfunction.

PRINCIPLES OF ANATOMY

The anatomic details of the various organ systems will be considered in Section Two, and this discussion will be confined to some general principles, primarily of nomenclature. The body traditionally is oriented in the erect posture, with the arms at the sides and the thumbs facing away from the body. All anatomic terms of direction are taken from this position.

Three planes divide the body (Fig. 1.1). The median one is a vertical plane that divides the body into right and left halves. It passes through the sagittal suture of the skull, and planes parallel to it are referred to as sagittal planes. Frontal planes are vertical planes at right angles to the median plane. One frontal plane passes through the coronal suture of the skull, so these are also called coronal planes. Transverse planes cut across the body horizontally, at right angles to the frontal and sagittal planes.

"Ventral" and "dorsal" refer to the front and back of the body respectively. The palmar surface of the hand is referred to as the volar and the sole of the foot as the plantar surface.

"Cranial" and "caudal" indicate the head and tail respectively, and in the erect human are synonymous with superior and inferior.

"Median" refers to structures in the midline of the body or of a limb. "Medial" and "lateral" indicate structures nearer to or further from the median plane.

"Superficial" and "deep" indicate the relative depth from the surface, and "proximal" and "distal" direction toward or away from the attachment of a limb, origin of a structure or center of the body.

The body consists of a musculoskeletal framework containing cavities (Fig. 1.2). The cranial, thoracic and abdominal cavities contain (in an oversimplification) the brain, heart and lungs, and gastrointestinal and genitourinary tracts respectively. The circulatory system binds these three cavities together and supplies nourishment to the viscera. The largest organ of the body is the skin, which envelops the entire package and acts as a buffer against the outside world. Regulation of the various organ systems is the province of the nervous and endocrine systems. The anatomy, histology (microscopic anatomy), function and dysfunction of these organ systems, and the effect of and on cultural factors, will be considered in the following chapters.

ANATOMIC DIVERSITY IN HUMANS

Physical anthropology traditionally has been concerned with variations in external characteristics such as racial features, skin and eye color, and hair color and distribution. Physical parameters of height, weight and size, and various bodily and skeletal indices have

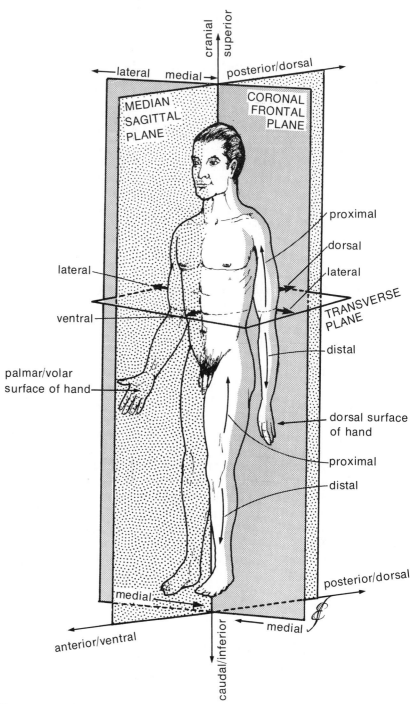

Figure 1.1 The anatomic planes of the human body, with the terms of position and direction.

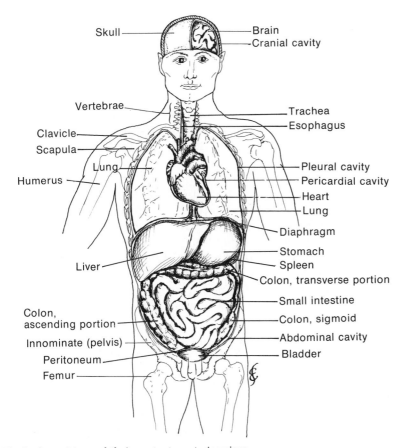

The body cavities and their contents, anterior view.   **Figure 1.2**

also been of interest, particularly in relationship to environmental stress (Frisancho et al., 1973; Malik and Singh, 1978). More recently, biochemical variations, especially genetic polymorphisms such as blood groups, have come to be of interest to anthropologists. The medical anthropologist must also be aware of the wide range of variations seen in the internal anatomy. On occasions, as in genetic counseling (McKusick, 1969), decisions must be made as to whether a variation is of sufficient magnitude or disturbs function to the point of being considered pathologic.

Such variations can be manifested any time in an individual's life, even though they may be present at birth (**congenital**) or acquired later in life. Congenital defects may be hereditary or acquired before birth, that is, *in utero*. For example, rare individuals are born with their organs reversed from right to left (*situs inversus*). This genetically determined condition is of no functional significance (unless a diagnosis of appendicitis is missed because the pain is on the "wrong" side). Some are born with incomplete *situs inversus*. This condition usually is associated with abnormalities of the heart inconsistent with prolonged life — clearly a pathologic variation.

An example of a congenital variation acquired *in utero* is the condition of adenosis. In the 1950s and 1960s pregnant women threatening to abort were treated with diethylstilbestrol (DES), a synthetic estrogen. Many of these pregnancies were carried through to delivery, although it now appears unlikely that DES was a significant therapeutic factor. A high percentage of the female offspring of these pregnancies have been found to have adenosis (Antonioli and Burke, 1975), the presence of cervical type glands in the vagina. Such a variation would appear to be innocuous, but a certain small percentage of young women with adenosis develop cancer in these glands in their late teens or early twenties (Herbst et al., 1971; Lanier et al., 1973; Ulfelder, 1973).

This **iatrogenic** ("doctor-caused") disease has several features of cultural interest. In a broad sense, all iatrogenic diseases are culturally induced, as medicine is a cultural phenomenon. The anatomic variation and disease in this case affect only a limited part of the population; no comparable condition has been documented in the male offspring of DES pregnancies. The condition is limited in time, as DES is no longer used to prevent abortion (abortion is used in the medical sense of any interruption of pregnancy). Finally, DES clinics have been set up at many medical centers to follow this population at risk. The problems of attendance and follow-up at such clinics are as often cultural as medical ones. This is particularly so when the possibility of removal of the uterus (**hysterectomy**) is raised in a young woman, terminating the ability to bear children.

Other congenital variations include agenesis of organs, again of varying importance depending on the organs involved. Survival is possible lacking a spleen, one kidney or even one lung, but absence of the brain (**anencephaly**) is fatal. Minor variations such as cleft uvula (Heathcote, 1974) or dry versus wet earwax (Petrakis et al., 1971) are of interest as population markers. A surgeon may be faced with the variations of the blood supply and biliary drainage of the gallbladder in a very practical manner. Alternatively, the presence of five renal arteries is of little concern to the individual possessing them, but is of vital interest to the surgeon planning a renal transplant. Again, variation shades into pathology.

Acquired anatomic variations are generally less common. LeMay (1976, 1977) has shown cranial and cerebral asymmetries associated with handedness. Other variations usually are secondary to surgery or trauma. Certain diseases can lead to functional loss of organs, such as autosplenectomy in sickle cell anemia, but some vestige of the structure usually is left, and the condition is clearly pathologic rather than variant. These conditions will be considered in more detail in the following chapters.

REFERENCES

Anthony, C. P. and N. J. Kolthoff (1975): Texbook of Anatomy and Physiology. Mosby, St. Louis.

Antonioli, D. A. and L. Burke (1975): Vaginal adenosis. Analysis of biopsy specimens from 100 patients. Am. J. Clin. Pathol. *64*:625–638.

Block, H. (1977): Human dissection: epitome of its evolution. N. Y. State J. Med. 77:1340–1342.

Breasted, J. H. (1930): The Edwin Smith Surgical Papyrus. University of Chicago Press, Chicago.

Crouch, J. E. and J. R. McClintic (1971): Human Anatomy and Physiology. John Wiley, New York.

Frisancho, A. R., Sanchez, J., Pallardel, D. et al. (1973): Adaptive significance of small body size under poor socioeconomic conditions in southern Peru. Am. J. Phys. Anthropol. 39:255–262.

Garrison, F. H. (1917): An Introduction to the History of Medicine. Saunders, Philadelphia.

Gordon, B. L. (1949): Medicine Throughout Antiquity. F. A. Davis Co., Philadelphia.

Heathcote, G. M. (1974): The prevalence of cleft uvula in an Inuit population. Am. J. Phys. Anthropol. 41:433–438.

Herbst, A. L., Ulfelder, H. and D. C. Poskanzer (1971): Adenocarcinoma of the vagina: association of maternal stilbestrol therapy with tumor appearance in young women. N. Engl. J. Med. 285:90–392.

Lanier, A. P., Noller, K. L., Decker, D. G. et al. (1973): Cancer and stilbestrol. Mayo Clin. Proc. 48:793–799.

LeMay, M. (1976): Morphological cerebral asymmetries of modern man, fossil man, and nonhuman primate. Ann. N.Y. Acad. Sci. 280:349–366.

LeMay, M. (1977): Asymmetries of the skull and handedness. J. Neurol. Sci. 32:243–253.

Malik, S. L. and L. P. Singh (1978): Growth trends among male Bods of Ladakh — a high altitude population. Am. J. Phys. Anthropol. 48:171–176.

McKusick, V. A. (1969): Human Genetics, 2nd ed. Prentice-Hall, Englewood Cliffs, New Jersey.

Petrakis, N. L., Pringle, V., Petrakis, S. J. et al. (1971): Evidence for a genetic cline in earwax types in the Middle East and Southeast Asia. Am. J. Phys. Anthropol. 35:141–144.

Riesman, D. (1935): The Story of Medicine in the Middle Ages. Hoeber, New York.

Rogers, F. B. (1962): A Syllabus of Medical History. Little, Brown, Boston.

Siegal, R. E. (1968): Galen's System of Physiology and Medicine: An Analysis of His Doctrines and Observations on Bloodflow, Respiration, Humors, and Internal Diseases. Karger, Basel.

Sussman, M. (1967): Diseases in the Bible and Talmud. In Diseases in Antiquity. D. Brothwell and A. T. Sandison, eds. Charles C Thomas, Springfield, Ill., pp. 209–221.

Ulfelder, H. (1973): Stilbestrol, adenosis and adenocarcinoma. Am. J. Obstet. Gynecol. 117:794–800.

two

Physiology and Biochemistry

INTRODUCTION

Living organisms are operating systems of organic and inorganic chemicals characterized by their ability to maintain their discreteness from the environment. Sufficient energy is produced from metabolic processes to fulfill the life functions of survival, growth, repair and reproduction, and adaptation to environmental changes. In contrast, inanimate objects follow the law of entropy; they proceed, at varying rates, to a state of disorganization and loss of discreteness.

Physiology is concerned with the mechanisms by which living organisms carry out their vital processes, and the science can be regarded as the study of function. **Biochemistry** is the study of the chemical processes of living organisms, including the reactions that fuel, operate and regulate physiologic functions. The two disciplines are intimately related, and in fact biochemistry did not gain recognition as a separate discipline until the end of the 19th century. Physiology is of greater antiquity and historical interest.

THE HISTORY OF PHYSIOLOGY AND BIOCHEMISTRY

The separation of physiology as an entity from anatomy is relatively recent, and therefore it suffered from the erroneous concepts of the Galenists for many centuries. Much of the work of Vesalius had physiologic implications, but most historians mark the beginning of the modern era of physiology by Harvey's publication in 1628 of his discovery of the circulation of the blood.

12

The 17th and 18th centuries were remarkable for the discovery of many basic anatomic features, as noted in Chapter 1, and the beginning of the understanding of physiologic principles. The basic conflict of this period was between the mechanists, who held that reactions in the body followed the same laws as those of the physical sciences, and the vitalists, who claimed that living organisms were imbued with vital forces which made their reactions different from those in the test tube. An early example was Borell's description of muscular contraction as a shortening and thickening of individual muscle fibers. It had previously been held that muscles were expanded by "animal spirits" produced by the nerves.

The major contribution of the 18th century was the elucidation of the physiology of respiration. Joseph Priestly (1733–1794) demonstrated that the same component of air was required by animals as for burning, and was given off by green plants exposed to light. Lavoisier (1743–1794) gave oxygen its name and demonstrated its indispensable role in oxidation in living and inanimate systems. He showed that carbon dioxide was the product of oxidation and that oxidative processes in the body were the same as those in a flame.

Another important 18th century experimentalist was Galvani (1737–1798), who demonstrated the reactivity of living material to electricity. Others began to study digestion at this time, but modern knowledge in this field really dates from the 19th century work of William Beaumont, a military surgeon, on Alexis St. Martin. St. Martin had developed a permanent fistula between his stomach and abdominal skin in the healing of a shotgun wound. Beaumont was able to sample and have analyzed gastric juices and partially digested food. This study clarified the effects of emotions and other factors on digestion, and also suggested the experimental use of fistulae.

Most of the major advances in physiology, and the development of its offspring, biochemistry, have come since the mid-19th century. In contrast to earlier periods, dominated by a few men, the last century has been characterized by the application of techniques and evolution of concepts by many workers, only a few of whom can be mentioned in this brief review.

The structural basis of modern biologic science is the concept of the cell as the basic unit of all organisms. The existence of cells has been known since Robert Hooke, using crude lenses, described them in cork in 1655. Leeuwenhoek developed the microscope later in that century, but it was not until 1824 that R. J. H. Dutrochet concluded that cells were the structural and growth units of tissues. In 1838–39 Schleiden and Schwann determined that cells were self-sufficient entities, capable of maintaining an existence separate from the rest of the organism.

In 1858 Rudolf Virchow, a German pathologist, anthropologist and political figure, published *Cellular Pathology*, supporting the studies of Schleiden and Schwann and adding the concept of the origin of all cells from pre-existing cells. The cell theory was now complete: all living organisms are composed of one or more cells; each cell can maintain its vitality independently; and all cells arise only from other cells.

Vitalism remained a force in physiology well into the 19th century.

Virchow's text and the experiments of Pasteur did away with the concept of spontaneous generation, and the synthesis of urea by Wohler in 1828 demonstrated that organic compounds are created by ordinary chemical processes. Reactions that occur in the test tube over the flame of the Bunsen burner are possible at body temperature because of the catalytic effect of enzymes. Recognition of this critical distinction was due to the work of Justus von Liebig, a 19th century German chemist who said that fermentation was a chemical process, dependent on nonliving catalysts he called "ferments." Enzymes catalyze reactions that otherwise would require temperature or concentration gradients unattainable in the body.

Von Liebig is considered the father of physiologic chemistry, making him the grandfather of biochemistry. In the late 19th century Claude Bernard discovered glycogen, elucidated carbohydrate metabolism, and proposed the concept of the internal environment of the body. In 1939 W. B. Cannon developed the concept of homeostasis, the relative constancy of conditions within the body. More recent work in physiology has focused on neurologic and endocrinologic control systems, nutrition, acid-base balance and enzymology.

Yudkin and Offord (1975) have outlined the 20th century course of biochemistry in three consecutive investigative lines, beginning with the identification of the molecular components of living organisms. The smaller molecules were studied first; the study of macromolecules has awaited the development of more sophisticated experimental techniques.

Intermediary metabolism became the next major field of study. The breakdown of foodstuffs (carbohydrates, fats, proteins and nucleic acids) and the synthesis of the simple chemical components of the body (sugars, fatty acids, amino acids and nucleotides) were worked out in the midcentury period.

With the recent development of such techniques as chromatography and x-ray crystallography, the structure of macromolecules has been clarified. Their synthesis, interactions with each other and with small molecules, and role in reproduction and in regulation of metabolic reactions have become the current fields of interest in this young and active science.

PHYSIOLOGIC PRINCIPLES

Cells and Tissues

Atoms combine to form simple compounds such as amino acids, nucleotides, sugars and fats which in turn combine to form polymers (proteins, nucleic acids, polysaccharides and fatty acids). These combine to form organelles (subcellular units with a distinct function and morphology), nucleus and cytoplasm, which make up the cells.

The cell thus consists of the nucleus, which serves a genetic function, and the cytoplasm, the metabolic portion of the cell (Fig. 2.1). The

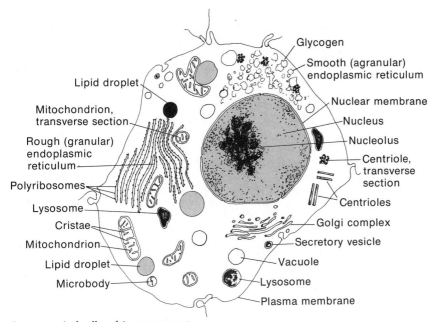

A prototypical cell and its components.

Figure 2.1

organelles are located in the cytoplasm, and it has been suggested (Thomas, 1974) that the organelles at one time were separate microorganisms that parasitized cells and became permanent symbiotic fixtures in the course of evolution.

The specific function of the nucleus is to replicate deoxyribonucleic acid (DNA), which carries the genetic information. DNA acts as a template for the formation of ribonucleic acid (RNA), which translates the genetic information by instructing the organelles to make specific proteins. Many of these proteins are enzymes that catalyze specific reactions, and this entire process determines the structure and function of the cell.

The cell is bounded by a membrane which is variably semipermeable, allowing some substances in and keeping others, usually larger molecules, out. Passive transfers across the membrane are regulated by concentration gradients and osmotic differences, and active transfers by pumping mechanisms. The active processes are those which require energy derived from the metabolic activities of the cells.

Cells are organized into several basic tissues that make up the organs of the body. **Epithelium** is the covering tissue which may be flattened (**squamous**), columnar (**glandular**) or intermediate (**transitional**) (Fig. 2.2). Epithelial surfaces are characterized by their having one free surface facing either the exterior or the cavity (**lumen**) of a hollow organ. These are the cells most exposed to the external environment, an important factor in their pathology.

Muscle is the contractile tissue of the body. There are three types (Fig. 2.3). **Skeletal,** or **striated** muscle is under voluntary control; **smooth** and **cardiac** muscle are involuntary. Smooth muscle, so called because it lacks the cross-striations seen microscopically in cardiac and

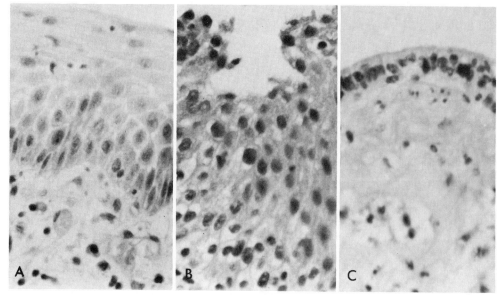

Figure 2.2   Epithelial surfaces. *A,* Stratified squamous epithelium, consisting of a basal layer and the progressively flattened cells of the prickle cell layer. Such epithelium is seen in the mouth, esophagus, vagina and anus. *B,* Transitional epithelium. Multiple layers of essentially identical polygonal cells. This epithelium lines the urinary system. *C,* Columnar epithelium. A single layer of columnar cells. Such epithelium lines the intestinal and respiratory tracts and their derivatives. Hematoxylin and eosin stains, × 400.

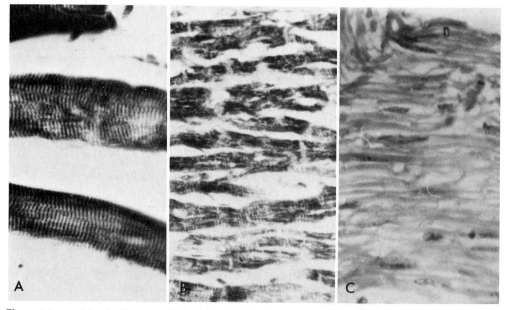

Figure 2.3   Muscle fibers. *A,* Skeletal muscle. The fibers are large with prominent cross-striations. Phosphotungstic acid hematoxylin stain, × 400. *B,* Myocardium. Thinner cross-striated fibers with intercalated bars. PTAH, × 400. *C,* Smooth muscle. Thin nonstriated fibers with elongate central nuclei. Hematoxylin and eosin stain, × 400.

skeletal muscle, is the major component of the walls of the intestines and blood vessels, and plays a major role in the control of flow through these and other tubular structures and hollow organs.

Nervous tissue consists of neurons with long processes for conducting nerve impulses throughout the body. **Connective** tissue (Fig. 2.4) is also widely scattered throughout the body, binding together the other tissues of the organism. Connective tissues elaborate a variety of

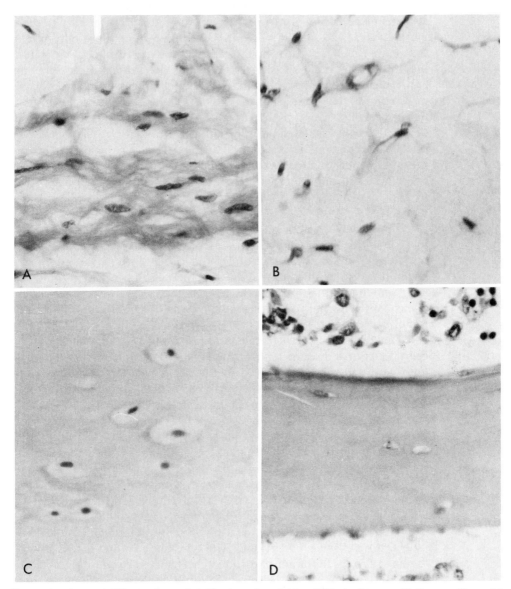

Connective tissue. *A*, Fibrous tissue. Spindle-shaped nuclei in a field of collagen, with ill-defined cell borders. *B*, Adipose tissue. Large cells distended with fat, with the nuclei pushed to one side. *C*, Cartilage. Small chondrocyte nuclei in lacunar spaces surrounded by a homogeneous chondroid matrix. *D*, Bone. Osteocytes in lacunae surrounded by an osteoid matrix, consisting in life of calcified collagen. The tissue has been decalcified for sectioning. Hematoxylin and eosin stains, × 400.

Figure 2.4

extracellular materials, such as **collagen, elastic tissue, cartilage** and **bone** for support, and **fat** for storage. Loose cells that wander through the body, such as the **blood cells,** are also connective tissue derivatives.

Organ Systems

These basic tissue types combine to form the organs and organ systems responsible for maintaining the vital functions of living organisms. In order to maintain their discreteness from the environment, organisms must extract elements and compounds from that environment and alter them for their own uses. Foodstuffs supply both the substrates for energy-producing (**catabolic**) processes and the basic materials for the synthesis (**anabolism**) of the compounds unique to living systems. Most of the organ systems are involved, directly or indirectly, in these **metabolic** processes. Since, for reasons not well understood, organisms are mortal and eventually run down and die, the other major function of the organism is reproduction. The role of the organ systems in these functions of maintenance and reproduction will be considered in an overview here, and in more detail in later chapters.

The **skeletal system** is the framework of the body, bound together by joints with their ligaments and associated muscles, and covered by the skin. The range of motion of the bones is determined by the anatomic form of the joints, the position of the ligaments and the arrangements of the muscles. Muscle contraction is due to the simultaneous contraction of the microscopic muscle fibers, excited by nervous impulses.

The **nervous system** consists of the **brain** and **spinal cord** (the **central nervous system**) and the **nerves** (the **peripheral nervous system**), and controls most of the bodily functions. The **sensory** nerves report on external conditions by vision, hearing, smell, taste and feel, and the **motor** nerves activate the muscles.

The **autonomic** nervous system regulates many of the internal processes of the body, by governing glandular and hormonal secretions and the contraction of smooth muscle. The heart rate is also regulated to some extent by these nerves.

The **cardiovascular** or **circulatory system,** consisting of the heart and the blood and lymphatic vessels, carries oxygen and nutrients to the tissues for metabolism or storage, wastes from the tissues to other organs for elimination, and endocrine hormones that regulate the activity of various tissues and organs. The **lymphatic** system is a secondary drainage system for larger particles such as bacteria and foreign materials. Along the lymphatic vessels, the **lymph nodes** act as filters for these materials. The lymph nodes also function in the immunologic system of the body, producing antibody-forming plasma cells when stimulated by antigens.

Oxygen is necessary for metabolic processes, and the function of the **respiratory system** is to extract oxygen from the inspired air, and to eliminate one of the products of metabolism, carbon dioxide, back into the expired air. In the smallest compartments of the lungs, the **alveoli,** only two thin membranes separate the blood cells from the air. Oxygen readily passes through, to be taken up avidly by **hemoglobin,** the oxygen-carrying compound in the red blood cells (**erythrocytes**). Transfer of carbon dioxide from the blood into the air to be expired is a passive process across a concentration gradient.

The digestion of carbohydrates, proteins and fats provides energy for organisms to grow, maintain, repair and reproduce themselves. The **digestive** or **gastrointestinal system** consists of the mouth, esophagus, stomach, and small and large intestines. The liver and pancreas are outgrowths of, and secrete their products into, the small intestine. After being swallowed, food is broken down in the stomach and digested in the small intestine, where nutrients are absorbed into the blood. The remainder of the intestinal contents are solidified as feces in the large intestine by the extraction of water.

Absorbed nutrients are passed from the small intestine to the liver, which is specialized for the transformation of nutrients into forms needed by the cells of the body for their metabolic processes. The liver stores fats, carbohydrates and proteins, and manufactures proteins, including the factors needed in blood coagulation and albumin, the major protein in blood serum. Bile made by the liver has a role as a digestive aid, and functions in the cycle of red blood cell breakdown and manufacture. In short, the liver is an indispensable organ of many functions.

The pancreas actually has two portions. The exocrine pancreas secretes digestive enzymes via a duct system into the small intestine. The endocrine portion regulates carbohydrate and fat metabolism throughout the body.

Metabolic rates are controlled to a large extent by the various glands of the **endocrine system**. These ductless glands secrete their products directly into the blood stream. Feedback mechanisms provide for adaptive responses over long periods, as compared to the relatively rapid action of nervous control. Secretions of the thyroid gland and adrenal medulla increase the rate of most metabolic processes. The ovaries and testes regulate the metabolism of the sex organs. Hormones produced by the adrenal cortex are important in protein and carbohydrate metabolism, and regulate some aspects of kidney function. Parathyroid hormones control the blood calcium level, using the bones as a storehouse.

The waste products of metabolism must be eliminated, and this role is filled by the **urinary** or **excretory system.** The kidneys have both active and passive mechanisms for removing wastes. In addition, they are the major regulatory organs for the level of hydration of the body and the concentration of various salts, all of which must be kept within narrow limits to maintain homeostasis.

The **reproduction** of animals is based on **meiosis,** the splitting of germ cells of the male to form spermatocytes and of the germ cells of the female to form ova with half the normal complement of chromosomes (Fig. 2.5). These cells, the **gametes,** combine to form a **zygote** with the full number of chromosomes. Errors in this process, producing abnor-

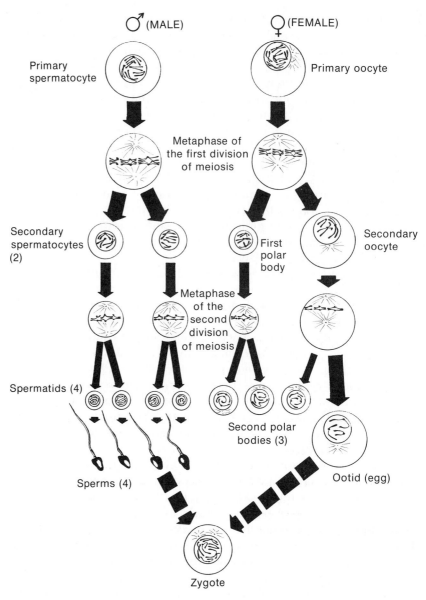

Figure 2.5   Gametogenesis and fertilization.

mal zygotes, account for many early abortions (Fantel, 1978). The zygote then normally divides by mitosis to form an **embryo,** which develops into the **fetus.** The fetus is supported on the wall of the uterus by the **placenta,** which functions as a combined respiratory and excretory system passing nutrients and oxygen directly into the fetal circulation and removing wastes. After the incubation period the fetus is expelled from the uterus. The extensive anatomic and physiologic changes necessary for existence in the outside world occur with remarkable regularity in the newborn.

METHODS OF STUDY

The study of physiologic processes is based on observation and experimentation. Observation has done much to clarify the function of organs, such as the heart as a pump, or the digestive action of the stomach. Attempts at understanding mechanisms have led to the development of modern experimental techniques. The effects of the removal of nonvital organs can be studied, and the vital organs can be temporarily incapacitated. Observation of the consequent changes gives information on function.

A removed organ can be replaced either mechanically, as by substituting an oxygenator for the lungs, or chemically, such as thyroxin for the thyroid gland. An alternative approach is to change the activity of an organism and look for changes in an organ. The simplest example is the hypertrophy of a muscle with an increased workload. Recalling the definition of physiology as the study of function, it is apparent that most knowledge of physiology is gained by observing or altering function.

BIOCHEMICAL PROCESSES

Chemical reactions can be categorized into those which produce energy — **exergonic** reactions, and those which require energy — **endergonic** reactions. In living cells exergonic reactions are those of the breakdown (**catabolism**) of foodstuffs, and endergonic reactions are those which synthesize the components of the cells (**anabolism**). Organisms have evolved in such a fashion that these reactions are coupled in a total metabolic system, allowing ingested food to be converted into the compounds required for the maintenance and reproduction of the cell and organism. (Alternatively, the linkage of the two processes has allowed the development of organisms.) The net result of these breakdown and synthetic reactions is referred to as **intermediary metabolism.**

Intermediary Metabolism

The energy supplied by the sun is made available to animals by the photosynthetic action of green plants. In a reaction catalyzed by chlorophyll and requiring the presence of light energy, carbon dioxide and water are combined to produce carbohydrate and oxygen. Animals ingest the carbohydrate, inspire the oxygen and oxidize the carbohydrate to release the energy they need to remain viable. The basic chemical mechanisms of this process are similar in all cells, so much so that much of our knowledge of metabolism has come from the study of microorganisms.

This simple scheme is the biochemical framework on which all the diversity of biochemical systems is constructed. Variations are seen in the foodstuffs, the metabolic pathways and the products synthesized. Variations occur from cell to cell and from organism to organism.

Foodstuffs consist of fats, proteins and nucleic acids in addition to carbohydrates. These are broken down into smaller components, absorbed in the intestine and transported to the liver, where they are either stored as glycogen or put to immediate use for the synthesis of new compounds. Glycogen is also synthesized by muscles for storage. Enzyme systems in these organs break glycogen down into glucose for energy production or for other syntheses.

The coupling of energy-producing and energy-dependent reactions is not direct, but proceeds through the mediation of high energy phosphate bonds. The energy produced by an exergonic reaction is used to couple the compound adenosine diphosphate (ADP) with inorganic phosphate (P_i) to form adenosine triphosphate (ATP), containing a high energy phosphate bond available for endergonic reactions (Fig. 2.6). Thus, the net effect of the oxidation of glucose to water and carbon dioxide in intermediary metabolism is the storage of energy in ATP as an available form for use in driving energy-dependent reactions, by coupling them to the hydrolysis of ATP.

There are two steps or pathways in the breakdown of glucose by animal cells. **Glycolysis** is an anaerobic mechanism for breaking glucose down into lactate. This process has a relatively low yield and is used primarily by red blood cells and skeletal muscle. The red cells do not use the oxygen they are carrying to the tissues for their own metabolism, and the muscles use glycolysis (also called the Embden-Meyerhof pathway) as an immediate short-term source of energy.

The complete oxidation of glucose to carbon dioxide and water is accomplished, primarily in the liver, by the **citric acid cycle (Krebs cycle, tricarboxylic acid** [TCA] **cycle).** This aerobic process is much more efficient than glycolysis. The details of these reactions are to be found in any of the standard biochemistry texts.

The ATP formed by the catabolism of foodstuffs is used for energy for motion and for the synthesis of new compounds for the organism. Of these, the most significant are the proteins (from the Greek *proteios* — primary). These include structural proteins and, more importantly, the enzymes, catalysts that activate and facilitate specific reactions. Enzymes are true catalysts in that they are effective in small amounts, reduce the amount of energy needed to start a reaction, and increase the rate of a reaction without affecting the equilibrium constant. Each biologic reaction has a catalytic enzyme, the specificity of which depends on the chemical, electrical and configurational characteristics of the enzyme and the materials being acted upon, the **substrates.** At physiologic levels, the rate of the reaction is directly proportional to the concentration of the enzyme. Adjustment of the amount

$$ADP + P_i + E \rightleftharpoons ATP$$

Figure 2.6   Energy produced by exergonic reactions is used to couple adenosine diphosphate and inorganic phosphorus to form adenosine triphosphate, containing a high energy phosphate bond.

and/or efficiency of specific enzymes, probably regulated by feedback mechanisms based on the concentration of the products, is the method by which the cell controls its metabolic activities.

This mechanism allows for the synthesis of amino acids into proteins, fatty acids into lipids, glucose into glycogen for storage, and nucleotides into nucleic acids. Again, the details are available in biochemistry texts, but a brief look at the last-named group is necessary. The nucleic acids, making up the chromosomes, are the carriers of genetic information in the cell, and are the targets of mutation and the other factors responsible for evolutionary change.

By the arrangement of their chemical structure, nucleic acids code the sequence of amino acids along the proteins being synthesized by the cell. This process determines the nature of the proteins, with the structural and enzymatic consequences outlined above. The nucleic acid of the chromosomes, deoxyribonucleic acid (DNA), is duplicated in mitotic cell division, a point at which error in replication (**mutation**) can occur. Even the most minimal changes in the genetic code may be of great significance. For example, the substitution of one amino acid for another, out of the hundreds in a hemoglobin molecule, is the sole difference between the hemoglobin of sickle cell anemia and normal adult hemoglobin. The genetic code carries not only the future of the individual but potentially that of the species.

REFERENCES

Anthony, C. P. and N. J. Kolthoff (1975): Textbook of Anatomy and Physiology. Mosby, St. Louis.

Brobeck, J. R. (1973): Best and Taylor's Physiological Basis of Medical Practice. Williams and Wilkins Co., Baltimore.

Carlson, A. J. and V. Johnson (1953): The Machinery of the Body. University of Chicago Press, Chicago.

Crouch, J. E. and J. R. McClintic (1971): Human Anatomy and Physiology. John Wiley, New York.

Dyson, R. D. (1975): Essentials of Cell Biology. Allyn and Bacon, Boston.

Fantel, A. G. (1978): Prenatal selection. Yearbook Phys. Anthropol. 21:215–222.

Ganong, W. F. (1973): Review of Medical Physiology. Lange, Los Altos, Ca.

Garrison, F. H. (1917): An Introduction to the History of Medicine. Saunders, Philadelphia.

Guyton, A. C. (1969): Function of the Human Body. Saunders, Philadelphia.

Horrobin, D. F. (1968): Medical Physiology and Biochemistry. Williams and Wilkins, Baltimore.

McGilvery, R. W. (1975): Biochemical Concepts. Saunders, Philadelphia.

Rogers, F. B. (1962): A Syllabus of Medical History. Little, Brown, Boston.

Siegal, R. E. (1968): Galen's System of Physiology and Medicine: An Analysis of His Doctrines and Observations on Bloodflow, Respiration, Humors, and Internal Diseases. Karger, Basel.

Thomas, L. (1974): Lives of a Cell: Notes of a Biology Watcher. Viking, New York.

Toporek, M. (1968): Basic Chemistry of Life. Appleton-Century-Crofts, New York.

Vander, A. J., Sherman, J. H. and D. S. Luciano (1970): Human Physiology: The Mechanisms of Body Function. McGraw-Hill, New York.

Yudkin, M. and R. Offord (1975): Biochemistry. Houghton Mifflin, Boston.

three

General Pathology

THE HISTORY OF PATHOLOGY: THE SEATS AND CAUSES OF DISEASE

Pathology did not become established as a recognized separate discipline in medicine until the 18th century, but even in antiquity physicians focused on the subject matter of pathology, the causes and anatomic manifestations of disease. These early inquiries were handicapped by many problems, including the absence of such basic disciplines as histology and microbiology, the lack of a systematic approach to performing and recording autopsies, and the lack of knowledge of such basic principles as the existence of the cell and the circulation of the blood. The development of pathology is thus bidirectional, with gradual refinement of the correlation between clinical disease states and pathologic anatomy, and a relatively sudden recognition of the cellular basis of disease after millennia of attempting to explain causation **(etiology)** on a generalized, humoral basis. Both lines of inquiry have reached their present state only through the use of the other disciplines mentioned above, in addition to experimental pathology.

In tracing the evolution of pathology, again one must first turn to the earliest medical records, the Egyptian medical papyri. The Edwin Smith papyrus is a New Kingdom (c. 1200 B.C.) copy of an earlier work. This document, dating in inspiration if not in actual fiber to the Old Kingdom (c. 2500 B.C.), reveals that trained physicians by that time had developed an anatomic approach to disease (Breasted, 1930). They speculated on etiology and the course of development of disease **(pathogenesis)**, and had specific modes of medical and surgical therapy. Modern paleopathologic investigations are consistent with many of these ancient observations.

The humoral theory of the etiology of disease is the contribution of the Greeks, specifically the Hippocratic school. This concept of pathology, which dominated medicine for centuries, drew analogies between

24

the four elements of Greek philosophy and the four humors of the body, as seen in the matrix of Figure 3.1.

Health was believed to depend on a normal balance of the humors, and such manifestations of disease as discharges or hemorrhages were considered to be efforts by the body to achieve balance. As the Greeks cremated their dead, no effort was made to correlate pathologic anatomy with the signs and symptoms of disease, but the clinical features of many diseases are easily recognized in the works of the Hippocratic authors, and in those of Celsus, a Roman layman of the period 30 B.C. to 38 A.D. Celsus gives us a clear picture of the medical practices of his day, but is of most interest in the context of this discussion for his description of the four cardinal signs of inflammation: redness, swelling, heat and pain.

The humoral approach as embellished by Galen in the 2nd century A.D. dominated medicine for the next 1,300 years. Galen and his medieval interpreters promulgated the concept of humoral imbalance as an explanation for all diseases and as justification for some truly remarkable therapeutic approaches; these included bleeding, purging by enemas and laxatives, and most notably polypharmacy, the notion that given enough medications the body will select those that will bring it back into balance (Ackerknecht, 1973). Galen remained the ultimate authority until the Renaissance, when autopsies were performed more frequently and the discrepancies between the humoral theory and the evidence of the organs became apparent.

This new orientation toward the organs as the seat of disease can be attributed in large measure to the work of Fernel in the 16th century, a French physician whose initial training in mathematics predisposed him to seek order in the apparent chaos of disease. He was the first to classify disease by the affected organs, and his text replaced Galen's in concept and usage.

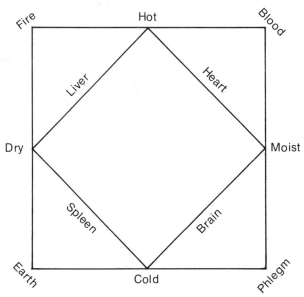

The four humors of the Hippocratic scheme, showing their attributes and sources.   **Figure 3.1**

The great advance of the next century was Harvey's discovery and publication in 1628 of the circulation of the blood. This concept is an absolute prerequisite to the understanding of almost all pathologic phenomena. Harvey's revelation led to the last gasp of the humoral theory, revived by Sylvius (1614–1672), who theorized (correctly, as it has developed) that acid and alkali were in balance in the blood in the healthy state. Sylvius' error was in building an entire superstructure on this factually correct but inadequate foundation. The by then almost routine use of autopsies made such a position untenable, and it did not long survive the death of Sylvius.

The true beginning of modern pathology is considered to be the publication in 1761 of *Seats and Causes of Disease* by Morgagni. This text was the first to provide extensive correlation between clinical history and pathologic findings. The pathology of the vascular system was covered in detail, as were the anatomic features of many diseases of other organ systems. Morgagni's great contribution was his thoroughness. Histology and bacteriology still lay in the future, and etiology for Morgagni remained in the miasma of the humoral approach.

By the 19th century pathology had become a recognized discipline. Bichat, in Paris, began the separation of general and histologic (tissue) pathology, and distinguished the various tissues of the body by fine dissection and physicochemical manipulations. His work and the meticulous autopsies of Rokitansky in Vienna led the way from organ pathology through tissue pathology to the cellular pathology of Rudolf Virchow, the single greatest name in the history of pathology. Virchow's contributions (in pathology, anthropology and politics) are too many to list in this brief review, but most important is his concept that cells develop from other cells. The entire field of modern anatomic pathology is built on this cellular foundation.

In contrast to the present clear understanding of the relationship of anatomic alterations to disease states, etiology remains obscure in many diseases, most notably in cancer. Microbiology developed in the 19th century, with investigators such as Pasteur and Koch pointing out the microbial causes of many diseases, and Krebs, Hansen, Ehrlich and many others integrating microbiology with pathology and the clinical branches of medicine. It is apparent that the focus of experimental pathology will remain on etiology, with continuing integration of other disciplines and techniques, and increasing emphasis on subcellular pathology.

CELLULAR REACTIONS TO INJURY

Principles

Modern pathology is based on the concept of the cell as the functional unit of tissues, organs and the body. The cells are classified by multiple separate, but to some degree overlapping, systems. One such classification is into somatic and germinal cells. Germinal cells have the potential to unite with those of the opposite sex and produce a new individual, whereas all somatic cells, those making up the various nongonadal tissues and organs of the body, die with the individual.

Another classification of cells is based on their reproductive capacities. Most cells possess the potential of replication. Each individual cell exists from the mitosis that formed it until its subdivision at the next mitosis into two new cells. Examples of such **intermitotic** cells are the basal cells of the skin and the primordial germ cells. Such cells do not die until the death of the organism as a whole. In contrast, highly specialized, or differentiated, cells lose the capacity for division, and age and die. Examples of **postmitotic** cells are those of the nervous system and superficial skin.

Cellular Adaptations to Stress

Tissues and their constituent cells are continually being exposed to internal and external stimuli and stresses. Individual cells have a limited but well defined capacity to adjust to these forces. Focal damage within a cell can be localized by sequestration of the damaged area within a vacuole, which eventually may be resorbed, extruded or permanently sequestered within the cell.

Cells can react to changes in the demands placed upon them in a variety of ways. One of these is an increase in the size of the cells, **hypertrophy.** An increased workload increases metabolic activity and in turn the actual size of the cell. Such adaptive changes are not necessarily beneficial, and may actually be maladaptive. An example is the hypertrophy of the heart seen in high altitude natives, whose hearts are stimulated to enlarge by the demands of pumping a less oxygenated and more viscous blood. The hypertrophy is primarily right-sided, increasing right ventricular work. A high incidence of a congenital anomaly, patent ductus arteriosus, is seen which, with pulmonary hypertension, has been implicated in the development of high altitude pulmonary edema (Mazess, 1970).

In contrast, a decrease in workload can lead to a decrease in cell size, **atrophy.** Other factors can have the same effect: denervation; decreased blood supply or nutrition; decreased hormonal stimulation. Examples are atrophy of a limb immobilized for fracture treatment, or postmenopausal changes in secondary sexual characteristics. Limbs denervated by poliomyelitis become atrophic; examples are seen in the mummies of ancient Egypt (Harris and Weeks, 1973; Mitchell, 1900).

Cells may divide excessively when stressed, **hyperplasia.** A well known example is goiter, the enlargement of the thyroid gland seen in individuals living in areas low in iodine, such as the Andes or Alps.

Cells may be replaced by others more resistant to stress, **metaplasia.** The lining of the respiratory tract in cigarette smokers changes to a squamous (skin-like) epithelium in reaction to chronic irritation. It is presumed that the superficial respiratory cells are killed by the smoke and the surviving basal cells replicate as more hardy squamous cells. This process suffers from a high cost/benefit ratio, however. The metaplastic squamous epithelium is incapable of clearing secretions from the air passages; hence, the "smoker's cough." Not infrequently the metaplastic process goes awry, with the development of abnormal cells, **dysplasia,** or malignant cells, **neoplasia.**

INFLAMMATION

Any injury beyond that which can be limited by an adaptive response at the cellular level calls forth a response at the tissue or organ level. In humans and other vertebrates this is an inflammatory reaction, defined by Robbins (1974) as ". . . the response of the body to tissue injury involving neurologic, vascular, humoral and cellular reactions within the site of injury." Inflammation acts to seal off the damaged area and initiate repair and, in vertebrates, is predominantly a vascular phenomenon. Vessels in the damaged area become dilated and congested, and plasma leaks out into the surrounding tissue, followed by red and white blood cells, **erythrocytes** and **leukocytes** (Fig. 3.2). This mixture of fluid and blood cells constitutes an **exudate,** as opposed to fluid passively leaking out of vessels, in a mechanical problem such as heart failure, termed a **transudate.**

The white cells that respond initially, in the acute phase of inflammation, are **polymorphonuclear** leukocytes, primarily **neutrophils,** which form pus. If the process continues for several weeks or longer it

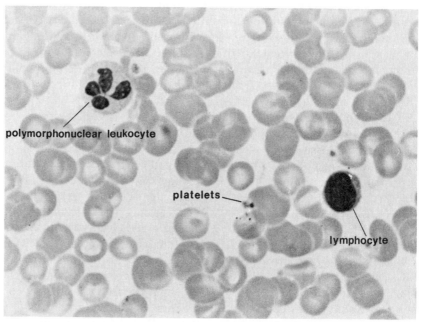

Figure 3.2   Blood cells. The red cells are anucleate biconcave discs. A polymorphonuclear leukocyte, a small lymphocyte and several platelets are seen. Wright's stain, × 1,000.

enters the chronic phase, and **lymphocytes, plasma cells** and **histiocytes** become the predominant cells. Dense fibrous tissue also develops in the chronic phase of inflammation. The polymorphs can be viewed as packages of proteolytic, destructive enzymes that ingest and attempt to digest bacteria and dead cells; the chronic phase cells are more important in immunologic reactions (particularly the antibody-forming plasma cells).

Special Types of Inflammation

Various special types of inflammation must also be considered. One type is **granulomatous.** In a teleologic sense, this reaction is to microorganisms or foreign bodies that are unchecked by the usual inflammatory mechanisms. Histiocytes enlarge to form so-called **epithelioid** cells and coalesce as **giant** cells, in an attempt to contain organisms causative of such diseases as tuberculosis, leprosy, syphilis and a variety of fungal infections. Similar reactions are seen to foreign bodies such as silica and oils. The end result of these processes is usually extensive scarring, with the inciting organism often remaining viable.

Ulceration is the loss of the lining or surface of an organ, with surrounding inflammation. Ulcers of the skin and intestinal tract are common, and the latter show some intriguing correlations with blood groups (Lechin et al., 1973). It must also be kept in mind that an ulcer can be superimposed upon a tumor.

An abscess is an accumulation of pus in solid tissue. These are mainly bacterial in origin, and consist of a central mass of bacteria, leukocytes and liquified tissue, surrounded by an acute inflammatory reaction. Abscesses are seen in the lung, liver, brain or any of the other solid tissues of the body. Until quite recently "abscess" was a general term connoting a local swelling, and this definition must be kept in mind when consulting the older medical literature.

The eventual course of an untreated abscess is that the pus burrows through tissue until it erupts at a surface, discharges and heals (if the resultant **sinus tract** is not life-threatening, or if the abscess is not in a vital organ such as the heart or the brain).

Allergic inflammation is to foreign proteins and requires previous sensitization. Thus, this reaction tends to be delayed and is characterized by the cells of chronic inflammation, particularly the plasma cell and one of the polymorphonuclear leukocytes, the **eosinophil.** There is a tendency to involve surfaces exposed to the environment. An example is the lining of the respiratory tract in bronchial asthma.

The Course of Inflammation

The initial reaction to injury is always an acute inflammatory response, but the subsequent course is determined largely by the nature of the injury. If the stimulus is terminated, there is subsidence of the acute reaction and, most often, healing and regeneration of the tissue, i.e., restoration to normal appearance and function. However, many highly differentiated tissues, which have limited or no power of regeneration, die (become **necrotic**) and are replaced by simpler tissues, usually scar tissue.

If the stimulus continues, or if the acute reaction is inadequate, the reaction enters the chronic phase. Repair is often attempted during chronic inflammation, by the ingrowth of highly vascular granulation tissue, and scarring is the almost inevitable result. Scarring usually decreases function, and regeneration can be atypical, resulting in anatomic and metabolic disorder, as in cirrhosis in the liver, or in certain types of lung cancer.

DISTURBANCES OF METABOLISM AND CIRCULATION

Damage to cells manifested by anatomic alterations is usually accompanied by changes in the metabolism of nutrients (fats, carbohydrates and proteins), minerals and pigments. Accumulation of fat can be generalized, as in obesity, or localized, in organs such as the liver or pancreas. If such fatty infiltration of the viscera is of sufficient degree, impairment of function of the organ will occur, as in fatty change of the liver, a common finding in alcoholism and other toxic states.

There are a number of abnormalities of carbohydrate metabolism, including the uncommon glycogen storage diseases and the very common diabetes mellitus. A variety of degenerative changes in tissue protein is also known. Uric acid is derived from nucleoproteins and can accumulate in the tissues in gout. An inadequate dietary intake of nutrients, minerals and vitamins results in specific deficiency diseases. These processes will be discussed in more detail in Section Two, under the appropriate organs.

The various disturbances of mineral metabolism will also be discussed in the specific pathology chapters, but mention should be made at this point of the abnormal deposition of calcium which can occur in many tissues, such as the blood vessels, lung, kidney and others. Such deposition can be due to elevated blood levels of calcium (usually due to parathyroid disease) or to local factors (such as necrosis in a focus of tuberculosis). Occasionally there is progression to the formation of bone in abnormal areas, **ectopic** bone formation. An example is the ossification of the thyroid cartilage seen so frequently in ancient skeletal remains.

Abnormalities of Pigment Metabolism

Pigments, both endogenous and exogenous, are extraordinarily persistent in ancient remains and thus of great interest to paleopathologists. In living persons the accumulation of exogenous pigments can indicate poisoning, which in turn may be related to industrial, environmental or cultural factors.

The endogenous pigments of importance are **melanin,** the coloring material of the skin, hair and eye, and those pigments derived from **hemoglobin,** the red blood cell pigment responsible for oxygen transport. Melanin can be increased physiologically, as in suntan, pregnancy and freckles, and in relatively rare pathologic conditions. Depigmentation may be localized, **vitiligo,** or generalized, **albinism.** Hemoglobin is broken down in the tissues to **hemosiderin.** If blood breakdown is ·excessive, as in hemorrhage or a hemolytic disease such as sickle cell anemia, there can be a marked fibrous reaction to the iron-containing hemosiderin, interfering with the proper function of the affected organ or organs.

Under normal circumstances, hemoglobin is metabolized by the liver, spleen and bone marrow to bile pigment, which eventually is excreted by the liver into the intestinal tract. If this system is disrupted, bile pigment, **bilirubin,** accumulates in excess and the person becomes **jaundiced.** Such an overload can occur because of excessive breakdown of blood (as in the hemolytic anemias), liver disease (such as hepatitis or replacement by tumor), or obstruction of the duct system (by stone or tumor). Chemical tests of the blood and urine (see Appendix 1) can distinguish these factors to a great extent, although there can be significant overlap, as when obstruction causes liver damage, or when the swelling in liver disease leads to intrahepatic obstruction.

An abnormal breakdown product of hemoglobin, **hematin,** is formed in malarial infections and is deposited in massive amounts in the liver and spleen.

Exogenous pigments can be deposited in the lung, in a condition referred to generally as **pneumoconiosis.** The specific diseases are caused by coal dust **(anthracosis),** silicon dioxide **(silicosis),** iron dust **(siderosis)** and asbestos fibers **(asbestosis).** Anthracosis and silicosis have been documented in virtually all civilizations, past and present. Anthracosis is usually due to the inhalation of smoke from open fires in the home or industrial sources. Sandstorms or mining activities have been shown to cause silicosis in modern and ancient times (Lanning, 1967; Tapp et al., 1965). The carbon pigment of anthracosis appears to be relatively inert, but the other pneumoconioses lead to inflammation and fibrosis, and predispose to other diseases. Silicosis is associated with tuberculosis, and asbestosis is linked to the development of cancer of the lining of the pleural cavity, **mesothelioma,** and of the lung itself.

Metallic poisons can also cause pigmentation of the skin and other organs. Lead poisoning is of particular interest, again both in modern times and in antiquity. Chronic lead poisoning has been postulated as a factor in the fall of ancient Rome and in the high incidence of gout in Victorian England (lead damage to the kidneys causing decreased uric acid excretion and elevated serum uric acid levels). In modern society, lead poisoning is a disease of children of the lower socioeconomic classes, who eat peeling, lead-based paint in older houses. The general term for abnormal appetites is **pica,** which in modern medical practice has come to be used almost exclusively for the ingestion of lead-based paint. The same mechanism probably accounts for the lead poisoning observed by Zook et al. (1973) in zoo primates.

Another culturally introduced pigment is that used in tattooing. The importance for the health professional is in the potential introduction of infectious diseases such as hepatitis or syphilis along with the pigment. Tattoo styles have also been useful in dating remains from archeologic populations; the tattoos on a 1,600-year-old Eskimo mummy studied by Smith and Zimmerman (1975) correlated in motif with those on implements of the Old Bering Sea archeologic phase, giving an excellent fit with radiocarbon dates on the mummy itself.

Circulatory Disturbances

As noted in the preceding historical review, knowledge of the circulation of the blood is a prerequisite to the understanding of most pathologic phenomena. Under normal circumstances an adequate amount of blood containing the proper amount of electrolytes and nutrients at the proper pressure is delivered to the tissues. Increases or decreases in the parameters of any of these factors results in pathologic changes in anatomy and function.

Edema is the accumulation of an increased volume of fluid in the tissues, outside of the cells and the vascular system. Edema fluid accumulations in the body cavities are referred to specifically as **hydrothorax, hydroperitoneum (ascites)** or **hydropericardium;** generalized edema of the body cavities and subcutaneous tissue is known as **anasarca** (or, in the older literature, **dropsy**).

Edema is caused by disturbances in fluid balance, such as blood pressure or osmotic discrepancies between the vascular system and the extravascular spaces, obstruction to blood and lymph flow, increased capillary permeability, or water and sodium retention. Frequently, multiple factors are involved simultaneously.

Congestion is an increased volume of blood in an organ, within dilated vessels, and can be acute or chronic. Active congestion is usually acute and due to increased arterial circulation, as seen in inflammation and in emotional states such as anger or blushing.

Passive congestion, in contrast, is due to decreased venous flow from an area. It tends to be chronic. Causes are gravitational pooling of blood or obstruction to flow, as by tumors, scars, tight bandages, etc. If it is prolonged, chronic passive congestion can result in edema, hemorrhage, necrosis of tissue and fibrosis. This process is particularly prominent in the lungs and liver, usually as a result of heart failure.

Hemorrhage refers to loss of blood from the heart and blood vessels, usually due to rupture. Hemorrhage can be secondary to trauma or spontaneous, and may be external or internal. When internal, the result is often a **hematoma,** a localized tumor-like collection of clotted blood. There are many terms specifying the area of hemorrhage, including **epistaxis** (nosebleed), **hemoptysis** (coughing of blood) and **hematemesis** (vomiting of blood).

Traumatic hemorrhage is common, and there are many causes of spontaneous hemorrhage. Diseases of the vessels, hypertension, and disorders of coagulation, such as hemophilia, are all causative factors.

Hemophilia affected many of the royal families of 19th and 20th century Europe. The disease is thought to have begun from a mutant gene in Queen Victoria, as she had no afflicted ancestors and bore one afflicted son and two carrier daughters (Winchester, 1972). The disease spread widely through the intermarriages of the various royal families. The Tsarevitch of Imperial Russia was afflicted and the apparent ability of Rasputin to control the disease, presumably by suggestion, was a major factor in his influence on the royal family. Historians have speculated on the role of Rasputin's excess in the fomentation of the Russian Revolution; in this case, as in many others, the disease of an individual may have altered history.

Pressure effects can result from internal hemorrhages. Surveys of mental hospitals have disclosed significant percentages of inmates to be suffering from old subdural hematomas compressing the brain and causing mental dysfunction. Penetrating wounds of the heart cause a **hemopericardium.** The blood in the pericardial cavity prevents filling of the heart and causes death by cardiac compression, **tamponade.**

Small hemorrhages can be completely resorbed, but larger hemorrhages become either encapsulated or replaced by fibrous tissue. As the red blood cells break down, hemosiderin pigment is released, producing the classic green-black discoloration seen in bruises or in a "black eye."

Massive hemorrhage has a systemic effect, **shock,** which is a clinical state characterized by loss of consciousness; pallor; a weak, rapid pulse; and decreased blood pressure. Many initiating factors for shock other than hemorrhage are known, and a considerable part of the clinical picture is due to an increase in the volume of the vascular system by dilatation, mediated by nervous impulses. Shock can be seen in trauma, infections, perforated organs and many other conditions, but whatever the cause the end result, insufficient blood flow to the tissues, is the same. Attempts by the body to compensate for the lowered blood pressure, by constricting certain vessels, can actually worsen the condition, causing necrosis of such organs as the liver and intestines. In general, treatment is that of the underlying condition, with replacement of lost blood, and a distinction is made between **reversible** and **irreversible** shock.

In certain conditions the blood stops flowing and coagulates in the vascular system of a living individual, a process referred to as **thrombosis.** The resultant mass in the heart or blood vessel is a **thrombus,** which has a characteristic structure differing grossly and microscopically from blood coagulated after death or outside the vessels, a **clot.** Thrombosis can be precipitated by changes in the vessel lining, decrease in flow, or increase in the coagulability of the blood. High altitude dwellers are **polycythemic** (having an increased number of red cells in the blood), and their more viscous blood is more liable to thrombosis. The results of this compensatory mechanism are particularly evident in the placenta, which shows many thromboses and is smaller than those in sea level pregnancies; the undernourished high altitude fetus starts life with the handicap of a lowered birth weight as a result (Grahn and Kratchman, 1963; McClung, 1969). This mechanism plays a major role in the generally decreased reproductive performance of high altitude natives (Abelson, 1976).

Thrombosis can occur anywhere in the cardiovascular system. Common sites are venous thromboses in the legs; arterial thrombi (secondary to atherosclerosis) in the aorta and arteries supplying the brain, kidneys and intestines; and coronary artery thrombi, often overlying areas of damage to the heart muscle, **myocardial infarction** ("heart attack"). In conditions such as malaria and sickle cell disease, thrombi form within capillaries.

Once formed, a thrombus can follow one of several different courses. If small, it can simply be dissolved. If larger, it will eventually be healed by **recanalization,** the ingrowth of fibroblasts and small blood vessels to form a new channel. An alternative is **embolization**; part or all of the thrombus can break loose and lodge in another part of the circulation. **Embolus** is a general term for any mass carried in the blood stream: thrombus, air, fat, bone marrow, foreign bodies such as bullets, etc. An embolism eventually lodges in the arterial circulation, where it produces the same effect as an arterial thrombus, deprivation of the flow of oxygenated blood to the affected organ. This decrease in blood supply is termed **ischemia,** and if the process causes tissue necrosis the result is a potentially fatal **infarct.** Infarcts can also occur in the absence of obstruction if the demand for blood exceeds the supply. There is a report in the literature of a marathon runner under extreme temperature and humidity stress who developed a massive myocardial infarction in the absence of coronary artery disease (Green et al., 1976).

A common cause of death is pulmonary infarction, usually due to embolism from venous thrombi in the legs. The thrombi detach and travel through the venous system and right side of the heart to lodge in the pulmonary arterial circulation. Myocardial and pulmonary infarcts often are immediately fatal, but these and infarcts in other organs can and do heal, frequently with scarring and functional impairment.

TRAUMATIC INJURY

The agents of trauma include physical force, cold, heat, chemicals and irradiation. The effects of physical force on the soft tissues are abrasions, lacerations, incisions and penetrating injuries; on the skeletal system the effects are sprains, dislocations and fractures. Penetrating injuries, such as arrow wounds and sword cuts, and fractures are the lesions most likely to be of interest to the archeologist. Immediately fatal wounds may be difficult to diagnose in skeletal material, as there would be no sign of healing (smooth or heaped-up bone at the edge of the wound) to differentiate pre- from post-mortem injury. An advantage of working with mummified material is that the identification of hemorrhage would clearly indicate premortem injury. Certainly the detailed instructions for the treatment of wounds in the Egyptian medical papyri bear witness to a significant incidence of trauma in ancient

Egypt (Ackerknecht, 1973; Risse, 1972). The full discussion of fractures is deferred to the consideration of the skeletal system in Section Two.

Exposure to excessive cold, **hypothermia,** can result in **frostbite,** with long-term changes of atrophy in the affected tissues, including the bones. Generalized hypothermia can cause death with minimal pathologic change.

Excessive heat, **hyperthermia,** produces local **burns** in which the tissue is coagulated much like a boiled egg. Such lesions heal by scarring. In generalized hyperthermia, death is due to pooling of blood in dilated superficial vessels and to leakage of potassium from damaged erythrocytes, provoking abnormal cardiac rhythms.

Many chemicals act as poisons, both acutely and chronically. Of these poisons, by far the most common is ethyl alcohol. The abuse of alcohol accounts for many deaths, both by its long-term effects, particularly on the liver, and in automobile accidents.

Chemical pollutants are becoming increasingly important poisons in modern societies. Environmental pollution can cause acute or chronic poisoning, and respiratory, mental and many other disorders. Since the 18th century, when Percival Pott diagnosed scrotal cancer in chimney sweeps as an industrial cancer, it has become apparent that those exposed to cancer-causing agents **(carcinogens)** are not only workers in specific industries but also the population at large. Pollution of air and water affects all. Attempts to solve this ecologic problem have encountered many difficulties, as can readily be seen in the daily newspapers.

Irradiation is of interest to the anthropologist in the context of the relationship of sunlight to skin pigmentation and such diseases as rickets and skin cancer. Melanin pigment formed by skin exposed to sunlight acts as a protective screen against carcinogenic ultraviolet rays. This system must maintain a delicate balance in relation to the amount of sun available, as a certain amount of ultraviolet light is necessary for the skin to produce a sufficient amount of vitamin D to prevent the development of rickets. Thus, blacks living in northern climates are more likely to develop rickets than are whites. Other cultural and environmental factors can upset this equilibrium. Rickets became a major problem during England's industrial revolution, as the living conditions in crowded tenements and the smoky skies acted synergistically to decrease sun exposure (Loomis, 1970). On the other hand, whites who work outdoors or migrate to a sunnier climate are much more liable to the development of skin cancer. White Australians have one of the highest rates of skin cancer in the world, whereas the disease is virtually nonexistent among Australian aborigines.

As fossil fuels are being exhausted and human society is inevitably turning to atomic power, the long-range effects of ionizing radiation may become of more importance, particularly to the worker in genetics. Some increase in the number of cases of cancers such as leukemia and lymphoma can be expected, but the real danger may be a subtle increase in the mutation rate. The effects of radiation are cumulative, and an increase in genetic defects and variations can be expected worldwide as exposure is increased.

INFECTION AND INFESTATION

General Considerations

The body can be invaded by bacteria, viruses, rickettsia, fungi, and single-celled **(protozoan)** and multicelled **(metazoan)** parasites (Fig. 3.3). Invasion by microorganisms such as bacteria and protozoa constitutes **infection,** and parasitism by macroorganisms, those visible to the eye such as worms or insects, is referred to as **infestation.** The local effect is the inflammatory reaction discussed above, which usually localizes infection.

Inflammation is not specific to or synonymous with infection. Physical agents and many sterile substances can cause an inflammatory reaction. Organisms differ from other inflammatory agents in several important ways. Bacteria, especially, given the proper conditions, can reproduce at a rapid rate in the body to produce a widespread and overwhelming infection. The production of toxins damages tissues, facilitating spread of microorganisms and altering the body's usual inflammatory response.

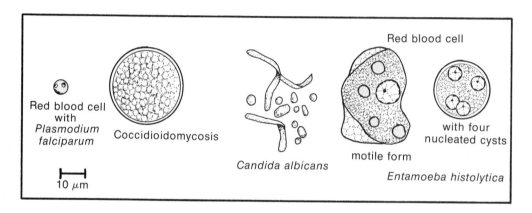

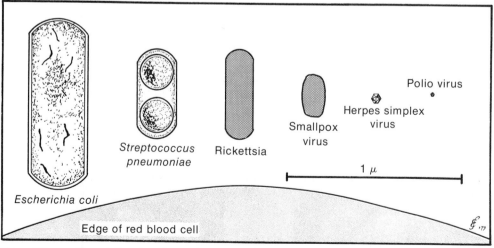

Figure 3.3   The relative size of some human pathogens.

The severity of the infection is related to the number and virulence, the **pathogenicity,** of the invading organisms. The portal of entry can be a crucial factor in the establishment of an infection. Certain microorganisms have adapted to specific portals, e.g., the genital tract in venereal diseases, whereas others such as the staphylococci can infect almost any tissue. Most parasites have highly evolved life cycles that are dependent on specific modes of transmission and routes of entry. Population size and density; cultural structures such as caste systems and subtler class distinctions affecting contact between groups; and patterns of migration and visiting, are all factors influencing the transmission of disease (Alland, 1970). Even age segregation in schools can play such a role, as has been shown in the transmission of rubella (German measles) (Mazzur, 1970).

The acute epidemic diseases (such as measles, smallpox and poliomyelitis) require a large population base in which to maintain themselves. Small or isolated communities have been shown to be exquisitely sensitive when such "crowd-type" diseases are introduced (Newman, 1976). It is unlikely that these diseases were present in the small groups of early man in the Old or New World (St. Hoyme, 1969), and equally unlikely that such pathogenic organisms could have exerted any selective influence on human genetic make-up until the recent advent of urbanized society (Black, 1975).

The resistance of the individual host is a major factor in preventing or limiting infection. Resistance is at several levels, including the integrity of the body's surfaces, the efficacy of the inflammatory reaction, physical barriers to the spread of infection, and immunologic (antibody) responses. Nutritional status also plays a role. It is generally believed that the debility of undernutrition fosters infection (Scrimshaw and Tejada, 1970), but Murray and Murray (1977) have suggested that starvation actually suppresses infection. They attribute the infections seen in times of famine to associated factors such as crowding and poor sanitation, and their animal studies appear to support this view.

Microorganisms usually show tissue specificity also, causing disease in some tissues but not in others. Certain bacteria grow optimally at temperatures below 37° C., and thus produce skin ulcers but not internal infections (Dubos, 1971). Leprosy is one such skin-adapted disease.

All these resistance factors can be greatly altered by treatment with antibiotics and vaccines, or by drugs that suppress the immune response, as in patients with kidney transplants or under treatment for cancer. It is fortunate that vaccines have been developed against many infectious diseases. Field archeologists and ethnologists should be particularly aware of the potential risk of disease in their travels. Wolfe (1976) has prepared an excellent review of the immunizations available to travelers.

Bacterial Infections

Bacteria are divided into a variety of overlapping categories. One classification is morphologic, into cocci, which are round; bacilli, which are rod-shaped; and spirochetes, which have a spiral shape. Bacteria are also classified by their reaction to the Gram stains as gram-positive (blue or purple) and gram-negative (red). Those which provoke purulent exudates, such as the staphylococci, streptococci, meningococci and gonococci, are referred to as pus-causing, **pyogenic,** bacteria.

Humans carry a large commensal population of bacteria on their skin, in their upper respiratory tract and in the intestinal tract. Disease results when the balance between bacteria and host is upset by local and/or systemic factors.

Among the most common bacteria are the staphylococci, gram-positive cocci that can cause skin and visceral abscesses, wound infections, pneumonia, bone infections **(osteomyelitis),** and many other lesions and diseases. A major problem has been the recent development of strains resistant to antibiotics, as an expression of the adaptive abilities of the organism, particularly in hospitalized patients on antibiotic therapy.

Streptococci are also common and have a similar potential for disease. These gram-positive microorganisms frequently infect the nasopharynx ("strep throat"); if this condition is untreated it can be complicated by involvement of the heart **(rheumatic fever)** or kidneys **(glomerulonephritis).** Erysipelas (infection of the subcutaneous tissues), scarlet fever and puerperal sepsis ("childbed fever") are all streptococcal infections which are thankfully rare in the modern day of antisepsis and antibiotics. One species, *Streptococcus pneumoniae* (formerly considered a separate genus, *Diplococcus pneumoniae*) is the causative agent of classic lobar pneumonia.

The *Neisseria sp.* are gram-negative cocci that cause significant disease. *N. meningitidis* is an occasional inhabitant of the nasopharynx, present in 2 to 5 per cent of the normal population. Under conditions of crowding, classically in military training camps, the percentage of carriers rises dramatically. Infections of the membranes covering the brain may develop, with the potential of epidemics of **meningitis** (the suffix "-itis" indicates inflammation). The disease often follows a fulminant clinical course, with death in a few hours.

In contrast, *N. gonorrhoeae,* similar morphologically, causes a disease that can be much more protracted, gonorrhea. Infection in the male is manifested as a purulent urethral discharge which usually results in the sufferer seeking prompt attention. Infection in the female is much more occult, often leading to chronic inflammation, particularly of the fallopian tubes, with abdominal pain, and potential ectopic pregnancies and sterility resulting.

Certain bacteria are important because of their elaboration of highly potent toxins which have generalized effects. These include: *Corynebacterium diphtheriae,* the agent of diphtheria; *Clostridium tetani,* the agent of tetanus ("lockjaw"); and *Clostridium botulinum,* the agent of botulism.

Tetanus is due to introduction of *C. tetani* spores into a wound, either traumatically or as a result of cultural practices. Tetanus of newborns is common in several areas of the world because of practices related to the umbilical cord (Hopps, 1977). In certain Pacific islands, dung poultices are applied to the umbilical stump, in Hong Kong ginger root, and in Peru cobwebs. In Nigeria the soil-dwelling organism is introduced when a freshly cut piece of bamboo is used to cut the cord. Contact between the newborn and iron, a symbol of the god of war, is prohibited here.

C. botulinum is another soil dweller that occasionally contaminates foodstuffs. This microorganism produces the most potent toxin known. Botulism is an important disease in ethnic groups that prepare food at home. Inadequate cooking or preservation can provide ideal conditions for the growth of the organism. Indeed, the term botulism derives from the Latin word for sausage.

An infection of considerable historical interest is plague, caused by the bacillus *Pasteurella pestis.* The bubonic plague or black death ravaged Europe from medieval times into the 19th century, the epidemic of the 14th century being estimated to have killed more than a quarter of the population. Biochemical studies have differentiated several varieties of the plague bacillus, and it has been possible to trace the path of spread of the bacilli from the Orient to Europe and the United States by this technique (Norris, 1977).

The organism is transmitted to man by the bite of an infected flea which has left its dying host, usually a rat. Genetic variation in susceptibility to the plague bacillus has been demonstrated in rats, although not in humans (Motulsky, 1971). A relationship has also been suggested between blood groups and susceptibility (Alland, 1970), the H antigen of type O individuals being similar to a bacterial antigen and thus decreasing resistance to the organism.

The organism infects the lymph nodes, causing large swellings **(bubos).** Occasionally, transmission is by inhalation of the organism, causing a rapidly fatal pneumonic form of the disease. Crowding facilitates this form of transmission. The lepers of medieval Europe, sequestered in crowded leprosaria, were virtually wiped out by the plague.

Prevention of the disease is best accomplished by separation of rats and humans. Foci of infections in wild rodents such as squirrels account for the sporadic cases reported in the Western United States.

The spirochetal disease of most significance for humans is **syphilis.** The origin of this venereal (transmitted by sexual contact) disease is a point of controversy. One school contends that the disease originated in the New World, and was brought to Europe by Columbus' sailors. Alternatively, it is said that the disease existed on both sides of the Atlantic but, for unknown reasons, became epidemic in Europe in the 16th century. It is probable that syphilis developed from nonvenereal spirochetal infections, as the use of clothing and sanitary facilities cut down on the direct contact necessary for the transmission of these rather delicate bacteria (Rosebury, 1971). It is unlikely that the exact development of the disease will ever be known, but there are some facts to consider. Syphilitic bones are known from both sides of the pre-Columbian Atlantic (Buikstra, 1977), but no cases have been described in ancient Egyptian material (Sandison, 1972). Modern Central American Indians seem to have a partial immunity to syphilis, particularly against involvement of the nervous system, suggesting a history of the disease long enough to allow an almost symbiotic relationship to have developed (Scrimshaw and Tejada, 1970).

There are two basic forms of the disease, acquired and congenital. The primary pathologic process, the destruction of blood vessels, is the same in both, but as might be expected there are marked differences in the respective clinical courses.

Acquired syphilis, if untreated, is a three-stage disease. The **primary** stage is a local ulcer, **chancre,** at the point of contact, which may be at any of a remarkable variety of anatomic locations, such as the genitalia or oral or anal mucosa. The lesion is hard, painless, self-healing and swarming with spirochetes in the early phase. The organisms spread rapidly to adjacent lymph nodes which become painlessly enlarged, **lymphadenopathy.** This stage resolves spontaneously, but the organisms spread throughout the body to produce the **secondary** stage, a diffuse skin eruption and lymphadenopthy, with general malaise. This stage also resolves spontaneously, usually in a few weeks, but from eight to 25 years after the initial infection the **tertiary** stage may develop. The disease is by now systemic, and many organs may be damaged. Most frequently involved are the cardiovascular system, the central nervous system, the skeleton, the skin and the upper respiratory tract. Destructive lesions, referred to as **gummas** (from the German word *gummi* — rubbery), occur in these organs. Involvement of the aorta causes ballooning of the vessel **(aneurysm)** with the potential of fatal rupture. Stretching of the aortic valve ring causes severe insufficiency of the valve, with massive hypertrophy of the heart, referred to as **cor bovinum**, and eventual heart failure. Involvement of the central nervous system leads to progressive dementia and paralysis.

A syphilitic mother may transmit the infection across the placenta to her offspring. If the fetus survives, and many do not, the infant is born in what amounts to a rapidly progressive secondary or tertiary stage of the disease. Characteristic deformities of the teeth **(Hutchinson's teeth),** legs **(saber shin)** and face **(saddle nose),** blindness and deafness are seen in the afflicted child.

Infected individuals develop relatively specific antibody reactions for which several tests are available. Treatment is with high doses of penicillin, effective even in advanced stages of the disease. The history of the treatment of syphilis is in itself an interesting cultural event. Syphilis was long held to be divine retribution for sins, and the sinners were expected to suffer as much from the therapy as from the disease. The early treatment was mercury, and the great English physician Sydenham was not satisfied unless the unfortunate sufferers developed evidence of mercury poisoning, such as the daily production of 4 liters of saliva (Ackerknecht, 1973). In this atmosphere the development by Paul Ehrlich of a "magic bullet," an organic arsenical, was greeted by some with less than open arms.

Leprosy is a disease of considerable interest to medical historians, because of (probably incorrect) Biblical references, and to paleopathologists, as the characteristic bone changes of the disease were first delineated in a study of medieval skeletons. Although the manifestations are external and it is often considered a skin disease, leprosy is actually a systemic disorder involving nerves, blood vessels, eyes, upper respiratory tract, testis and skeleton.

The leprosy bacillus, *Mycobacterium leprae,* is similar to *M. tuberculosis,* the agent of human tuberculosis, and one type of reaction to infection, the formation of microscopic granulomas, is also similar. Otherwise the infections are markedly different. Leprosy is acquired by prolonged direct contact with an infected person, either skin contact or from nasal discharge. The incubation period ranges from three to ten years, and the earliest detectable sign is that noted by Møller-Christiansen (1961) in the medieval lepers of his study — atrophy of the nasal spine. The organisms infiltrate the skin, causing nodular lesions. Two principal forms of the disease are recognized. In **lepromatous** leprosy, resistance is minimal and vast numbers of bacilli infiltrate the skin. Patients with more resistance develop **tuberculoid** leprosy, with a granulomatous reaction and more limited disease. The characteristic deformities are mostly secondary changes, due to loss of sensation in the affected areas. The skin lesions themselves are anesthetic, and the nerves are also affected. Deformities are due to repeated trauma, secondary infection and paralysis.

A considerable social stigma results from these deformities, affecting mating patterns (Smith and Guinto, 1977) and leading to discrimination against sufferers in life (Sigerist, 1970) and after death (Beidelmann, 1971). The Philippine government even made special coinage for leper colonies, to prevent contamination of the money used by the general population (Jarcho, 1973).

The disease spoken of in the Bible is a point of controversy (Verbov, 1976). The earliest skeletal evidence in Europe is medieval, and the diagnosis has been made by Sandison (1972) in an Egyptian Coptic Christian body. There is no paleopathologic evidence of the disease in the pre-Christian era.

Most other bacteria are highly tissue-specific and will be considered under the appropriate organ in Section Two.

Viral Diseases

Viruses consist of nucleic acids surrounded by a protective protein layer, and are much smaller than bacteria (Fig. 3.3). These organisms are intracellular parasites and increasingly are recognized as being responsible for human diseases. The viruses have been classified on the basis of the type of nucleic acid they contain. Deoxyribonucleic acid (DNA) viruses cause smallpox, chickenpox, warts, colds and other diseases. One member of the group, the herpes virus, has been implicated in the development of cancer of the uterine cervix. Ribonucleic acid (RNA) viruses cause mumps, measles, German measles, rabies, yellow fever, polio and other diseases.

Cultural factors operate in viral diseases as in others. For example, **kuru,** a degenerative neurologic disorder occurring in natives of New Guinea, has been found to be due to a "slow virus" (one with a prolonged incubation period) acquired through ritual cannibalism of deceased relatives (see Chapter 12).

The effect of the virus on its host cell can vary from a symbiotic relationship to cell death. The interaction between host and virus is conditioned by many of the same factors operative in bacterial infections. Infection is determined by the characteristics of the virus, including its tissue specificity and mode of transmission, and by the resistance of the host. An illustrative case is that of the **polio** virus.

The virus is normally a harmless intestinal commensal. In societies lacking modern sewage disposal facilities, exposure to the polio virus occurred very early in life, when the protection afforded by passively acquired maternal antibodies could restrict the virus to the intestinal tract. Children begin to make their own antibodies at about 6 months of age, and thus could continue to confine the virus. With modern separation of man and sewage the infection, when it occurs, is later in life. By this time the protective effect of the maternal antibodies, which only last for a few months, is lost. Before the individual can develop his own antibodies, the organism spreads, doing particular damage to the nervous system. This mechanism accounted for the polio epidemics that occurred in the western world in the first half of the 20th century, until the development of an adequate vaccine. It is of interest that the mummy of the Pharaoh Siptah, of the XIXth Dynasty, shows a leg deformity characteristic of poliomyelitis (Harris and Weeks, 1971). The Pharaoh would have been one individual separated from the masses (and their sewage) early in life.

The effects of viruses on nonimmune populations have been demonstrated repeatedly. Measles has been responsible for the virtual elimination of isolated communities such as those of Eskimos. Even today, isolated populations in the South Pacific show almost total susceptibility to measles (Willis and Warburton, 1974). Yellow fever caused explosive epidemics in the New World aborigines after its importation along with African slaves (Carter, 1931; Wolf, 1959). Smallpox, together with plague and tuberculosis, also played a major role in the depopulation of America (Cook, 1973; Stearn and Allen, 1945).

Rickettsial Diseases

Rickettsia are insect-transmitted organisms intermediate in size between bacteria and viruses (Fig. 3.3). They cause systemic diseases characterized by skin rashes and severe constitutional signs, i.e., fever, chills, prostration and, in the case of **typhus,** up to a 50 per cent mortality rate. Typhus, caused by *Rickettsia prowazekii,* is the most important of these diseases. The organism is louse-borne and has repeatedly caused epidemic disease under conditions of war. The reader is referred to Zinsser's classic **Rats, Lice and History** (1963) for a full discussion of the impact of this disease on human history.

Fungal Infections

The fungi are plants that produce chronic infections in man. Some of these infections are superficial but so widespread in the population as to be of major clinical importance. This group of diseases includes athlete's foot, ringworm, and moniliasis (candidiasis or "thrush"), a common infection of the oral or female genital mucosa. Two deep infections are of importance in that they are endemic in certain areas of the United States and that they resemble tuberculosis clinically and pathologically.

Coccidioidomycosis is common in the southwest, particularly in California's San Joachim Valley, where it is known as "valley fever." The organism is in the soil, and caused a small epidemic in archeology students excavating in the Valley in 1970 (Werner et al., 1972). Archeologists should be aware of this occupational hazard. A finding of particular importance was that half of these cases showed skin lesions. Two were misdiagnosed as contact dermatitis and treated with corticosteroids, exactly the wrong treatment for any infection.

Histoplasmosis is a similar disease that also provokes a granulomatous reaction simulating tuberculosis. The fungus is found all over the world and is very common in the upper Mississippi and Ohio River Valleys. Bird and bat excreta have been implicated in the transmission of the disease. Diagnosis of both these fungal diseases is by chest x-ray, skin tests, and identification of the organism in tissue section or by culture.

Many other fungi can cause infection, especially in patients debilitated by cancer or made more vulnerable by anticancer or immunosuppressive therapy. All fungal diseases are much more common in the tropics, where heat and humidity foster the growth of fungi in nature.

Protozoal Infections

Infections by these single-celled animals are of great interest to workers in underdeveloped or tropical countries. The single most widespread disease of man is probably **malaria,** to which it has been estimated that half of the deaths in human history have been related. The debility caused by malaria is thought to have played a role in the decline of the classic Greek civilization and its conquest by Rome, and in the fluctuations of settlement in the area around Rome (the Roman Campagna) (Sigerist, 1970). The importation of malaria to the New World by the African slaves of the Spaniards also played a role in the decimation of the aboriginal population mentioned above (Wolf, 1959).

As nonhuman primates are liable to malarial infection and transmission to humans has been demonstrated (Coatney et al., 1971), it is likely that the human disease has evolved from an anthropoid infection, although the details of the process are unclear (Cockburn, 1967; Weiner, 1971). Human malaria is caused by four species of the genus *Plasmodium* and is transmitted by female mosquitos of the genus *Anopheles.* The parasite has a sexual reproductive cycle in the mosquito and is injected into man in the mosquito's saliva. In man the organism parasitizes erythrocytes, in which it undergoes asexual reproductive cycles of characteristic duration for each species. The cycle terminates with the rupture of the parasitized (and, for reasons which are unclear, many nonparasitized) erythrocytes. The parasites, their metabolic products and hemoglobin are liberated into the blood, causing the well-known clinical picture of periodic chills and fever.

Malaria is virtually the only disease in which an understanding of the interaction of culture, disease and genetic polymorphism has been worked out well. The most severe form of the disease, falciparum malaria, had a relatively recent evolution in Africa, when land clearing for agricultural use produced an environment favorable to the species of mosquito which happens to be a more effective vector for *Plasmodium falciparum* (Tobias, 1974). The result was an increase in this type of malaria and a decrease in the other forms of the disease (Weisenfeld, 1967). In African blacks there has been selection for the sickle cell gene, which in the heterozygous state increases resistance to malarial infection (Allison, 1954; Livingstone, 1969). Infected heterozygous cells sickle more rapidly and thus are removed more quickly from the circulation, with their parasites, than are normal cells (Roth et al., 1978). Of course, the price of this protection is that homozygous individuals suffer the ill effects of sickle cell disease, including premature death. As the selective pressure of malaria does not affect American blacks, the prevalence of the gene has shown a dramatic decrease in this group.

Another example of the complex interrelation between culture and malaria was seen in an epidemic of the disease in Sri Lanka (then Ceylon) in 1967–68. The island was on the verge of eliminating malaria when a woman discovered a sapphire in her garden. The news of the find brought hordes of prospectors, by the tens of thousands, from all parts of the island. Mining activity led to pools of stagnant water which became breeding grounds for mosquitos. Some of the prospectors were malaria carriers, and the others became infected and spread malaria throughout the island when they returned home (Hopps, 1977).

A less common but still important protozoan disease is **amebiasis,** a primary infection of the colon that can spread to the liver, lung and brain. The organism, *Entamoeba histolytica,* causes ulceration of the colon with a clinical picture of a nonspecific diarrhea, with abdominal pain and occasional bloody stools. Travelers to foreign countries, such as anthropologists on field trips, often develop such a clinical picture. Usually such dysentery is simply due to a change in the bacterial flora of the colon and is self-limiting. Because of the potential of extra-intestinal involvement by *E. histolytica,* it is essential that amebiasis be ruled out by appropriate laboratory tests in these individuals.

Amebiasis is a serious disease in Durban, South Africa, with high morbidity and mortality. Three hundred miles north, the same Bantu population group showed the same prevalence of infection, but the disease was much less severe. Elsdon-Dew (1946) has suggested that urbanization, with a change to a diet rich in refined sugars, allowed the infection to develop into a much more severe disease.

There are other protozoan diseases of importance, particularly in the tropics. **Leishmaniasis** is a disease transmitted by the bite of the sand fly and which may affect the liver and spleen ("visceral leishmaniasis" or **kala-azar**) or skin and oral mucosa ("oriental sore," **espundia** or **uta**). There are marked geographic differences in the expression and course of the disease. **Trypanosomiasis** ("sleeping sickness") is transmitted by the bite of the African tsetse fly. The trypanosomes infect the blood and cause a generalized lymphadenopathy, with involvement of the central nervous system in advanced stages. American trypanosomiasis is caused by the bite of large biting bugs of the genus *Triatoma.* These bugs bite at night, hiding in cracks in walls during the day, and thus are found in poverty areas. The disease damages many organs.

A disease distributed worldwide is **toxoplasmosis.** The organism is transmitted in the feces of the house cat. When a pregnant woman is infected, the organism can cross her placenta, causing a congenital infection that can result in mental retardation or death of the infant.

Helminthic Disease

Diseases caused by helminths (worms) are relatively uncommon in temperate climates but are of vital importance in the subtropical and tropical countries of Africa, the Middle and Far East, and Latin America. It has been estimated that the population of China harbors 130,000 tons of intestinal worms (Dubos, 1971). Those helminths with major economic impact will be considered here, after some general remarks on parasitism. Other parasites will be covered in Section Two.

Worms are classified morphologically as roundworms, the **nematodes,** flatworms, the **cestodes** ("tapeworms") and flukes, the **trematodes.** Most helminths have evolved rather elaborate life cycles, often requiring intermediate hosts and almost always involving the ingestion by the definitive host of viable eggs **(ova)** or encysted **larvae.** Some larval forms can penetrate the skin directly. Many worms parasitize the intestinal tract, and one vital step in their life cycle is exposure of the new host to the feces of the carrier. Cultural practices such as the use of human feces as fertilizer ("night soil") and inadequate washing and cooking of foodstuffs clearly facilitate such infestations.

A final point is the variability of the effect on the host. Some parasites cause profound debilitation whereas others are much more benign in their course. It is tempting to suggest that the latter are better adapted to their host, as it is, after all, to the advantage of the parasite for the host to be in relatively good health. Death of the host means, at best, a search for a new home and, at worst, death for the parasite. The effects of the parasite on the host may be a rough indication of the time over which the genera have been associated.

An exception to the generally tropical distribution of parasitic diseases is **trichinosis,** which is found worldwide. Man acquires the parasite by ingesting larvae, usually in undercooked pork. As with botulism, ethnic groups that prepare food at home are most liable to disease, although the general population is at the mercy of careless commercial food preparers in this respect. Another ethnic group at high risk is the Indians of northern Canada and Alaska, much of whose diet is bear meat. The bears have a high infection rate, and the meat is undercooked because of the scarcity of firewood in these northern climates (Hopps, 1977).

Man is actually an accidental, dead-end host for *Trichinella spiralis,* as continuation of the life cycle is dependent on the ingestion by a new host of muscle-encysted larvae. In man, the larvae encyst throughout the body, and the symptoms are referable to the involved organs and are relative to the severity of the infection and the resistance of the host.

Hookworms are intestinal roundworms which have taken advantage of another cultural practice, that of going barefoot (or more properly, disdain of the cultural artifact, shoes). This ancient disease, which has been identified in pre-Columbian Peruvian mummies (Allison et al., 1974), is widespread in the New and Old World. The life cycle consists of the passage of the ova with the feces, the hatching of the ova and eventual development of infective larvae in the soil, and the infection of the new host through the skin of the feet.

The symptoms of infection are those of blood loss, i.e., iron deficiency anemia and physical and mental retardation. Cultural and geographic factors play important roles in the expression of the disease, however. If iron intake is high enough, anemia does not develop. Bushmen absorb enough iron from their iron cooking pots to prevent the development of anemia, even in pregnant women (Baumslag and Petering, 1976). In Ethiopia, grain is thrashed by placing it on the ground and having oxen trample it. The grain, low in iron itself, is contaminated by the soil, which has a high iron content. In contrast, the soil of the Amazon River basin has been leached of most of its minerals, and manioc, the vegetable which is the major food source for most of the Indians of this region, is very low in iron. As a result, anemia is profound in hookworm disease, with a high death rate.

Prevention of the disease is accomplished by separation of humans and sewage, and by the wearing of shoes. Such measures have virtually eradicated the disease in the southern United States, but it remains common elsewhere.

The **tapeworms** are large (up to 20 feet long), flat worms that inhabit the intestinal tract and occasionally invade the viscera. The worms are acquired by the ingestion of larvae in the undercooked meat of an intermediate host. Ethnic dietary practices play a major role in the distribution of the beef, pork and fish tapeworms. Devout Moslems and Jews eat no pork, and are liable only to accidental infestation by the pork tapeworm. Home preparers of sausage may not cook the meat adequately and acquire a parasite in this fashion, as may those who eat **beef tartare.** Ingestion of raw fish, such as the Japanese **sushi,** can lead to a fish tapeworm *(Diphyllobothrium latum)* infestation. The symptoms of infestation are abdominal pain, diarrhea and anemia. The fish tapeworm specifically absorbs large amounts of vitamin B_{12}, causing a type of pernicious anemia that is not responsive to replacement therapy.

A smaller tapeworm is *Echinococcus granulosus,* which usually affects sheep and dogs and is an accidental parasite of man. Human infection usually represents a termination of the worm's life cycle. However, in Africa, certain tribes such as the Masai believe death brings bad luck to a dwelling, and the dying are placed in the bush to be disposed of by jackals and other scavengers. The jackals ingest the worms and then deposit contaminated feces as they follow the Masai cattle herds. These cattle represent the wealth of the Masai and are rarely slaughtered, but the Masai do drink their blood, mixed with milk. To stop the bleeding, they scoop up earth in their hands, mix it with saliva, and apply it to the bleeding skin wounds. This technique leads to ingestion of eggs deposited on the ground by the jackals and perpetuation of the parasite life cycle (Hopps, 1977).

Another ancient disease is **schistosomiasis.** Schistosomes are blood flukes, the various species of which infest the blood vessels of the intestinal tract and/or urinary system. The disease has been documented in Ancient Egypt on philologic grounds by Jonckheere (1944).

The hieroglyphic term ⸺ (aaa) occurs frequently in the medical papyri, referring to a disorder marked by blood in the urine, **hematuria,** a characteristic sign of schistosomal involvement of the urinary tract. Even more conclusive is the demonstration of schistosome ova in the intestinal tract and liver (Reyman et al., 1976), and the kidneys (Ruffer, 1910) of several Egyptian mummies. The etiology of the disease remained unknown until established in 1851 by Bilharz; hence, the alternative name of bilharzia or bilharziasis.

The life cycle of the schistosome, three species of which infect man, is an extremely complex one. The ova are passed in urine or feces and hatch in water into free-swimming larval forms, **miracidia,** which then enter an aquatic snail intermediate host. In the snail the larvae develop into **cercariae,** which pass through the skin of the snail into the water. This free-swimming form is infective for man, by penetrating the skin directly. The cercariae migrate by the blood stream to the liver and then travel against the blood flow to their sites of preference. Although there is some overlap, in general *S. japonicum* resides in the inferior mesenteric veins, *S. mansoni* in the superior mesenteric veins, and *S. haematobium* in the vesical (bladder) and inferior mesenteric veins. In these locations the organisms develop into adult worms, male and female living in intimate association for up to 30 years. Many thousands of ova are produced and extruded out of the vascular system. Some enter the bladder or intestinal lumen for passage out of the body, to complete the life cycle.

Chronic anemia results from the leakage of blood that accompanies the extrusion of the ova, but the pathologic effects of schistosomiasis are predominantly due to those ova which remain in the tissues and embolize throughout the body rather than passing out via the intestinal or urinary tracts. A foreign body reaction is provoked in the tissues, and the inflammation and subsequent fibrosis compromise organ function.

Involvement of the liver produces cirrhosis. There is considerable individual variation in the progress of the disease, and Bina et al. (1978) have shown that Brazilian blacks are relatively resistant to the development of cirrhosis in the face of severe schistosomal infection. These investigators postulate a genetic factor preventing hepatic fibrosis, but this hypothesis is difficult to reconcile with the propensity of blacks to develop excessive fibrosis in other anatomic sites (Polednak, 1974).

Individuals with schistosomal cirrhosis are liable to all the complications of that disease (see Chapter 6). The Egyptian mummy reported by Reyman et al. (1976) was that of a teenaged boy who probably died of a ruptured spleen secondary to schistosomal cirrhosis.

The cirrhotic liver is unable to metabolize the small amounts of estrogen normally produced in the adrenal glands. In countries with high rates of schistosomiasis, enlargement of the breasts in males, **gynecomastia,** is common, and cancer of the male breast is not the rarity that it is in temperate climates. It is intriguing that the ancient Egyptian god of the Nile, Hapi, is usually depicted on papyri and temple walls as a male with breasts.

Involvement of the urinary bladder predisposes to bladder cancer, another common tumor in Egypt. Other environmental factors may be operating, however, as other areas of endemic schistosomiasis do not show an increased bladder cancer rate.

The highly evolved life cycle of the schistosomes is dependent on very specific environmental and cultural features, being geared to a population that spends much of its time immersed in water. The irrigation civilizations of China and Japan and the flood-based agricultural system of ancient Egypt clearly fit this picture. It is attractive to postulate the evolution of human schistosomiasis from parasites affecting water fowl. Modern duck schistosomes are capable of penetrating human skin, but do not go into the deeper tissues. They cause only a local reaction, the "swimmer's itch" well known to midwestern Americans.

Control of the disease can be achieved by proper sanitation (with the usual problems that this seemingly simple approach engenders). Snail control is possible, but in Egypt the recent building of the Aswan Dam has created a vast breeding area for aquatic snails and has allowed for perennial irrigation. Avoidance of infected water prevents the disease, but the use of the Nile for drinking water, sewage disposal, washing and agricultural purposes ensures exposure of humans to parasites. The infection has increased in incidence to an almost universal level (Halpern, 1970). The outlook for control, in the face of established customs and practices, is dim. The effect of this chronic debilitating disease on the population, economy and history of Egypt and other countries is virtually incalculable.

NEOPLASIA

Neoplasm means "new growth" and this class of diseases is among the most important in modern societies, being responsible in its malignant form, **cancer,** for the deaths of over 300,000 Americans each year. The word "tumor," strictly defined, means a swelling of any type, but in practice has come to refer only to neoplasms. There are many other terms used synonymously or euphemistically for cancer, such as mitotic lesion, CA, etc.; in this respect modern medicine is in accord with the ancient Egyptian principle that the name is as evil as the reality.

The basic subdivision of neoplasms is into benign and malignant forms. Benign tumors grow slowly, remain localized and rarely cause anything other than cosmetic problems. Malignant tumors, or cancers, grow rapidly and have the ability to invade locally and to spread throughout the body, **metastasize,** and kill the individual.

Benign tumors are generally named by adding the suffix "-oma" to the cell type of tumor. Thus we have **fibromas** (fibrous tissue), **myomas** (muscle tissue), etc. This system works well for tumors derived from the soft tissues, but is less useful for the more common epithelial-derived benign (and malignant) tumors, which usually are named on the basis of their macroscopic or microscopic appearance. Examples are glandular tumors, **adenomas,** and papillary tumors, **papillomas.**

Malignant tumors follow a similar scheme. Those deriving from the mesenchymal tissues are called **sarcomas,** e.g., fibrosarcoma, osteosarcoma, etc. Malignant epithelial tumors, again much more frequent, are called **carcinomas.** The most common of these tumors are: **squamous cell** carcinomas, composed of cells similar to those seen on the skin surface, and arising in sites such as the skin or lung; and **adenocarcinomas,** malignant glandular tumors, usually arising in the gastrointestinal tract. Any tissue of the body is a potential site of tumor development.

The criteria of malignancy generally are well defined, although problems can arise in assessing individual tumors. Macroscopically, a tumor is usually seen as a discolored (often white or yellow) area replacing the normal structure, or a growth protruding from a normally flat surface. Microscopically, the malignant cells tend to grow in an unorganized fashion, producing what amounts to a parody of the appearance of the normal tissue. The individual cells of a tumor have large irregular nuclei which contain more nucleic acid than normal, and hence are dark staining **(hyperchromatic).** An important point is related to the rapid growth of malignant tumors. Many more mitotic figures are seen than is normal, and many of these mitoses are abnormal in appearance. These various cytologic criteria have become more important with the development of the Papanicolaou (Pap) smear. Tumor cells are less cohesive than normal cells. They are shed easily from surfaces such as the uterine cervix and can be examined for the cytologic evidence of malignancy (Papanicolaou and Traut, 1943).

Occasionally, tumors originate from two germ cell layers, **mixed tumors,** or all three layers, **teratomas.** Again, these may be benign or malignant.

Behavior of Neoplasms

Benign tumors, as noted above, remain localized. Such lesions cause damage only under special conditions. If they are in a critical location, they may obstruct the flow of bile or cerebrospinal fluid. The tumor may elaborate products that can be life-threatening if present in excess, such as certain hormones.

Although malignant tumors have the potential for local invasion and distant metastasis, such growth can be very erratic. Some tumors, such as certain lung cancers, bone tumors or acute leukemias, grow and kill in a matter of weeks or a few months, whereas carcinoma of the cervix appears to have a latent period of 10 to 15 years between its inception and the development of a clinically apparent lesion. Still other tumors, such as thyroid, kidney or breast cancer, can be removed and yet reappear many years later.

Tumors metastasize to other organs via the lymphatics or blood vessels. Generally, carcinomas spread through the lymphatics and sarcomas by the blood vessels, but either cancer can spread by either route. The sites most frequently involved are local lymph nodes, the lung and the liver. Again, there are idiosyncrasies of individual tumors. Breast cancer spreads to the bone and the ovaries, lung cancer to the adrenals, and so on. Metastases to the spleen are quite rare, despite its rich blood supply. The reasons for these predilections are poorly, or not at all, understood. The important fact is that once distant metastases are present, a tumor is generally beyond surgical treatment.

Carcinogenesis

A number of agents have been experimentally identified as causing cancer in animals or proposed as causing cancer in humans. These include viruses, chemicals, irradiation, nutritional factors, hormones, trace elements and chronic irritation. The suspected etiologic factors in a wide variety of human cancers are covered in a comprehensive review by Higginson (1977). Hereditary factors also seem to be involved in certain tumors.

Geographic differences in tumor incidence suggest causation or a modifying influence by environmental factors. Lung cancer is the most common fatal cancer in the United States and England, but is much less common in Iceland and Japan, where half the cancers in men originate in the stomach. Half of the cancer deaths among the Bantu are due to liver cancer, a rare disease in Europe and the United States. Variations within counties and between social groups also implicate environmental factors (Dubos, 1971). The Bantu of southern Africa make a potent snuff by adding the ashes of plants to powdered tobacco, and the soil and plants have been found to contain high levels of chromium, a known carcinogen (Baumslag and Keen, 1972). It is not surprising that cancer of the maxillary sinus (which communicates with the nose) is the commonest respiratory tract cancer of the Bantu (Keen, 1964).

Respiratory and skin cancer mortality in the United States is highest in counties in which the petroleum industry is most concentrated (Blot et al., 1977). It is also discouraging that asbestos, another known carcinogen, has been found to be widely distributed in home repair materials (Rohl et al., 1975), and that cancer mortality in Louisiana is positively associated with drinking water obtained from the Mississippi River (Page et al., 1976).

A final point is that spontaneous tumors are rare in nonhuman primates and virtually unheard of in the great apes (McClure, 1973; Siebold and Wolf, 1973). The current working hypothesis is that there is no single etiology of cancer in man, and that a cancer can be due to any one of the agents listed above or to the synergistic action of several of them.

There is much evidence that cancer is a relatively modern disease. Tumors are mentioned in the Egyptian medical papyri, but have been interpreted by some authorities as simply swellings or perhaps varicose veins. Cancer's crab-like nature was noted by the Greeks c. 200 A.D., but the first reports in the scientific literature of a number of distinctive tumors have been only in the relatively recent past. These include Hodgkin's disease in 1832 (Holleb, 1973), multiple myeloma in 1840 (Clamp, 1967), cancer of the nasal passages in snuff users in 1761 (Redmond, 1970) and cancer of the scrotum in chimney sweeps by Pott in 1775 (Shimkin, 1975). Sir Percival Pott's discovery of the relationship of soot to scrotal cancer is considered to be the first recognition of an environmentally determined tumor.

Comparative and paleopathologic evidence also point in the direction of cancer being a "new" disease. As mentioned above, tumors are rare in apes. Gross diagnoses of cancer in archeologic human skeletal material have been made but not verified microscopically. Only three microscopic diagnoses of tumors in mummified tissue have been made, and two of these were benign skin tumors (Sandison, 1967; Zimmerman, 1976, 1977a). Malignant melanoma, a skin cancer, has been tentatively (and not very convincingly) diagnosed in several Peruvian mummies (Urteaga and Pack, 1966); this constitutes the sole microscopic evidence for cancer in antiquity.

It has been suggested that the short life span of individuals in antiquity precluded the development of cancer. Although this statistical construct is true, many persons did live to a sufficiently advanced age to show other degenerative diseases, such as atherosclerosis, Paget's disease of bone and degenerative joint disease. In addition, it must be remembered that, at least in modern populations, tumors such as osteosarcoma and leukemia primarily afflict the young.

Another explanation offered for the lack of tumors in ancient remains is that tumors might not be well preserved. Experimental studies have demonstrated that mummification preserves the diagnostic features of malignancy, and that tumors are actually better preserved than normal tissues (Zimmerman, 1977b). In spite of this experimental finding, examination of hundreds of mummies from all areas of the world has not yet yielded one convincing case of cancer.

Recent statistics indicate that approximately 17 per cent of deaths in the United States are due to cancer (Schottenfeld, 1975). In an ancient population, lacking surgical intervention, evidence of cancer should be present in essentially all cases. The virtual absence of malignancies in ancient tissues must be interpreted as indicating their rarity or perhaps absence in antiquity. It has been estimated that up to 75 per cent of human cancers are related to environmental factors (Lilienfeld et al., 1967), and these historical studies suggest that such factors are limited to societies affected by modern industrialization.

REFERENCES

Abelson, A. E. (1976): Altitude and fertility. Hum. Biol. *48*:83–92.

Ackerknecht, E. H. (1973): Therapeutics from the Primitives to the 20th Century. Hafner, New York.

Alland, A., Jr. (1970): Adaptation in Cultural Evolution: An Approach to Medical Anthropology. Columbia University Press, New York.

Allison, A. C. (1954): Protection afforded by the sickle cell trait against subtertian malarial infection. Br. Med. J. *1*:290–294.

Allison, M. J., Gerszten, E. and H. P. Dalton (1974): Paleopathology in preColumbian Americans. Lab. Invest. *30*:407–408.

Allison, M. J., Pezzia, A., Hasegawa, I. I. et al. (1974): A case of hookworm infestation in a preColumbian American. Am. J. Phys. Anthropol. *41*:103–106.

Baumslag, N. and P. Keen (1972): Trace elements in soil and plants and antral cancer. Arch. Environ. Health *25*:23–25.

Baumslag, N. and H. G. Petering (1976): Trace metal studies in Bushman hair. Arch. Environ. Health *25*:254–257.

Beidelmann, T. O. (1971): The Kaguru: A Matrilineal People of East Africa. Holt, Rhinehart and Winston, New York.

Bina, J. C., Tavares-Neto, J., Prata, A. et al. (1978): Greater resistance to development of severe schistosomiasis in Brazilian negroes. Hum. Biol. *50*:41–49.

Black, F. L. (1975): Infectious diseases in primitive societies. Science *187*:515–518.

Blot, W. J., Brinton, L. A., Fraumeni, J. F. et al. (1977): Cancer mortality in United States counties with petroleum industries. Science *198*:51–53.

Breasted, J. H. (1930): The Edwin Smith Surgical Papyrus. University of Chicago Press, Chicago.

Buikstra, J. E. (1977): Biochemical dimensions of archeological study: a regional perspective. *In* Biocultural Adaptation in Prehistoric America. R. L. Blakely, ed. University of Georgia Press, Athens, Georgia, pp. 67–84.

Carter, H. R. (1931): Yellow Fever: An Epidemiological and Historical Survey of its Place of Origin. Williams and Wilkins, Baltimore.

Clamp, J. R. (1967): Some aspects of the first recorded case of multiple myeloma. Lancet *2*:1354–1356.

Coatney, G. R., Collins, W. G., McWilson, W. et al. (1971): The Primate Malarias. National Institutes of Health, Bethesda, Md.

Cockburn, T. A. (1967): Infectious Diseases: Their Evolution and Eradication. Charles C Thomas, Springfield, Ill.

Cockburn, T. A. (1971): Infectious diseases in ancient populations. Curr. Anthropol. *12*:45–62.

Cook, S. F. (1978): The significance of disease in the extermination of the New England Indians. Hum. Biol. *45*:485–508.

Curran, R. C. and D. G. Harnden (1972): The Pathological Basis of Medicine. Saunders, Philadelphia.

Dubos, R. (1971): Man Adapting. Yale University Press, New Haven.

Elsdon-Dew, R. (1946): Some aspects of amebiasis in Africa. S. Afr. Med. J. *20*:580, 620.

Grahn, S. and J. Kratchman (1963): Variations in neonatal death rate and birthweight in the United States and possible relations to environmental radiation, geology and altitude. Am. J. Hum. Genet. *15*:329–352.

Green, L. H., Cohen, S. I. and G. Kurland (1976): Fatal myocardial infarction in marathon racing. Ann. Intern. Med. *84*:704–706.

Halpern, M. (1970): The Politics of Social Change in the Middle East and North Africa. Princeton University Press, Princeton.

Harris, J. E. and K. Weeks (1973): X-Raying the Pharaohs. Scribner's, New York.

Higginson, J. (1977): The role of the pathologist in environmental medicine and public health: a review. Am. J. Pathol. *86*:460–484.

Holleb, A. I., ed. (1973): Classics in oncology: Thomas Hodgkin (1798–1866). CA *23*:52–60.

Hopps, H. C. (1977): Geographic pathology. *In* Pathology, 7th ed. W.A.D. Anderson and J. M. Kissane, eds. Mosby, St. Louis, pp. 692–736.

Jarcho, S. (1973): Medical numismatic notes, IX: coins of the leper colony at Culion and of the Philippine Health Service. Bull N.Y. Acad. Med. *49*:156–159.

Jonckheere, F. (1944): Une Maladie Egyptienne: L'Hematurie Parasitaire. Fond. Egypt. R. Elisabeth, Brussels.

Keen, P. (1964): Carcinoma of the antrum in the South African Bantu. UICC Monogr. Ser. *1*:95–100.

Lanning, C. P. (1967): Peru Before the Incas. Prentice-Hall, Englewood Cliffs, New Jersey.

Lechin, F., Van der Dys, B., Pena, C. et al. (1973): A study of some immunological and clinical characteristics of gastritis, gastric ulcer, and duodenal ulcer in three racial groups of the Venezuelan population. Am. J. Phys. Anthropol. *39*:369–374.

Lilienfeld, A. M., Pedersen, E. and J. E. Dowd (1967): Cancer Epidemiology: Methods of Study. Johns Hopkins Press, Baltimore.

Livingstone, F. B. (1969): Gene frequency lines of the B hemoglobin locus in various human populations and their simulation by models involving differential selection. Hum. Biol. *41*:223–236.

Long, E. R. (1928): A History of Pathology. Williams and Wilkins, Baltimore.

Loomis, W. F. (1970): Rickets. Sci. Am. *223*, no. 6:76–91.

Mazess, R. B. (1970): Cardiorespiratory characteristics and adaptations to high altitudes. Am. J. Phys. Anthropol. *32*:267–278.

Mazzur, S. (1970): Behavior and disease: a possible approach. Am. J. Phys. Anthropol. *32*:309–314.

McClung, J. (1969): Effects of High Altitude on Human Birth: Observations on Mothers, Placentas and the Newborn in Two Peruvian Populations. Harvard University Press, Cambridge.

McClure, H. M. (1973): Tumors in nonhuman primates during a six-year period in the Yerkes Primate Center Colony. Am. J. Physiol. *38*:425–430.

Mitchell, J. K. (1900): Study of a mummy affected with anterior poliomyelitis. Trans. Assoc. Am. Physicians *15*:134–136.

Møller-Christiansen, V. (1961): Bone Changes in Leprosy. Munksgaard, Copenhagen.

Motulsky, A. G. (1971): Metabolic polymorphisms and the role of infectious diseases in human evolution. *In* Human Populations, Genetic Variation, and Evolution. L. N. Morris, ed. Chandler, San Francisco, pp. 222–252.

Murray, M. J. and A. B. Murray (1977): Starvation suppression and refeeding activation of infection: an ecological necessity? Lancet *1*:123–125.

Newman, M. T. (1976): Aboriginal New World epidemiology and medical care, and the impact of Old World disease imports. Am. J. Phys. Anthropol. *43*:667–672.

Norris, J. (1977): East or west? The geographic origin of the black death. Bull. Hist. Med. *51*:1–24.

Page, T., Harris, R. H. and S. S. Epstein (1976): Drinking water and cancer mortality in Louisiana. Science *193*:55–57.

Papanicolaou, G. and H. F. Traut (1943): Diagnosis of Uterine Cancer by the Vaginal Smear. Commonwealth Fund, New York.

Polednak, A. P. (1974): Connective tissue responses in negroes in relation to disease. Am. J. Phys. Anthropol. *41*:49–58.

Redmond, E. D. (1970): Tobacco and cancer — the first clinical report, 1761. N. Engl. J. Med. *282*:18–23.

Reyman, T. A., Barraco, R. A. and A. Cockburn (1976): Histopathological examination of an Egyptian mummy. Bull. N.Y. Acad. Med. *52*:505–516.

Riesman, D. (1935): The Story of Medicine in the Middle Ages. Hoeber, New York.

Risse, G. B. (1972): Rational Egyptian surgery: a cranial injury discussed in the Edwin Smith Papyrus. Bull. N.Y. Acad. Med. *48*:919–929.

Robbins, S. L. (1974): Pathologic Basis of Disease. Saunders, Philadelphia, p. 55.

Rohl, A. N., Langer, A. M., Selikoff, I. J. et al. (1975): Exposure to asbestos in the use of consumer spackling, patching, and taping compounds. Science *189*:551–553.

Rosebury, T. (1971): Microbes and Morals. Viking, New York.

Roth, E. F., Friedman, M., Ueda, Y. et al. (1978): Sickling rates of human AS red cells infected in vitro with *Plasmodium falciparum* malaria. Science *202*:650–652.

Ruffer, M. A. (1910): Note on the presence of "*Bilharzia haemotobia*" in Egyptian mummies of the twentieth dynasty (1250–1000 B.C.). Br. Med. J. *1*:16.

St. Hoyme, L. E. (1969): On the origins of new world paleopathology. Am. J. Phys. Anthropol. *31*:295–302.

Sandison, A. T. (1967): Diseases of the skin. *In* Disease in Antiquity. D. Brothwell and A. T. Sandison, eds. Charles C Thomas, Springfield, Ill., pp. 449–456.

Sandison, A. T. (1970): The study of mummified and dried human tissues. *In* Science in Archaeology, 2nd ed. D. R. Brothwell and E. Higgs, eds. Praeger, New York, pp. 490–502.

Sandison, A. T. (1972): Evidence of infectious disease. J. Hum. Evol. *1*:213–224.

Schottenfeld, D. (1975): Introduction — the magnitude of cancer. *In* Cancer Epidemiology and Prevention: Current Concepts. D. Schottenfeld, ed. Charles C Thomas, Springfield, Ill., pp. 3–28.

Scrimshaw, N. S. and C. Tejada (1970): Pathology of living Indians as seen in Guatemala. *In* Handbook of Middle American Indians, Vol. 9: Physical Anthropology. T. D. Stewart, vol. ed. University of Texas Press, Austin, pp. 203–225.

Shimkin, M. D. (1975): Some historical landmarks in cancer epidemiology. *In* Cancer Epidemiology and Prevention: Current Concepts. D. Schottenfeld, ed. Charles C Thomas, Springfield, Ill., pp. 60–74.

Siebold, H. R. and R. H. Wolf (1973): Neoplasms and proliferative lesions in 1065 nonhuman primate necropsies. Lab. Anim. Sci. *23*:533–539.

Sigerist, H. E. (1970): Civilization and Disease. University of Chicago Press, Chicago.

Sigerist, H. E. (1971): The Great Doctors. Dover, New York.

Smith, D. G. and R. S. Guinto (1977): Leprosy and assortative mating on Mactan Island, Philippines. Med. Anthropol. *1*, #4, pt. 4:76–86.

Smith, G. S. and M. R. Zimmerman (1975): Tattooing found on a 1600 year old frozen mummified body from St. Lawrence Island, Alaska. Am. Antiq. 40:434–437.

Stearn, E. W. and E. Allen (1945): The Effect of Smallpox on the Destiny of the Amerindians. Humphries, Boston.

Strouhal, E. (1976): Tumors in the remains of Ancient Egyptians. Am. J. Phys. Anthropol. 45:613–620.

Tapp, E., Curry, A. and C. Anfield (1975): Sand pneumoconiosis in an Egyptian mummy. Br. J. Med. 2:276.

Tobias, P. V. (1974): An anthropologist looks at malaria. S. Afr. Med. J. 48:1124–1127.

Urteaga, O. and G. T. Pack (1966): On the antiquity of melanoma. Cancer 19:607–610.

Verbov, J. L. (1976): Skin diseases in the Old Testament. Practitioner 216:229–236.

Weiner, J. S. (1971): The Natural History of Man. Universe Books, New York.

Werner, S. B., Pappagianis, D., Heindl, I. et al. (1972): An epidemic of coccidioidomycosis among archeology students in Northern California. N. Engl. J. Med. 286:507–512.

Wiesenfeld, S. L. (1967): Sickle-cell trait in human biological and social evolution. Science 157:1134–1140.

Willis, M. F. and M. F. Warburton (1974): Measles susceptibility in two Pacific atoll populations; epidemiological factors and response to live attenuated measles virus. Med. J. Aust. 1:780–793.

Winchester, A. M. (1972): Genetics: A Survey of the Principles of Heredity, 4th ed. Houghton Mifflin, Cambridge, Mass.

Wolf, E. R. (1959): Sons of the Shaking Earth. University of Chicago Press, Chicago.

Wolfe, M. S. (1976): Management of the traveler to exotic places. Milit. Med. 141:831–836.

Zimmerman, M. R. (1976): A Paleopathologic and Archeologic Investigation of the Human Remains of the Dra Aba el-Nagu Site, Egypt: Based on an Experimental Study of Mummification. Ph.D. Thesis, University of Pennsylvania, Philadelphia.

Zimmerman, M. R. (1977a): The mummies of the tomb of Nebwenenef: paleopathology and archeology. J. Am. Res. Center Egypt 14:33–36.

Zimmerman, M. R. (1977b): An experimental study of mummification pertinent to the antiquity of cancer. Cancer 40:1358–1362.

Zimmerman, M. R. and G. S. Smith (1975): A probable case of accidental inhumation of 1600 years ago. Bull. N. Y. Acad. Med. 51:828–837.

Zinsser, H. (1963): Rats, Lice and History. Little, Brown, Boston.

Zook, B. C., Sauer, R. M., Bush, M. et al. (1973): Lead poisoning in zoo-dwelling primates. Am. J. Phys. Anthropol. 38:415–424.

Section Two

ORGAN SYSTEMS IN HEALTH, DISEASE AND CULTURAL CONTEXT

four

The Cardiovascular System

ANATOMY AND PHYSIOLOGY

The cardiovascular system (Fig. 4.1) consists of the heart and its attendant blood and lymphatic vessels. The mammalian body has a double circulatory system, being divided into the **systemic** (left-sided or greater) and **pulmonic** (right-sided or lesser) circulations. Accessory to these circuits are the **portal venous system,** flowing from the intestinal tract to the liver, and the **lymphatics,** a drainage system for acellular lymphatic fluid which parallels the blood vessels and empties into the venous system.

Venous blood, deoxygenated and containing metabolic waste products, including carbon dioxide, is drained from the head by the superior vena cava and from the rest of the body by the inferior vena cava. The venae cavae empty into the right atrium of the heart. From this thin-walled collecting chamber the blood passes through the tricuspid valve into the right ventricle, a muscular chamber which forcibly ejects the blood through the pulmonic valve into the pulmonary artery and on into the lungs. Within the lungs carbon dioxide is lost and oxygen acquired. The oxygenated blood returns to the heart via the pulmonary veins, draining into the left atrium. After passing through the mitral valve, the blood enters the left ventricle, is ejected through the aortic valve and enters the aorta, the major vessel exiting from the heart. Branching from the aorta are the smaller arteries and arterioles which pass the blood on to the capillaries in the tissues. In these thin-walled microscopic vessels oxygen and glucose are extracted from the blood, and carbon dioxide and metabolic wastes are taken up, for eventual disposition by lungs, kidneys and liver. The capillaries coalesce to form venules and veins, completing the circuit by draining into the venae cavae.

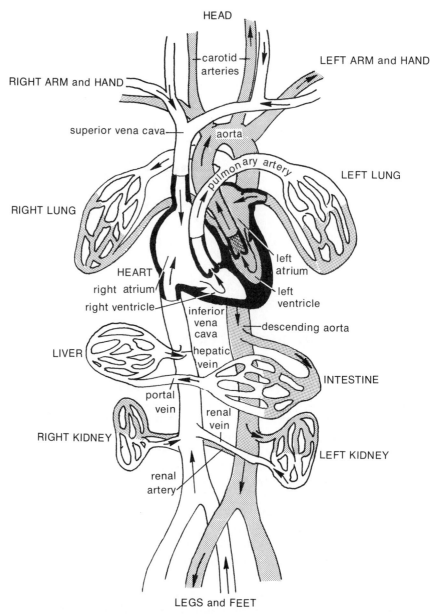

Figure 4.1   Schematic diagram of the human circulatory system. The shaded area indicates oxygenated blood. The arrows indicate the direction of blood flow.

The action of the heart is that of a muscular pump driving the blood through the arterial side of the circulatory system, abetted by elastic tissue in the arteries. Venous return is accomplished by a combination of gravity, compression of veins by skeletal muscles, and simple semilunar valves controlling the direction of flow. The valves within the heart also direct flow and prevent regurgitation of the blood, unless pathologically altered.

The output of the heart is dependent on the heart rate and on the volume of the heart. Both of these factors may increase when extra physiologic or pathologic demands are made on the heart. In addition, the actual force of contraction may increase.

Blood Pressure is divided into a **systolic** and a **diastolic** phase. The former is, roughly, a measure of the contractile effort of the heart; the latter is related to the expansive capacity of the aorta and large arteries, and the degree of peripheral resistance in the arterioles. The normal value is usually given, in millimeters of mercury (mm. Hg.), as 110/70, but there is a wide range dependent on age (increase with increased age) and sex (females are lower). Hypertension is diagnosed if the systolic pressure is over 140 or the diastolic over 90. An elevated diastolic blood pressure is an indication of serious vascular disease, whereas an elevated systolic pressure is of less clinical significance.

The blood supply to the heart itself is by the coronary artery system. When the blood is pumped from the left ventricle to the aorta in **systole,** the contraction phase of the heart, the aortic valve leaflets are pushed open. In the relaxation phase, **diastole,** the rebound of the elastic aorta forces the blood both further on and back toward the heart. The semilunar cusps of the aortic valve catch this back flow and are closed by the diastolic pressure. At the base of two of the cusps are the openings, the **ostia,** of the two coronary arteries, and the diastolic pressure fills these vessels. In this fashion the coronary system is filled while the heart is in a relaxed state. A much higher pressure would be necessary if the coronary arteries had to be filled during systole. Such a higher pressure would greatly increase the likelihood of the development of coronary arteriosclerosis.

The portal venous system drains blood from the intestines, rich in nutrients, to the liver, where the nutrients are metabolized. Because of the high volume of the portal venous flow, the liver gains a significant proportion of its oxygen via this route.

Tissue fluids drain into the lymphatic system, a network of fine vessels roughly paralleling the veins. Along the lymphatics are lymph nodes, which act as filters for bacteria and other particulate matter, including tumor particles. The lymphatics are thus of obvious concern in cancer surgery. They eventually drain into the **thoracic duct,** which empties into the venous system in the neck.

PATHOLOGY

Congenital Heart Disease

The embryology of the heart involves the twisting of a straight tube and the development of valves to produce a four-chambered organ with two inflows and two outflows. This complicated mechanism can be affected by both genetic and environmental factors to produce a great variety of anomalies. Some conditions, such as defects in the septa between the right and left sides of the heart, are thought to be purely genetically determined. Intrauterine environmental hazards such as rubella (German measles) and drugs such as thalidomide and cortisone are also well known, and may act either directly or synergistically with genetic factors in causing congenital heart disease.

The specific types of cardiac defects are too numerous to be covered in this brief review, but a consideration of the changes in cardiopulmonary circulation at birth will clarify some of the clinical consequences of certain congenital defects. The fetus does not needs its lungs, the placenta assuming the function of oxygenation of the fetal blood. Circulation to the fetal lung is shut off to a large extent by two mechanisms: constriction of the pulmonary arterial bed, raising the blood pressure in the lungs; and a connection between the pulmonary artery and the aorta, the **ductus arteriosus.** The major portion of the outflow from the right heart is thus directed not through the lungs, but rather through the ductus to the systemic circulation. At birth the airways and vascular system of the lungs open, dropping the pulmonary blood pressure and allowing flow into the lungs. Shortly after birth the ductus becomes obliterated, completing the shift to the extrauterine circulatory pattern.

In some individuals the ductus remains open after birth. As the pressure in the systemic circulation is higher than in the pulmonary circuit, the result of this abnormal communication is a "left-to-right" shunt, i.e., blood flowing from the aorta to the pulmonary artery, to be recycled through the lung. Initial symptoms are weakness, usually expressed in children by squatting, due to an insufficient amount of blood reaching the tissues. If the disorder is uncorrected, the large volume of blood going to the lungs under systemic pressure eventually raises the pulmonary blood pressure, to the point where there can be reversal of flow in the ductus, a "right-to-left" shunt. If this shunt becomes severe, the amount of unoxygenated blood in the systemic circulation will rise to the point at which **cyanosis** (blue discoloration of the lips and extremities) will develop.

Operative therapy consists simply of ligating the ductus early in life, before the lungs have been damaged. This is a simple procedure in a society with a modern health care system.

Certain other anomalies cause a right-to-left shunt and cyanosis from birth, the so-called "blue babies." Again, operative therapy is available for most of these conditions.

Coronary (Ischemic) Heart Disease

The muscle of the heart, the **myocardium,** is dependent on the coronary artery system for its blood supply, as no oxygen is extracted from the blood within the chambers. Narrowing of the coronaries, in western society usually secondary to atherosclerosis (Fig. 4.2A), reduces the blood supply of the myocardium, **ischemia. Atherosclerosis** is a progressive process, the complications of which account for over half of all deaths in the United States. If the course is protracted, diffuse scarring **(fibrosis)** of the myocardium results. Clinically the

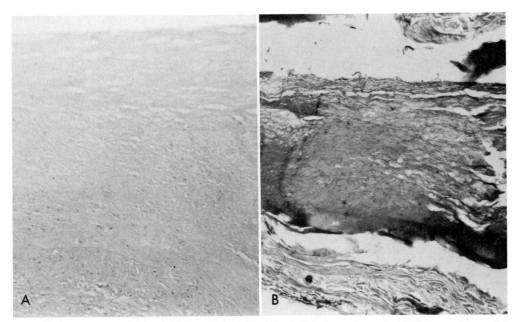

Atherosclerosis, in *A*, a contemporary individual and *B*, an Eskimo woman who died c. 400 A.D. The pathologic change is identical in both cases. Cholesterol has accumulated in the vessel walls. As the cholesterol washes out in processing, it is represented in the section as empty clefts. Hematoxylin and eosin stain, × 100.

Figure 4.2

condition is referred to as **arteriosclerotic heart disease** (ASHD), arteriosclerosis being a more general term for any disease causing narrowing of arteries, including the atherosclerotic deposition of cholesterol and lipids.

Angina pectoris is pain in the chest due to a transient coronary insufficiency. Severe coronary insufficiency can lead to death, **necrosis,** of heart muscle and a "heart attack" or **myocardial infarction.** The clinical diagnosis is by the characteristic crushing chest pain; specific changes in the electrical activity of the heart, as determined by the electrocardiogram (ECG); and finding leakage of myocardial enzymes into the circulation. Myocardial infarction is a lethal disease, with a five-year survival of only 50 per cent; approximately 25 per cent die within six weeks.

The traditional view that myocardial infarction is secondary to coronary thrombosis has been challenged recently by those (Roberts and Buja, 1972) who feel that the basic process is an increased need for blood flow that cannot be met by a sclerotic coronary system. An infarct results and thrombosis is considered to be a secondary phenomenon. Supportive evidence for this view is seen in the fact that the longer patients survive after infarction, the higher a percentage show coronary thrombosis at autopsy.

Whatever the pathogenetic sequence, the changes in the heart are the same. The muscle becomes necrotic, with a surrounding acute inflammatory reaction. Within a week the inflammation becomes chronic, and healing starts to become evident at about ten days.

Healing is by scar formation and is usually complete by about six weeks.

There are a number of complications of myocardial infarction. The most serious is acute loss of the normal cardiac rhythmic contractions, **arrhythmia,** which may cause markedly decreased cardiac output, shock and death. This sequence accounts for most of the acute deaths seen.

A variety of longer-term complications occur. The tissues surrounding the heart, the **pericardium,** also become inflamed, and this **pericarditis** occasionally resolves by fibrous adhesions that can restrict flow into and out of the heart. The blood in the left ventricle, where most infarcts occur, may stagnate and coagulate on the endocardial surface overlying the infarct. Fragments of this **mural thrombus** have the potential of embolization with the development of infarcts in other organs, such as the brain, kidney and spleen. An infarct can rupture, causing a hemopericardium, cardiac tamponade and death. Occasionally such a rupture is into the right ventricle or through a valve, causing an acute but not catastrophic heart failure amenable to surgical intervention. Finally, the weakened wall of an old infarct can balloon out as an aneurysm, often complicated by mural thrombosis. Again, surgical treatment is available.

There are striking and intriguing geographic, environmental and racial differences in the incidence of ASHD. The disease is several times more prevalent in the United States, Europe, Australia and New Zealand than in Japan, Africa and South America. As Africans adopt western living standards, their rate of ASHD rises toward the Caucasian level (Somers, 1976). City dwellers are afflicted more frequently than rural populations. In the United States, Caucasians have much higher rates than others, and in Israel males of European birth have higher rates than those born in Africa or Asia (Yodfat, 1972). However, it is apparent that a pure racial phenomenon is not involved. Chinese living in the United States have a rate closer to American Caucasians than to Chinese living in China. In general, males are affected earlier and more seriously than females.

Although genetic and environmental factors have been implicated in these differences, the focus is on environment as an area which can be modified. Peacock (1973) has categorized determinant factors for ASHD as personal (sex, age and heredity), behavioral (diet, smoking and exercise), those related to other disease (hypertension, diabetes) and environmental (temperature, noise, air pollution, soft drinking water and many others). Hypertension, obesity, hypercholesterolemia and cigarette smoking have all been clearly demonstrated to be associated with a markedly increased rate of ASHD. The role of the many other factors suggested is much less clear. Even coffee drinking has been implicated as a factor in ASHD (Jick et al., 1973), but the association has been refuted by other studies, for example that of Hennekens et al. (1976). It is likely that the coincidental cigarette is responsible for the apparent association. Another factor in ASHD appears to be a sedentary life style, although the data is epidemiologic and controversial (Enselberg, 1970).

The stress of modern life has also been suggested as a causative factor. Several studies have demonstrated a higher incidence of ASHD in more crowded populations, not only in humans but in crowded zoo populations as well (Dubos, 1971). On the other hand, there is ample evidence of the antiquity of atherosclerosis. Indeed, Nye (1971) has postulated the evolution of ASHD as a population control measure in early human groups, the disease culling out those men who had already fulfilled their reproductive potential and were competing for food and females with the younger men. This postulate is probably unprovable, but paleopathology does give evidence of atherosclerosis. The sudden death of Weshptah, a vizier of the Vth Dynasty of ancient Egypt, as described in his tomb inscription, has been diagnosed as a cerebrovascular accident ("stroke") by Rowling (1961), and Breutsch (1959) interpreted a sudden death depicted on another Egyptian tomb relief as evidence of coronary atherosclerosis and myocardial infarction. This historical evidence is well substantiated by the finding of atherosclerosis in many Egyptian mummies, as summarized by Sandison (1962). Smith (1908) noted severe atherosclerosis of the aorta in the Pharaoh Merneptah, verified microscopically by Shattock (1909). Ruffer (1911) found involvement of all arteries, large and small, to be very common in the hundreds of mummies he examined. Long (1931) demonstrated not only coronary artery disease but also myocardial fibrosis and the renal arteriolar sclerosis of hypertension in a mummy of 1000 B.C. Shaw (1938) noted involvement of the superior mesenteric artery in the mummy of Harmose, of the XVIIIth Dynasty.

More recent studies have yielded similar results. Reyman et al. (1976) demonstrated aortic atherosclerosis in an Egyptian mummy histologically. Radiologic surveys by Gray (1967) and Vyhanek and Strouhal (1975) have shown evidence of the disease, and Harris and Weeks (1973), in a radiologic survey of the Pharaohs in the Cairo Museum, saw calcification of the leg arteries of Amenhotep II and Ramses II.

Atherosclerosis has also been seen in New World mummies. An Aleutian mummy examined by Zimmerman et al. (1971) showed severe involvement of the aorta. An Eskimo body frozen for 1,600 years showed coronary artery disease (Fig. 4.2B) (Zimmerman and Smith, 1975). This pathology was consistent with an atrophic uterus and breasts in considering this woman to have been postmenopausal; atherosclerosis is rare in women during the reproductive years. Williams (1927) diagnosed atherosclerosis in two Peruvian mummies, but Allison's group (1974) have noted this condition to be rare in the Chilean and Peruvian mummies they have examined, suggesting a lower incidence in ancient South America than in modern populations.

In spite of this evidence of antiquity, the medical concept of ASHD and myocardial infarction is clearly a 20th century one (Levenstein, 1975). There is some evidence that Leonardo da Vinci suggested that death might be due to coronary occlusion (Buchwald et al., 1974) but it was not until the 1920s that the death certificate entry of "acute indigestion" was replaced by "acute myocardial infarction."

Hypertensive Heart Disease

Hypertension, as defined above, can be transient, as in physical or psychological stress, or prolonged. If chronic, the eventual effect on the heart is a marked hypertrophy of the left ventricle. The condition is more common in females, the overweight, American blacks, and the offspring of hypertensive parents. Environmental stress also appears to play a role in pathogenesis.

Eventually the hypertrophied myocardium is unable to keep up with the demands placed upon it, and cardiac failure results. The clinical picture of heart failure is primarily due to the accumulation of fluid in the lungs (pulmonary congestion and edema). There is difficulty in breathing, **dyspnea,** particularly when lying down, **orthopnea,** since this position increases the return from the legs to the heart. ASHD frequently complicates the picture.

In contrast to myocardial infarction, **congestive heart failure (CHF)** has been known for centuries. Squill, a plant containing a glycoside that acts on the heart, was used as a medicine by the ancient Egyptians. It is mentioned in Papyrus Ebers (Dawson, 1967) and was used as a diuretic by the Romans (Goodman and Gilman, 1975). Digitalis, the drug of choice in CHF, was mentioned by Welsh physicians in 1250, and first recommended for the treatment of "dropsy" in 1785 by Withering, an English physician and botanist (Ackerknecht, 1973). Withering noted that he had acquired the medication as a family secret from an old woman in Shropshire; the drug represents one of many instances in which a folk remedy has become integrated into the medical armamentarium.

Rheumatic Heart Disease

Rheumatic heart disease (RHD) is one manifestation of a systemic disease that illustrates the potential changes in the interaction between host and parasite. Infection by the streptococcus can produce a variety of clinical pictures, depending to a large extent on the organ involved. Direct infection of the skin causes **erysipelas.** Involvement of the pharynx causes local symptoms ("strep throat") and, as the bacterial toxins are absorbed into the blood stream, an acute febrile illness with a characteristic skin rash, **scarlet fever.** Streptococcal pharyngitis may be followed by arthritis, **chorea** (involuntary movements), or involvement of the heart, **rheumatic fever.** The long history of these diseases is evident in their association with saints, dating back to medieval Europe. Erysipelas is known as St. Anthony's fire, and chorea as St. Vitus' dance.

The myocardial involvement is a hypersensitivity phenomenon. Based on animal studies, it is believed that the streptococcus forms a complex with connective tissue proteins which acts as a foreign material in the body. The result is an autoimmune reaction, with destruction of myocardium and endocardium.

The myocardium may be involved acutely, causing sudden cardiac failure or fatal arrhythmias. The heart valves are often affected in chronic disease, allowing regurgitation, **insufficiency,** or restricting flow, **stenosis.** With aging of the individual, scarring compounds the valvular defects. The typical clinical picture is that of a woman in her 40s or 50s presenting with progressive heart failure. Usually a childhood history of acute rheumatic fever or St. Vitus' dance can be elicited. Relentlessly progressive heart failure, often complicated by infection of the abnormal valves or thrombosis in the dilated cardiac chambers, leads to an early demise.

For several reasons, RHD is of decreasing importance in the western world, although it remains common elsewhere, accounting for 30 per cent of all cardiovascular deaths in Africa (Somers, 1976). Rheumatic fever is less frequently seen now, for unknown reasons. Antibiotic therapy for throat infections has certainly played a role in this changing pattern, but the decline antedates the introduction of antibiotics. As the preantibiotic population ages and dies off, RHD is becoming ever more rare. Those individuals with valvular disease now have available the option of surgical replacement of their valves, a procedure with a remarkably high success rate. Thus, medical and surgical therapy has dramatically changed the picture of an infection already noted to be in a state of evolution.

Bacterial Endocarditis

Normal humans have defense mechanisms capable of quickly clearing relatively large numbers of bacteria from the blood, with little or no ill effects. If there is a damaged site somewhere in the vascular system, bacteria may lodge there and cause an infection. The deformed valves of RHD are a choice site for such an infection. Virulent bacteria are capable of infecting normal valves, and drug addicts, constantly injecting bacteria into their blood stream, are also liable to infection. Most cases of endocarditis are secondary to infections established elsewhere, although dental manipulations and the saprophytic bacteria of the intestinal tract can cause bacteremia and endocarditis.

The infection results in bulky **vegetations** on the surface of the valves. The mitral valve is involved most frequently, then the aortic. In drug addicts, the tricuspid valve is often affected.

The vegetations disrupt flow, causing an abnormal heart sound, a **murmur.** These murmurs are usually of changing character and are superimposed on the murmur caused by the abnormal valve. Complications include perforation of the valve leaflet, causing insufficiency, or extension of the infection through the myocardium to produce a pericarditis. Fragments of the vegetations can break off and embolize to other sites, causing abscesses in the heart (via the coronary arteries), brain, kidneys, spleen, etc. If blood flow is obstructed by the embolus, an infected **septic infarct** results. Emboli may lodge in the blood vessels of the brain, weaken the vessel walls and produce an infected **mycotic aneurysm,** which is liable to fatal rupture. Finally, the kidney may be involved in an allergic type of inflammation.

Treatment is by antibiotic therapy. In drug addicts the infected tricuspid valve may be excised, a procedure which is tolerated surprisingly well. As the right side is a low pressure system, there is minimal regurgitation. When all evidence of infection has cleared, these patients are candidates for surgical valve replacement.

Syphilitic Heart Disease

As noted in Chapter 3, the tertiary stage of syphilis is characterized by involvement of the nervous system and heart, usually some 20 years after the initial infection. The spirochetes have a predilection for the aorta and aortic valve ring, where they cause a necrotic and inflammatory reaction that occludes the small nutrient arteries of these regions. The elastic tissue of the aortic valve ring undergoes ischemic necrosis, and the pressure of systole dilates the valve ring, causing aortic insufficiency (AI). AI results in marked cardiac hypertrophy up to four or five times normal size, **cor bovinum,** with rapidly fatal cardiac failure.

The thoracic aorta undergoes the same pathologic process, and may develop an aneurysm that erodes through surrounding structures and may rupture, with a fatal outcome.

With the control of syphilis by penicillin, syphilitic heart disease has become rare. The recent rise in incidence of syphilitic infection noted by public health authorities may mean an increase in tertiary syphilis in the future.

Miscellaneous Cardiac Diseases

There are many other diseases affecting the heart, but these are all statistically uncommon. Some are worth mentioning in passing. **Tuberculous pericarditis** can result in dense scarring and fibrous obliteration of the pericardium, with obstruction of flow in and out of the heart (**constrictive** pericarditis). There are many **myocardiopathies,** including infiltration by fat or leukemic cells, involvement by diphtheria, typhoid fever and scarlet fever, trichinosis, Chagas' disease, and nutritional and alcoholic cardiomyopathies.

Tumors of the heart are exceedingly rare.

DISEASES OF THE BLOOD VESSELS

Congenital disorders

The vascular system is remarkable for the regularity of its complex development. Occasional variations from normal anatomy are usually of importance only during surgical procedures, when dissection may have to be altered. An example is seen in gallbladder surgery, in which variations in the blood supply to the gallbladder can lead to inadvertent ligation of vessels supplying the liver.

An important anomaly is the "berry" aneurysm of the cerebral vessels (Fig. 4.3). These saccular outpouchings occur in approximately 2 per cent of individuals and are found at branch points, the weakest points of the vessels. Although present from birth, they do not cause any clinical problem until the third to fifth decade of life, when rising blood pressure may cause rupture and, in almost 50 per cent of cases, fatal hemorrhage. Occasionally these aneurysms are amenable to surgical excision.

A generalized connective tissue disorder, Marfan's syndrome, affects the skeletal, visual and cardiovascular systems. Affected individuals are tall and thin, with weak ligaments producing loose-jointedness. Various visual abnormalities are recorded, and heart valves may be abnormal. Aneurysms of the aorta are common, with rupture causing premature demise. Sudden death in more than one young basketball player has been due to this syndrome.

Marfan's syndrome has been traced through the lineage of Abraham Lincoln for nine generations to the present day (Schwartz, 1964). Lincoln's habitus fits well with the clinical picture. It has been suggested that this condition was responsible for the decline in Lincoln's health noted in the period before his assassination (Schwartz, 1972), and that his sons, including Tad who died at 18, were also affected.

Arteriosclerosis

Arteriosclerosis means "hardening of the arteries" and refers to thickening of arterial walls, with loss of elasticity. The most common variant, **atherosclerosis,** is the accumulation of fatty material, including cholesterol, on the intimal surface and in the walls of the arteries. Fibromuscular thickening of small arteries and arterioles, **arteriolosclerosis,** and Mönckeberg's **medial sclerosis,** are two other variants. These three forms of the disease are thought to vary in etiology and are of differing clinical signifance.

Atherosclerosis is virtually a universal disease, the complications of which account for most deaths in the United States. The same factors discussed in relation to ASHD apply to the systemic disease. Incidence increases with age, is lower in premenopausal woman, and is positively correlated with obesity, hypertension, cigarette smoking, urbanism, stress, a high calorie/high fat intake, and probably with lack of physical exercise.

The etiology of atherosclerosis is unknown, and a number of explanatory theories have been advanced. The aging hypothesis suggests that senescent deterioration of the walls of arteries leads to fatty degeneration. Hemorrhages into the walls of arteries or surface thromboses have been proposed as causative factors, but are more likely to play roles in the progression of the disease than in the onset. The currently most-favored hypothesis is that a diet with an excess of calories and fats, particularly saturated animal fats, results in disordered fat metabolism in the arteries and atherosclerosis. It is possible that any one of these hypotheses is correct, and more likely that more than one factor operates to produce atherosclerosis.

The lesions of atherosclerosis consist of fatty plaques seen on the intimal surface of the large arteries. As these progress they enlarge and ulcerate the intima. Mural thrombus may be superimposed, hemorrhages occur into the plaques, and fibrosis and calcification can eventually convert the elastic arteries into rigid pipes. The lesions themselves are asymptomatic, but can cause clinical manifestations by: (1) gradual narrowing of the lumen, causing ischemia; (2) thrombotic occlusion of the lumen, causing infarction of the organ or gangrene of the limb supplied; (3) embolization from the mural thrombus or plaque itself; and (4) aneurysmal dilatation of the weakened arterial wall (Fig. 4.3). Such **fusiform** aneurysms occur most commonly in the abdominal aorta. Mural thrombosis is frequent, with the dangers of subsequent embolization. A significant number of aneurysms rupture, with fatal results. Occasional aneurysms are of the **dissecting** type, in which hemorrhage extends through the wall of the aorta. Eventual rupture of the aorta, or pinching off of vital branches such as the renal arteries, causes death. Rarely, a dissection leads back into the lumen, with survival.

The other forms of arteriosclerosis are of somewhat less clinical significance. Medical calcinosis is important only in that it appears to predispose to atherosclerosis. Arteriolosclerosis is more important in that involvement of the small vessels of the kidney is associated with hypertension. Several different pathologic variants are described, associated with mild, "essential" hypertension or with a more severe and rapidly progressive "malignant" hypertension.

Veins

Dilatation and occlusion of veins are common disorders of this

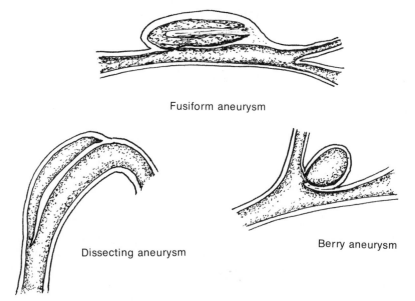

Fusiform aneurysm

Dissecting aneurysm

Berry aneurysm

Figure 4.3   The three major types of aneurysm.

anatomic weak link in the body. Drainage of the veins, particularly of the lower extremities, is passive, and the veins are poorly supported. Conditions that increase the intraluminal pressure, such as prolonged standing or obstruction to flow, or factors that decrease support, such as obesity, lead to elongation and dilatation of the veins, **varicose veins.** The impaired circulation of such veins affects the skin, causing **stasis dermatitis** and ulceration. Thrombosis occurs, but is of minimal clinical significance. In contrast, thrombosis of deeper veins carries a significant hazard of embolization. **Pulmonary embolus** is the immediate cause of death identified in approximately 10 per cent of autopsies.

Tumors of Blood Vessels

Tumors arise from the lining cells, **endothelium**. Benign tumors, **hemangiomas,** are fairly common and of little clinical importance other than cosmetically. Malignant vascular tumors, **angiosarcomas,** are rare, although they have recently been noted to occur with increased frequency in the liver of vinyl chloride workers (Block, 1974; Spiritas and Kaminski, 1977). Such tumors are rapidly fatal.

BLOOD AND BONE MARROW

Approximately 55 per cent of blood, by volume, is the proteinaceous fluid, **serum,** and 45 per cent consists of the formed elements: **red** and **white blood cells** and **platelets.** Red cells carry oxygen, white cells are important in inflammation, and platelets are subcellular fragments that function in coagulation. Disorders of the blood are characterized by either an excess or a deficiency of these elements.

Red Blood Cells

The formation of red blood cells, **erythrocytes,** is stimulated by the oxygen tension in the tissues, mediated by a hormone, **erythropoietin,** produced primarily by the kidneys. Occasionally tumors of other tissues produce erythropoietin, causing an excessive number of erythrocytes in the blood, **polycythemia.** Polycythemia is also a response to the lowered oxygen tension of high altitude, although this physiologic response enacts a toll of a higher incidence of thrombosis. The blood becomes more viscous when the **hematocrit,** the percentage of formed elements in the blood, is elevated. Experimental studies on mice (Aggio et al., 1972) show that survival under hypoxic conditions is based on respiratory and metabolic changes, and that polycythemia is probably an overcompensatory liability. Occasionally the condition is spontaneous, **polycythemia vera,** and can develop into leukemia.

The active element in erythrocytes is **hemoglobin,** an iron-containing organic compound that takes oxygen from the lungs and delivers it to the tissues. A deficiency of hemoglobin is referred to as **anemia,** and is due to either a decreased concentration of hemoglobin or a decrease in the total red cell mass. The life of the erythrocyte is about 120 days, so the marrow must manufacture 1/120th of the red cell volume each day, or more if there is abnormal blood loss. Anemia results if marrow activity is depressed, or if the production of erythrocytes, **erythropoiesis,** is incapable of matching blood loss.

The most commonly encountered anemia is that due to **blood loss.** The marrow is capable of a remarkable expansion in erythropoiesis, but is limited in hemoglobin production by the amount of iron available. A normal diet provides iron far in excess of the daily loss of less than 1 mg. (the iron in senescent red cells is scavenged and recycled). Cultural differences are important in the production of these anemias. Abnormal diets can reduce the intake of iron below adequate levels. The "milk-baby syndrome" is one in which an infant is fed almost exclusively on cow's milk, which is very low in iron. This condition is particularly prevalent in those segments of society in which bottle feeding is regarded as superior to nursing. Combined with a delayed introduction to solid foods, the result is an obese, pale infant, the "milk baby."

The paleopathologic equivalent of the milk baby is the infant skeleton exhibitng a characteristic thickening and pitting of the vault of the skull, **porotic hyperostosis,** or of the roof of the orbits, **cribra orbitalia,** or both. The radiologic picture is a "hair-on-end" appearance, seen in modern patients with congenital hemolytic anemias. The red cells of patients with diseases such as sickle cell anemia or thalassemia do not survive for the usual 120 days. The bone marrow becomes hyperplastic in an effort to maintain a normal number of circulating red cells. The proliferating marrow actually expands and erodes the bone in this peculiar fashion. Ancient skulls show this change in geographic regions where thalassemia is known today (Angel, 1966).

Similar changes are seen in archeologic specimens from the New World, where there are no hereditary hemoglobinopathies. Such cases of porotic hyperostosis and cribra orbitalia have been explained on the basis of iron deficiency, due to several different mechanisms. Trinkaus (1977) reported a pathologic child's skull from coastal Peru and suggested that iron deficiency was due to a diet of certain molluscs with a copper- rather than iron-based respiratory system. Cases occurring among the Indians of British Columbia are considered to be due to societal disruptions interfering with nutrition (Cybulski, 1977). Examples of the lesion from the southwestern United States are common in the skeletons of children from prehistoric Indian agricultural populations. The lesions are correlated with periods of stress, determined both physically, as in rapid growth periods, and culturally, as in weaning (Lallo et al., 1977). These populations subsisted on a maize diet, which not only is low in iron (El-Najjar, 1976; El-Najjar et al., 1976) but contains phytate that specifically binds iron and hinders intestinal absorption. Infectious diseases also promote the development of porotic hyperostosis, which is properly viewed not as a single disease but rather as the manifestation of a whole constellation of developmental, cultural and pathologic factors.

At the other end of the age spectrum, the elderly of contemporary society, especially those living alone, often do not prepare or cannot afford proper meals, live on tea and toast, and develop iron deficiency anemia.

Blood loss may be physiologic (as in menstruation) or pathologic. Again, cultural and geographic factors are important. In the western world, occult cancer is the major consideration, whereas in less-developed areas parasitism is the usual underlying cause.

Another type of blood loss is due to premature destruction of blood cells, the **hemolytic anemias.** The shortened survival time can be the result of intrinsic defects of the red cells, extrinsic abnormalities, or combinations of the two. Of the many intrinsic defects of red cells, one is of particular anthropologic interest, **sickle cell anemia.**

The disorder is a hereditary abnormality of the hemoglobin molecule. Under conditions of low oxygen tension, the red cells of homozygotes develop a sickle shape which renders the cells liable to rupture **(hemolysis)** and thrombosis. The net result is a markedly shortened life span for the cells and the individual. The reasons for the persistence of this abnormality, in relation to the interaction between culture, environment and disease, have been discussed in Chapter 3.

White Blood Cells

In contrast to erythrocytes, disorders of **leukocytes** are almost all of excess production, **the leukemias.** Deficiency of white cells, **leukopenia,** is much less common, and is usually caused by an idiosyncratic drug reaction. If severe and prolonged, death due to infection occurs.

Leukemias can be acute or chronic, and may be of any of the white cell types (neutrophils, eosinophils and basophils, named for their staining characteristics, lymphocytes, or monocytes). There is a remarkable age distribution, in that children and young adults are primarily affected, with a second smaller peak of incidence in the elderly. The disease is usually acute in children, and an adequate therapeutic regimen has recently been developed. Acute leukemia in adults runs a fulminant, refractory course. Over-all, approximately 50 per cent of cases are acute. The incidence has shown a dramatic rise in the 20th century, approximately fivefold in the past 50 years. An association with ionizing radiation has been clearly demonstrated. Before this danger was known, radiologists showed an elevated rate of leukemia, as did patients given repeated x-ray treatment for ankylosing spondylitis. Suggested factors for the recent increase in leukemia include antenatal irradiation of the fetus during maternal x-ray examination, and the accumulation in the bones of strontium[90] from nuclear tests. Exposure to hydrocarbons is also thought to be significant. An intriguing fact is that in the case of children dying of leukemia (and other malignancies), a significant excess of fathers work in hydrocarbon-related industries (Fabia and Thuy, 1974). Chromosomal abnormalities and viruses are also thought to play a role. Children with mongolism (Down's syndrome, an extra chromosome 21) have an elevated incidence of leukemia, and many animal leukemias have been shown to be transmissible, virally-induced diseases.

The pathologic effects of leukemia are due to the massive infiltration of normal structures by the neoplastic cells, the clinical presentation usually being enlarged lymph nodes. Marrow involvement produces anemia and a hemorrhagic state secondary to decreased platelets, **thrombocytopenia.** The circulating white blood cells are abnormal in function and these patients are liable to the same types of infections as those with leukopenia. Failure of other organs is rare, as the cells push apart the functional elements, the **parenchyma,** rather than destroying them. The invasion is between the cells, in the **stroma,** the supportive tissues of the organs.

Leukemia in the elderly is usually chronic, running a prolonged and indolent course. These patients often die of some other, unrelated disease, although they occasionally terminate as an acute leukemia.

Blood Clotting

Platelets **(thrombocytes)** and a large number of serum factors are necessary for blood clotting, and deficiencies result in bleeding tendencies or, if severe, frank hemorrhage. Deficiency of a component called **Factor VIII, antihemophilic globulin,** results in hemophilia, the most widely known clotting deficiency. The disorder is transmitted by a sex-linked recessive gene on the X chromosome, and is thus manifested when a male has the defective gene on his single X chromosome. The homozygous state is rare in females. Heterozygous females are clinically normal but are carriers of the trait. As discussed in Chapter 3, the condition affected many of the royal families of Europe in the 19th and 20th centuries.

The pathologic effects are due to hemorrhage secondary to trauma, often of a minimal nature. Bleeding is often into closed areas, such as joints, causing considerable pain and dysfunction. As patients age, they learn to protect themselves from trauma and have a better prognosis. Modern therapy with fresh-frozen plasma is adequate treatment.

THE LYMPHATIC SYSTEM

The lymphatic system consists of the lymphatic vessels, lymph nodes and spleen. Many infections involve the lymphatics and lymph nodes secondarily, producing nonspecific reactive changes. A specific infection of the lymphatic system is **filariasis.** This mosquito-borne disease is caused by a nematode, *Wuchereria (Filaria) bancrofti.* The life cycle involves the maturation of injected microfilaria in the large lymphatics. The adults, females 100 mm. long and the males 30 mm. long, copulate and produce numerous microfilaria, which enter the blood stream via the thoracic duct to complete the life cycle by being taken up in a mosquito's blood meal.

The disease itself is due to an intense inflammatory reaction to dead parasites in the lymphatics, with eventual scarring and obstruction. Chronic edema, thickening of subcutaneous fibrous tissue and thickening of the skin produce the classic picture of **elephantiasis,** usually complicated by secondary bacterial infection.

There is a periodicity to the production of microfilaria, either at midnight or at dawn and twilight, keyed to the feeding habits of the vector at that particular locale. It is of interest that the Trukese believe that filariasis is due to the "bad souls" or ghosts of ancestors, which are thought to be active in the early morning or late afternoon. This, of course, is the feeding time of mosquitos of Truk (Goodenough, n.d.).

Lymph Nodes

The diseases of concern in the lymph nodes are the primary tumors, the **lymphomas.** The broadest classification separates these into **Hodgkin's disease** (HD) and the **non-Hodgkin's lymphomas** (NHL).

Hodgkin's disease is distinctive both histologically and clinically. The enlarged nodes of HD are infiltrated by a variety of cells: lymphocytes, atypical histiocytes, eosinophils, plasma cells, and the specific and diagnostic Reed-Sternberg cells, large cells with characteristic double nuclei. In contrast, the infiltrate of the NHL group is monomorphic.

The clinical and epidemiologic differences between the two diseases are remarkable. The marked clustering of cases of HD (Newell and Rowlings, 1972; Vianna and Polan, 1973) suggests an infectious etiology. HD is generally amenable to medical treatment and some forms are even considered curable. NHL is a sporadic disease that follows a progressive course refractory to treatment. Both these diseases invade other organs, metastasizing and killing in the same fashion as other malignancies and occasionally terminating as leukemias.

Burkitt's Lymphoma. Burkitt and O'Connor (1961) reported a destructive lymphoma common in young children in tropical Africa. The tumor affected the jaw and abdomen and rarely terminated as leukemia. The geographic distribution and seasonality (Williams et al., 1974) suggest an insect vector and a viral etiology. The Ebstein-Barr virus has been isolated from the tumors, and Burkitt's lymphoma patients do have antibodies against the virus, but the virus is worldwide, is known to cause mononucleosis and is found in normal individuals. Other viruses isolated have not been shown to be pathogens, and the only virally-induced tumor known in man remains the common wart.

Metastatic Tumors. Lymph nodes commonly are involved by secondary tumors, and this is the rationale of radical tumor surgery. The hope is to excise tumor which has spread beyond its origin but has been entrapped by regional lymph nodes.

Spleen

The spleen is affected by many of the same processes as the lymph nodes, including the lymphomas. Certain other lesions are peculiar to the spleen, however.

The spleen is liable to enlargement secondary to congestion, due to either cardiac failure or cirrhosis. One of the functions of the spleen is the removal of aged cells from the blood. An enlarged spleen may become overexuberant at this task, causing anemia, leukopenia and/or thrombocytopenia, with attendant clinical consequences.

Many other conditions, such as mononucleosis, leukemia or malaria, cause splenic enlargement, **splenomegaly.** Such enlarged spleens are liable to rupture with minimal trauma.

Infarcts of the spleen are common, either secondary to embolization (usually from the heart) or thrombosis. In sickle cell disease, repeated infarcts lead to autosplenectomy, with functional and virtually complete anatomic loss of the spleen.

Secondary tumors of the spleen, other than the lymphomas, are exceedingly rare. The reason for the resistance of the spleen to metastasis, in spite of its rich blood supply, which would seem to favor tumor deposition, is unknown.

REFERENCES

Ackerknecht, E. H. (1973): Therapeutics from the Primitives to the 20th Century. Hafner, New York.

Aggio, M. C., Montano, J. J., Bruzzo, M. T. et al. (1972): Possible inefficiency of polycythemia in tolerance to high altitude. Acta Physiol. Lat. Am. 22:123–128.

Allison, M. J., Gerszten, E. and H. P. Dalton (1974): Paleopathology in pre-Columbian Americans. Lab. Invest. 30:407–408.

Angel, J. L. (1966): Porotic hyperostosis, anemias, malarias, and marshes in the prehistoric eastern Mediterranean. Science 153:760–763.

Block, J. B. (1974): Angiosarcoma of the liver following vinyl chloride exposure. J.A.M.A. 229:53–54.

Breasted, J. H. (1930): The Edwin Smith Surgical Papyrus. University of Chicago Press, Chicago.

Breutsch, W. L. (1959): The earliest record of sudden death possibly due to atherosclerotic coronary occlusion. Circulation 20:438–441.

Buchwald, H., Moore, R. B. and R. L. Varco (1974): Surgical treatment of hyperlipidemia. Circulation 49, Suppl. 1:1–37.

Burkitt, D. and G. T. O'Connor (1961): Malignant lymphoma in African children. Cancer 14:258–269.

Cybulski, J. S. (1977): Cribra orbitalia, a possible sign of anemia in early historic native populations of the British Columbia Coast. Am. J. Phys. Anthropol. 47:31–40.

Dawson, W. R. (1967): The Egyptian medical papyri. In Diseases in Antiquity. D. Brothwell and A. T. Sandison, eds. Charles C Thomas, Springfield, Ill., pp. 98–114.

Dubos, R. (1971): Man Adapting. Yale University Press, New Haven.

El-Najjar, M. Y. (1976): Maize, malaria and the anemias in the pre-Columbian New World. Yearbook Phys. Anthropol. 20:329–337.

El-Najjar, M. Y., Ryan, D. J., Turner, C. G. et al. (1976): The etiology of porotic hyperostosis among the prehistoric and historic Anasazi Indians of the Southwestern United States. Am. J. Phys. Anthropol. *44*:477–488.

Enselberg, C. D. (1970): Physical activity and coronary heart disease. Am. Heart J. *80*:137–141.

Fabia, J. and T. D. Thuy (1974): Occupation of father at time of birth of children dying of malignant disease. Br. J. Prev. Soc. Med. *28*:98–100.

Goodenough, W. H. (n.d.): Personal communication.

Goodman, L. S. and A. Gilman (1975): The Pharmacological Basis of Therapeutics, 5th ed. Macmillan, New York.

Gray, P. H. K. (1967): Radiography of ancient Egyptian mummies. Med. Radiogr. Photogr. *43*:34 44.

Harris, J. E. and K. Weeks (1973): X-Raying the Pharaohs. Scribner's, New York.

Hennekens, C. H., Drolette, M. E., Jesse, M. J. et al. (1976): Coffee drinking and death due to coronary heart disease. N. Engl. J. Med. *294*:633–636.

Jick, H., Miettinen, O. S., Neff, R. K. et al. (1973): Coffee and myocardial infarction. N. Engl. J. Med. *298*:63–67.

Lallo, J. W., Armelagos, G. J. and R. P. Mensforth (1977): The role of diet, disease and physiology in the origin of porotic hyperostosis. Hum. Biol. *49*:471–483.

Levenstein, J. H. (1975): Historical perspective of myocardial infarction. S. Afr. Med. J. *49*:1585–1590.

Long, A. R. (1931): Cardiovascular renal disease: report of a case three thousand years ago. Arch. Pathol. *12*:92–94.

Mazess, R. B. (1970): Cardiorespiratory characteristics and adaptation to high altitudes. Am. J. Phys. Anthropol. *32*:267–278.

Newell, G. R. and W. Rowlings (1972): Evidence for environmental factors in the etiology of Hodgkin's disease. J. Chronic Dis. *25*:261–267.

Nye, E. R. (1971): Natural selection and degenerative cardiovascular disease. *In* Natural Selection in Human Populations. C. J. Bajema, ed. Wiley, New York.

Peacock, P. B. (1973): Atherosclerotic heart disease and the environment. Trans. N. Y. Acad. Sci. *35*:631–635.

Reyman, T. A., Barraco, R. A. and A. Cockburn (1976): Histopathological examination of an Egyptian mummy. Bull. N.Y. Acad. Med. *52*:505–516.

Roberts, W. C. and L. M. Buja (1972): The frequency and significance of coronary arterial thrombi and other observations in fatal acute myocardial infarction: a study of 107 necropsy patients. Am. J. Med. *52*:425–443.

Rowling, J. T. (1961): Pathological changes in mummies. Proc. R. Soc. Med., Sect. Hist. Med. *54*:409–425.

Ruffer, M. A. (1911): On arterial lesions found in Egyptian mummies (1580 B.C.–525 A.D.). J. Pathol. Bacteriol. *15*:453–462.

Sandison, A. T. (1962): Degenerative vascular disease in the Egyptian mummy. Med. Hist. *6*:77–81.

Schwartz, H. (1964): Abraham Lincoln and the Marfan syndrome. J.A.M.A. *187*:473–479.

Schwartz, H. (1972): Abraham Lincoln and aortic insufficiency: the declining health of the President. Calif. Med. *116*:82–84.

Shattock, G. S. (1909): Report on the pathology of King Merneptah. Lancet *1*:319.

Shaw, A. F. B. (1938): A histological study of the mummy of Har-mose, the singer of the 18th dynasty (circa 1490 B.C.). J. Pathol. Bacteriol. *47*:115–123.

Smith, G. E. (1908): The unwrapping of Pharaoh. Br. Med. J. *1*:342–343.

Somers, K. (1976): Cardiology: Africa versus Australia. Med. J. Aust. *1*:60–63.

Spiritas, R. and R. Kaminski (1977): Angiosarcoma of the liver in vinyl chloride/polyvinyl chloride workers. J. Occup. Med. *20*:427–429.

Trinkaus, E. (1977): The Alto Salaverry child: a case of anemia from the Peruvian preceramic. Am. J. Phys. Anthropol. *46*:25–28.

Vianna, N. J. and A. K. Polan (1973): Epidemiologic evidence for transmission of Hodgkin's disease. N. Engl. J. Med. *289*:499–502.

Vyhanek, L. and E. Strouhal (1975): Arteriosclerosis in Egyptian mummies. Anthropologie *13*:219–221.

Williams, E. H., Day, N. E. and A. G. Geser (1974): Seasonal variation in onset of Burkitt's lymphoma in the West Nile District of Uganda. Lancet *2*:19–22.

Williams, H. U. (1927): Gross and microscopic anatomy of two Peruvian mummies. Arch. Pathol. *4*:26–33.

Yodfat, Y. (1972): The prevalence of cardiovascular disease in different ethnic and socioeconomic groups in Beit Shemesh, Israel. Isr. J. Med. Sci. *8*:1685–1694.

Zimmerman, M. R. and G. S. Smith (1975): A probable case of accidental inhumation of 1600 years ago. Bull. N. Y. Acad. Med. *51*:828–837.

Zimmerman, M. R., Yeatman, G. W., Sprinz, H. et al. (1971): Examination of an Aleutian mummy. Bull. N. Y. Acad. Med. *47*:80–103.

five

The Respiratory System

ANATOMY AND PHYSIOLOGY

The respiratory system consists of two functional units, the **air passages** and the lung (**pulmonary**) **alveoli**. The air passages include the **nose** and **mouth, trachea, bronchi** and **bronchioles**, making up a system of ever smaller tubes bringing air to the alveoli for oxygen and carbon dioxide exchange. During its passage the air is warmed to body temperature and fully hydrated to provide optimal conditions for gas exchange. The alveoli consist of simple epithelial sacs with capillaries in their walls. Hemoglobin, the oxygen-carrying component of the erythrocyte, is separated from the oxygen in the alveoli only by the red cell membrane, the endothelial lining of the capillary, and the epithelial cells of the alveolus. This minimal separation allows for easy gas diffusion. In addition, a specific mechanism operates for the acquisition of oxygen. The affinity of hemoglobin for oxygen is high when hemoglobin is exposed to high concentrations of oxygen, and drops dramatically when the ambient oxygen tension is low, in a sigmoid curve (Fig. 5.1). Thus, hemoglobin is "programmed" to take up oxygen when it is available, as in the alveoli, and give it up where needed, as in the tissues.

The lungs, divided into three right and two left lobes, are situated in the **pleural cavities**, this arrangement determining the mechanics of respiration. In inspiration the chest is expanded by the intercostal muscles and diaphragm, creating a negative pressure in the cavities, expanding the lungs and drawing in air. When these muscles are relaxed, the passive process of expiration occurs. The elastic recoil of the lungs forces the air out.

Although there is some degree of voluntary control of respiration,

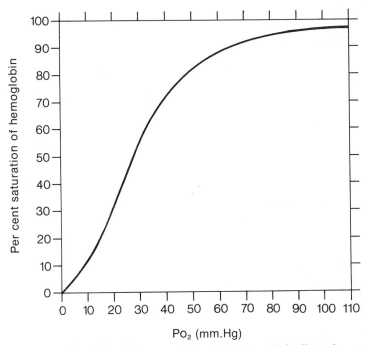

The oxygen-hemoglobin dissociation curve. Hemoglobin has a high affinity for oxygen in an oxygen-rich environment but readily gives up oxygen in an oxygen-poor setting.

Figure 5.1

the process is primarily involuntary and regulated by receptors for carbon dioxide, oxygen and pH. If, for any reason, carbon dioxide concentration goes up, oxygen concentration goes down or the pH goes down, respiration is increased. If these factors change in the opposite direction, respiration decreases, correcting the abnormality. These physiologic controls may pose some therapeutic hazards, as administration of oxygen to patients with respiratory difficulty can actually depress respiration.

Above the trachea are situated the larynx, containing two vocal cords, and pharynx. The anatomy of this area allows for the human voice. The basic frequencies are produced by passing air through the tensed vocal cords, and the quality of the voice is largely determined by the shape of the pharynx.

In 1971 Lieberman and Crelin published a reconstruction of the Neanderthal vocal mechanism which they interpreted as indicating that Neanderthals were incapable of sophisticated vocalization, being limited to the level of chimpanzee or newborn human communication. The accuracy of their reconstruction has been challenged (Falk, 1975), and radiologic studies have found modern men with similar anatomy who speak very well (LeMay, 1975). A rebuttal by Lieberman (1976) provides a good review of the reconstruction problem. Lieberman points out that *any* vocal deficiencies in Neanderthals would have been an evolutionary disadvantage (although the existence of such deficiencies is probably unprovable).

PATHOLOGY

Congenital Lesions

Cysts of the lung are of importance only as sites for infection. Rarely, cysts can take up an entire lobe, causing the "vanishing lung" syndrome.

Inflammatory Diseases

Asthma.   **Bronchial asthma** is characterized by spasm of the bronchi caused by allergy, usually to inhaled dust or pollen, or to certain foods. A significant minority of patients cannot be shown to have a specific allergy. In all cases other factors such as cold, emotional stress, fatigue and exposure to irritants are important, and there is a considerable hereditary component. Psychogenic factors are well recognized, but asthma clearly predates psychiatrists. The ancient Maya were familiar with the disease, and treated it with pepper, which aids the expulsion of mucus plugs (Roys, 1931).

The major anatomic lesion in asthma is obstruction of the bronchi by these mucus plugs. Inspiration is hindered and, on expiration, the combination of bronchospasm and the normal passive constriction of the bronchi makes the release of air extremely difficult. The result is a wheezing patient with hyperexpanded lungs. The attack is resolved by the expectoration of the mucus plugs.

Mild forms of the disease are bothersome, but severe forms may feature prolonged attacks, **status asthmaticus**, which may be fatal in themselves or if complicated by secondary infection.

Bronchiectasis.   Chronic infection of the bronchi can lead to dilatation, **bronchiectasis** (ectasia = dilatation). The condition starts in childhood and becomes a long-term chronic process. There is some controversy over whether the ectasia or the infection is primary, but it is clear that childhood onset shortens the duration of life. Lung abscesses, pneumonia and metastatic brain abscesses are recognized life-threatening complications.

Bacterial Pneumonia.   Inflammation of the lungs, **pneumonia** or **pneumonitis**, can be classified on the basis of the etiologic agent or the anatomic pattern of the disease. **Lobular** pneumonia, or **bronchopneumonia**, has a patchy distribution usually located around the bronchi or bronchioles. Bronchopneumonia may become confluent to produce a **lobar** pattern, diffuse involvement of one or more lobes.

Classic lobar pneumonia is pneumococcal in origin, caused by *Streptococcus pneumoniae*, and is acquired outside of the hospital, whereas bronchopneumonia is usually acquired in the hospital (a **nosocomial** infection), and generally is caused by species of staphylococci or the enteric bacteria. Considerable overlap is seen in this picture, however.

In either case, the pathologic changes are similar. The lung is consolidated by hemorrhage and an infiltrate of leukocytes, filling the alveoli and producing a gross appearance similar to that of the liver, referred to as **hepatization**. If treatment is successful, the process resolves and the normal lung structure is preserved.Occasionally, lung tissue has been destroyed, and healing is by scar formation. With modern antibiotic therapy, lobar pneumonia usually is successfully treated on an outpatient basis. Bronchopneumonia, on the other hand, is often a terminal process in a patient debilitated by another disease.

Before the development of antibiotics, lobar pneumonia was a much more serious disease, even in previously healthy individuals. Fatal cases have been described in ancient remains (Shaw, 1938; Zimmerman et al., 1971) and the mortality rate remained high even in the first half of the 20th century.

Complications of pneumonia include scarring and abscess formation. Scarring presents another danger, in that alveolar lining cells entrapped within a scar may become irritated and develop into a malignancy. In the not too distant past, these "scar cancers" were virtually the only type of lung cancer seen in women. With the increase in smoking by females, they now have the same types of lung cancer as those seen in males and the frequency is fast approaching that in males.

Tuberculosis.　Along with malaria, **tuberculosis** still ranks as one of the leading causes of death, on a worldwide basis. Owing to improvements in therapy, the death rate from tuberculosis has dropped extraordinarily in the western world. However, the death rate from tuberculosis in the great cities of the United States and Europe had fallen from 500/100,000 in 1850 to 40/100,000 by 1947, the year the first effective drugs were isolated. Public health measures were in part responsible, such as prohibitions on spitting in public conveyances, and improved living conditions. It is likely that the organism, *Mycobacterium tuberculosis*, had decreased somewhat in virulence, as the decrease began before the discovery of the tubercle bacillus, let alone curative drugs (Dubos, 1971). An element of natural selection also plays a role, with susceptibles dying out of the population (Motulsky, 1971).

The tubercle bacillus infects man by two routes. The lung is the usual site of initial infection, owing to inhalation of infected sputum droplets from other humans. The intestinal tract may be infected by milk from tuberculous cows, containing *M. bovis.* Other sites may be involved secondarily, including the kidneys, bone, breast, meninges, fallopian tubes, pericardium and others. Pulmonary infection is the most common, and will be discussed as a model for the other sites.

The initial infection is a bronchopneumonia, almost always at the apex of the lung. The initial inflammatory reaction is incapable of destroying the tubercle bacilli, probably because of the protective effect of the lipid in the bacterial cell wall, and the process rapidly proceeds to necrosis of the lung and inflammatory cells. The necrosis is of a characteristic cheese-like consistency, referred to as **caseation.** The necrosis and surrounding inflammatory reaction, along with similar changes in the draining lymph nodes, makes up the **primary complex**. The course of the disease seems to depend on the state of resistance of the host.

Most simply wall off the lesion and it remains as a scar. A few infants and children show little resistance, and the proliferating organisms cause a full-blown tuberculous pneumonia, leading to widespread dissemination of the disease and rapid death (the "galloping consumption" of 19th century novelists). Such cases have been documented in antiquity, including the mummy of a 5-year-old from New Kingdom Egypt, dead of pulmonary hemorrhage secondary to tuberculosis (Zimmerman, 1977).

In contrast to childhood disease, adult (**secondary** or **reinfection**) tuberculosis is almost always a serious disease of lethal potential. It is unclear whether reinfection is from an exogenous source or by reactivation of an endogenous focus, but the pathologic process of progressive destruction of lung tissue is well documented. The lung becomes cavitated and the many tubercle bacilli found in such a lesion invade the blood stream to spread to other organs. The kidneys and reproductive organs may be involved. Spread to the bone produces the characteristic hunchback deformity of Pott's disease. As fungal infections can produce similar skeletal pathology, the paleopathologist must use archeologic and paleoepidemiologic evidence in assessing such lesions (Buikstra, 1976; Katzenberg, 1976).

Disseminated disease can also occur in the form of multiple small granulomas spread throughout the body, roughly the size of millet seeds, **miliary tuberculosis**. This form is a manifestation of failure of resistance; such patients are often incapable of even mustering a positive skin test to a tuberculous antigen. If untreated, the condition is rapidly fatal.

At present, effective chemotherapy means that less than 10 per cent of patients with active tuberculosis die of the disease. However, treatment must be consistent with cultural practices. Tuberculosis remains a highly fatal disease among the Zulus of South Africa. Treatment involves hospitalization, which the Zulus fear. Delay in reporting for treatment results in a high proportion of advanced cases. The inevitably high death rate reinforces the fear of hospitalization (Cassel, 1976).

Influenza.   Influenza is an upper respiratory infection caused by any one of several viruses. Clinically the disease is characterized by a rapid onset of fever, cough, prostration, muscle pain and nasal discharge. Most patients have an uneventful recovery, but considerable mortality has been seen in the past, primarily as a result of superimposed bacterial pneumonia. The virus shows periodic changes in antigenic structure, making production of an effective vaccine difficult (Schulman, 1978).

Great epidemics of influenza have swept across the world in the 20th century. In the pandemic of 1918-19, half a million deaths were recorded in the United States alone. Another serious epidemic occurring in 1957 was marked not only by lower mortality, attributable in part to antibiotic therapy, but also by a shift in the pattern of mortality in the United States. Those dying in the earlier epidemic were previously healthy young adults; in 1957 children and the aged were the victims. Katz (1974) relates this phenomenon to the presence in early 20th century America of a single cohort of susceptible immigrants from rural areas of Europe, who were clustered together in the large cities of their new land. The combination of their lack of immunity because of previous isolation and the poor living conditions in the urban tenements explains the high mortality observed. By 1957, this group was no longer a major component of the United States population.

Paragonimiasis. This is a parasitic disease caused by the lung fluke, *Paragonimus westermani.* This tropical and Far Eastern disease is acquired by ingestion of ova. The ova hatch, and the liberated cercaria penetrate the intestinal tract and migrate to the lungs, causing severe destruction, with a clinical picture of a cough productive of blood (**hemoptysis**) and brown sputum. Secondary involvement of other organs, including the brain, is possible. Eventually, pulmonary function is severely compromised and secondary cardiac disease, **cor pulmonale,** with failure, can develop.

For many years an inexplicable association was noted between paragonimiasis and measles epidemics in Korea. Finally it was learned that the Koreans were attempting to prevent the eye damage seen occasionally in measles by applying a folk medicine, the tissue juices of freshwater crabs, to the eyes of children with measles. Many of the crabs were found to be infected with *P. westermani* (Hopps, 1977).

Vascular Disturbances

Congestion and Edema. Heart failure leads to pooling of blood in the lungs and the escape of serum from the capillaries into the alveoli, **pulmonary edema**. The heart failure may be of any cause, a weakened myocardium in ASHD and valvular deformities being the most common. The accumulation of this proteinaceous fluid in the alveoli inhibits respiratory function and predisposes to the development of pneumonia, often as the terminal event in serious heart disease.

Embolism, Hemorrhage and Infarction. Pulmonary emboli, usually arising from thromboses of the deep leg veins, are common and a frequent cause of death. Prolonged bed rest favors the development of such thromboses.

Sudden death may occur in pulmonary embolism, presumably owing to obstruction of blood flow through the lungs. In such cases the lungs themselves show little pathologic change. It must be remembered that the lung has a double blood supply, the pulmonary circulation from the right ventricle and the bronchial circulation arising from the aorta. The bronchial arteries alone can keep the lung in a viable state, even if the pulmonary flow is occluded. However, if the patient's cardiovascular status is such that the bronchial flow is marginal, the result of a pulmonary embolus is a hemorrhagic infarct of the lung, a condition that may also be fatal. As in most diseases, the best cure is prevention — early ambulation of postsurgical patients, for example.

Disturbances of Lung Expansion. The lungs can be underinflated or overinflated. Failure of inflation, **atelectasis**, is congenital or acquired. The fetal lung is normally uninflated, and occasionally newborns, particularly in prematurity, are incapable of lung expansion, a condition incompatible with extrauterine existence.

Acquired or secondary atelectasis, collapse of alveoli that had been expanded, is due either to airway obstruction or external compression of the lung. If airflow is completely occluded, as by mucus, tumor or foreign body, the air in the alveoli is absorbed and the lung collapses. Alternatively, compression of the lung, as by air in the pleural cavity, **pneumothorax**, may collapse the lung. Pneumothorax is usually traumatic in origin and, before the discovery of effective drugs, was surgically induced in the therapy of tuberculosis, to "rest" the lung and allow scar formation.

Atelectasis, like edema, is reversible and is a predisposing factor for pneumonia. Overexpansion of the lung is almost always accompanied by destruction of lung tissue, the complex comprising **emphysema**. This is a disease of the aged, and cigarette smoking and air pollution are significant etiologic factors. The pathology involves dilatation of the alveoli and destruction of the elastic tissue in the alveolar walls. These changes have two effects. Oxygen exchange takes place at the periphery of the alveoli, and increase in the size of the alveoli increases the amount of dead space unavailable for gas exchange (Fig. 5.2). Second, expiration is normally a passive process based on the elastic recoil of the lung. Emphysematous patients must expel air actively, by using accessory muscles, thus increasing the metabolic cost of respiration.

The distended lungs of emphysema result in a barrel-shaped chest, easily recognizable in skeletal remains. Evidence of air pollution in antiquity is clear. Many diagnoses of anthracosis, the deposition of carbon pigment in the lungs, have been made in mummies, but anthrocotic pigment is relatively inert and few cases of ancient emphysema are seen.

Lung Tumors.   The most common primary tumor of the lung, and one showing a rapidly rising incidence, is **bronchogenic carcinoma**. Statistical, clinical and experimental evidence all indict cigarette smoking as the major causative factor in what has become the most common cancer in males and an increasingly frequent cancer in females. The ratio of lung cancer between smokers and nonsmokers is on the order of 30 to 1, and the extraordinary rise in incidence over the past 60 years cannot be attributed entirely to improved diagnosis. Increases in lung

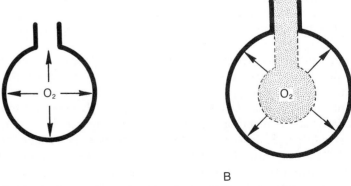

A   B

Figure 5.2   Central alveolar dead space in emphysema: *A*, normal; *B*, emphysema.

cancer are seen about 20 years after periods of increase in cigarette sales, such as wars.

Ionizing radiation can also be a carcinogenic factor. Over half the miners of Joachimstal, where the uranium ore used by the Curies was mined, died of lung cancer, presumably owing to the high concentration of radon in the air. Chemicals may also play a role; nickel workers suffer an excess of lung and upper respiratory cancers.

As the name indicates, these tumors arise from the mucosal lining of the major bronchi. Chronic irritation results in squamous metaplasia of the normally columnar mucosa, and in a significant number of individuals there is progression to squamous carcinoma or less differentiated cancers. These lesions can obstruct and patients may present with emphysema, atelectasis, abscess or pneumonia. The tumor may invade or compress the superior vena cava, brachial plexus or recurrent laryngeal nerve, producing symptoms of dysfunction referable to these structures. Distant metastases are common and may be responsible for the presenting complaints. The usual course is rapidly downhill, with a five-year survival rate of 5 to 20 per cent.

Secondary tumors of the lung are more common than primary cancers, as the lung acts as a filter for the entire circulatory system. Generally, the presence of such tumors means that the primary tumor can no longer be cured surgically, although occasional solitary metastases are amenable to surgical excision.

Pleura.   The lining of the pleural cavity is liable to involvement by many of the infections and tumors affecting the lung. A specific tumor of the pleura, **mesothelioma**, was rare but has become somewhat more common recently. An association with asbestos has been well documented. Almost all patients with mesothelioma either worked in asbestos factories or in the insulation industry, had relatives in such employment, or lived within half a mile of an asbestos factory. Exposure for as little as five weeks appears to be sufficient to cause the disease (Curran and Harnden, 1972).

Mesothelioma is inevitably and rapidly fatal, the tumor growing rapidly to encase the lung and cause respiratory insufficiency.

REFERENCES

Allison, M. J., Mendoza, D. and A. Pezzia (1973): Documentation of a case of tuberculosis in preColumbian America. Am. Rev. Resp. Dis. *107*:985–991.

Buikstra, J. E. (1976): Differential diagnosis: an epidemiological model. Yearbook Phys. Anthropol. *20*:316–328.

Cassel, J. (1976): A comprehensive health program among South African Zulus. *In* Health, Culture and Community. B. D. Paul, ed. Russel Sage Foundation, New York, pp. 15–42.

Curran, R. C. and D. G. Harnden (1972): The Pathological Basis of Medicine. Saunders, Philadelphia.

Dubos, R. (1971): Man Adapting. Yale University Press, New Haven.

Falk, D. (1975): Comparative anatomy of the larynx in man and the chimpanzee: implications for language in Neanderthal. Am. J. Phys. Anthropol. *43*:123–132.

Hopps, H. C. (1977): Geographic pathology. *In* Pathology, 7th ed. W. A. D. Anderson and J. M. Kissane, eds. Mosby, St. Louis, pp. 692–736.

Katz, R. S. (1974): Influenza 1918-1919: a study in mortality. Bull. Hist. Med. *48*:416–422.

Katzenberg, M. A. (1976): An investigation of spinal disease in a Midwest aboriginal population. Yearbook Phys. Anthropol. *20*:349–355.

LeMay, M. (1975): The language capability of Neanderthal man. Am. J. Phys. Anthropol. *42*:9–14.

Lieberman, P. (1976): Structural harmony and Neanderthal speech: a reply to LeMay. Am. J. Phys. Anthropol. *45*:493–496.

Lieberman, P. and E. S. Crelin (1971): On the speech of Neanderthal man. Ling. Inquiry *2*:203–222.

Motulsky, A. G. (1971): Metabolic polymorphisms and the role of infectious diseases in human evolution. *In* Human Populations, Genetic Variation, and Evolution. L. N. Morris, ed. Chandler, San Francisco, pp. 222–252.

Roys, R. L. (1931): The Ethno-Botany of the Maya. Tulane University, New Orleans.

Schulman, J. L. (1978): Epidemiology of influenza. Am. J. Clin. Pathol. *70*, Suppl.:141–145.

Shaw, A. F. B. (1938): A histological study of the mummy of Har-mose, the singer of the eighteenth dynasty (circa 1490 B.C.). J. Pathol. Bacteriol. *47*:115–123.

Zimmerman, M. R. (1977): The mummies of the tomb of Nebwenenef: paleopathology and archeology. J. Am. Res. Center Egypt *14*:33–36.

Zimmerman, M. R., Yeatman, G. W., Sprinz, H. et al. (1971): Examination of an Aleutian mummy. Bull. N. Y. Acad. Med. *47*:80–103.

six

The Digestive System: Metabolism and Nutrition

ANATOMY, PHYSIOLOGY AND BIOCHEMISTRY

The **oral cavity** is of course the site of ingress for food and water, and also has important digestive functions. The teeth grind the food into particles small enough for swallowing and digestion. It is important to remember that the teeth are metabolically active in their developmental stage and can reflect a variety of environmental stresses. As mature teeth are markedly resistant to postmortem degradation, they constitute an important source of information on these environmental factors. Dentition analyses have been related to nutritional patterns, with a variety of interpretations (Perzigian, 1977), and to socioeconomic status (Garn et al., 1973).

Digestion of starches is initiated in the mouth. Digestive enzymes in the saliva split carbohydrates into smaller components, called **dextrins.**

The **esophagus** forms a connection between the oral cavity and the stomach, through the thorax and diaphragm. It consists of a muscular tube lined by stratified squamous epithelium, for protection, and has no secretory or digestive function.

The **stomach** is a saccular organ just below the diaphragm, in the left upper quadrant of the abdominal cavity. Its function is to provide a storage place for food, regulating the flow into the small intestine, and to begin the digestion of protein. Certain cells of the gastric mucosa secrete **pepsinogen,** which is activated to **pepsin,** a proteolytic enzyme, by hydrochloric acid, which is secreted by other cells in the mucosa. Still other cells, the most superficial, secrete mucin, which protects the stomach from autodigestion. The stomach also secretes **intrinsic factor,** necessary for the absorption of vitamin B_{12}.

The pH of the gastric juices is about 1, and is neutralized by the bolus of food itself. This rise in the pH decreases the action of pepsin, which is further counteracted by the alkaline secretion of the pancreas in the small intestine.

Most absorption of food is from the **small intestine.** Only small molecules pass through the gastric mucosa into the blood stream. Of these, the most significant is alcohol.

The small intestine, divided into the **duodenum, jejunum** and **ileum,** is remarkably adapted for absorption. The surface of the mucosa shows many gross folds and there are microscopic mucosal **villi** that result in a surface area of about 10 square meters. **Microvilli,** minute projections on the surface of the mucosal villi, increase the area still further.

The secretions of the small intestine, and the liver and pancreas (which drain into the duodenum), contain the enzymes necessary for the final breakdown of foodstuffs into compounds small enough to be absorbed and enter metabolic pathways. The pancreatic secretion contains enzymes that break down proteins, nucleic acids, fat and carbohydrates to simpler compounds. The secretion of the intestine itself completes the digestion of proteins into amino acids and carbohydrates into simple sugars.

There are genetic variations in these enzymes. **Lactase,** the enzyme that splits the milk sugar, lactose, is present almost exclusively in northern Europeans. Most Chinese and Africans are lactase-deficient, and when they ingest milk the undigested lactose causes abdominal distention and diarrhea. Milk is not used as food in large parts of Africa and Asia, perhaps because of genetic intolerance of milk by the inhabitants of these areas. This mechanism may also account for the development of yoghurt in Asia and Eastern Europe. Yoghurt is fermented milk, i.e., predigested by bacteria of the genus *Lactobacillus.* It has also been suggested that the interaction was in the opposite direction, that cattle could not be raised in these areas, perhaps because of insect-borne disease, and that lactase deficiency might not have been a disadvantage, or may even have conferred some unknown selective advantage and increased in frequency (McKusick, 1969).

Bile produced by the liver emulsifies fats and makes them soluble in water for ease of absorption. Bile is manufactured continuously by the liver, from the breakdown of aged erythrocytes, and is stored in the **gallbladder** until food enters the duodenum. Fats in the duodenum cause the release of **cholecystokinin,** which stimulates the gallbladder to contract.

Sugars, amino acids and salts are absorbed actively; water follows osmotically and the water-solubilized fats enter passively. Vitamins and minerals are also actively absorbed.

The **large intestine** consists of the **cecum** (with the **appendix**), **colon, rectum** and **anus.** The colon ascends from the cecum, traverses the abdomen in the upper midline and descends to the **sigmoid** portion, which becomes continuous with the rectum.

The colon's function is to absorb water from the stool and solidify the feces. The upper gastrointestinal tract is sterile, but many microorganisms live in the colon in a symbiotic relationship with the host, deriving nutrition from the colonic contents and in turn supplying some vitamins and amino acids.

Not all ingested material is digested, and enough material is present in the stool to give a good idea of dietary intake. Such studies are useful in examining archeologic specimens of excrement, **coprolites.** Heizer and Napton (1969) for example, have rehydrated and examined coprolites in reconstructing the diet of prehistoric Great Basin American Indians.

The **liver** is the heaviest gland of the body, elaborating many products of great importance, as well as being a major metabolic organ. A major role in digestion is the secretion of bile into the small intestine, where it assists in the digestion of fats. Most of the bile is resorbed and returned to the liver via the portal vein. The small portion of bile that is excreted gives the feces their characteristic brown color. In bile duct obstruction, the feces are gray-white and the bile backs up into the blood and tissues, producing **jaundice.**

The liver also functions as a storehouse, for glycogen, vitamins A, D and B_{12}, and for iron. In the fetus, and under certain pathologic conditions in adults, the liver acts as a major source of blood cells. The phagocytic cells lining the sinusoids play a major role in destroying old erythrocytes throughout life. Detoxification of drugs and hormones is another important function. An example of the importance of this function has already been seen, in schistosomal cirrhosis (Chapter 3).

The **pancreas,** an elongate organ situated under and dorsal to the stomach, is a mixed endocrine and exocrine gland. The pancreas of lower animals is known to gourmets as sweetbread. The exocrine portion of the gland secretes bicarbonate and digestive enzymes into a ductal system that usually joins the bile duct just before terminating in the duodenum.

The endocrine portion consists of the islets of Langerhans, which secrete **insulin** and **glucagon** directly into the blood stream. Insulin facilitates the entry of glucose into the cells of all tissues (except the brain), thus lowering the blood glucose concentration. Insulin also stimulates the synthesis of glycogen, proteins and triglycerides. A deficiency of insulin is associated with the clinical state of **diabetes mellitus.**

Glucagon acts in opposition to insulin by stimulating the breakdown of glycogen and triglycerides and the formation of glucose from amino acids. Glucagon deficiency has been postulated as a cause of low blood sugar, **hypoglycemia,** and an excess may be a factor in diabetes mellitus.

PATHOLOGY

Oral Cavity

The mouth is subject to most of the diseases that affect the remainder of the body. Unique lesions are associated with the teeth.

Heavy **dental wear** is seen in prehistoric skeletal populations and in many extant primitive groups, primarily as a result of abrasive diets. Not even Pharaohs were exempt. The mummy of Rameses II showed heavy wear (Harris and Weeks, 1973), undoubtedly owing to a highly abrasive bread. Leek (1972) subjected bread found in ancient tombs to radiologic and mineralogic analysis, and demonstrated sufficient abrasive material to account for the attrition seen in ancient Egyptian teeth. Cultural factors, including dietary specialization and division of labor, have been noted to account for differences in attrition between groups and between sexes within groups in modern populations (Molnar, 1971).

Another example of the effect of cultural practices on teeth is seen in the mutilated teeth of pre-Hispanic Mexicans reported by Romero (1970). Teeth were filed, and they occasionally used inlays of semiprecious stone. This custom appears to have been widespread, and Romero feels that it cannot be used as an indicator of social status.

Cavities (caries) affect virtually all members of modern populations. Dental **calculus** ("tartar" or "plaque") is present on the teeth, consisting of a calcific mass of bacteria, fungi and food debris. It is thought that ingested carbohydrates are fermented by the bacteria, the acids produced destroying the tooth enamel and producing caries.

Periodontal disease (pyorrhea) is the primary dental disease of adults. Inflammation at the junction of gum **(gingiva)** and tooth spreads to the bone, causing resorption of the bone, with loosening and eventual loss of the tooth.

Both caries and pyorrhea are ancient (Smith, 1978). The antiquity of caries is well attested to by the Rhodesian Pleistocene Neanderthal skull, in which the number of caries exceeds the number of teeth (Pycraft et al., 1928). Despite this early extreme example, caries was not frequent until Neolithic times, and is presumed to be related to the introduction of refined sugars and flours into the human diet (Brothwell, 1965). Marked population differences in the incidence of caries have been noted in antiquity (Elzay et al., 1977; St. Hoyme and Koritzer, 1976) and contemporary times (Dubos, 1971), demonstrating the cariogenic effect of a carbohydrate-rich diet. In contrast, periodontal disease has probably decreased in frequency, the softer modern diet being less traumatic to the gingiva.

Esophagus

Congenital Lesions.   The most important congenital lesion is **atresia,** the presence of a segment consisting only of a thin solid cord, often associated with an abnormal connection to the trachea, a **tracheoesophageal fistula.** Ingested food passes into the respiratory tract, causing coughing, vomiting, and suffocation or pneumonia. Anomalies of the heart or the remainder of the intestinal tract are often associated. The condition is incompatible with life but amenable to reconstructive surgery.

Hiatal hernia is a protrusion of the stomach through the diaphragm into the chest, disrupting the normal mechanisms preventing reflux of gastric contents into the esophagus, and causing heartburn and difficulty in swallowing, **dysphagia.** These lesions are usually seen in the elderly. A hiatal hernia, with fatal intestinal strangulation, has been described in the mummy of a young Chilean, dated to 1550 A.D. (Munizaga et al., 1978). The hernia was probably related to excessive physical labor in colonial mines. These miners all died at an early age, being literally worked to death by their Spanish masters.

Inflammation. There are many causes of esophageal inflammation, including corrosives such as lye ingested in suicide attempts. Other causes are prolonged vomiting, which often results in actual tears of the esophagus, with hemorrhage, and infection by microorganisms. As terminally ill patients are kept alive by modern therapy, unusual infections such as fungi (often of the genus *Candida*) are being seen increasingly.

Esophageal Varices. If blood flow through the liver is obstructed, most commonly by cirrhosis, the portal flow bypasses the liver and goes through the esophageal vessels. These submucosal veins become dilated and tortuous **(varices)** and are liable to hemorrhage, a common mode of death in alcoholics.

Cancer. Carcinoma is a relatively rare but highly lethal tumor. It is much more common in males, presumably being related to alcohol and cigarettes. Marked geographic differences have been noted in the incidence of this tumor. Very high rates are found in areas of Iran (Kmet and Mahboubi, 1972), possibly owing to deficiencies of trace elements. High rates are also found in central Africa and among Africans living in London. Exposure to carcinogenic hydrocarbons has been postulated as the underlying problem, as the Africans in both sites drink beer made with water contaminated by storage in old oil drums (Wapnick et al., 1972).

The course of esophageal cancer is insidious, with gradually worsening obstruction. There is a tendency for the victim to alter his diet toward liquid foods, and it is only too common for a patient to present with complete obstruction by an inoperable tumor. Even if surgery is possible, survival rates are low, under 10 per cent for five years.

Stomach

The stomach is the organ most often responsible for clinical disease of the digestive tract. Three conditions, gastritis, ulcer disease and carcinoma, account for most of the pathology.

Gastritis. **Acute** and **chronic gastritis** are somewhat blanket terms used to cover a wide range of abdominal discomfort. It is clear that the condition is incited by a number of agents, including alcohol, aspirin, caffeine and spicy foods.

The acute form of the disease is usually transient, and repeated episodes may lead to chronic gastritis. In the chronic condition, atrophy of the stomach results in impaired elaboration of a factor necessary for the absorption of vitamin B_{12}, producing **pernicious anemia** (PA). Gastric atrophy appears to be an aging change and PA is most common in the elderly. The condition is called "pernicious" because it was untreatable until the discovery of the gastric intrinsic factor, and led to progressive neurologic deficits and death. Gastric carcinoma was also a complication.

An interesting variant of PA in the past was seen in Jewish housewives, who would acquire fish tapeworm infestations by tasting the raw fish used in the preparation of *gefilte* fish (chopped fish and spices). *Diphyllobothrium latum,* the fish tapeworm, preferentially absorbs vitamin B_{12}, causing a PA-like picture, but in this case a treatable disease.

Ulcer Disease.   Acute ulcers can develop in patients with burns or stress, or on steroids. These lesions are small and painful, and can cause bleeding. Chronic, or **peptic,** ulcers can develop in any part of the digestive tract exposed to the action of gastric acid and digestive enzymes. Such ulcers occur more frequently in the duodenum than in the stomach. Although the pathology of gastric and duodenal ulcers is essentially identical, ethnic differences in incidence suggest that pathogenetically these are two different diseases (Lechin et al., 1973). For convenience, the two lesions will be discussed together.

Ulcers occur somewhat more frequently in males, and the incidence in both sexes has clearly been on the rise. Persons of blood group O have an increased tendency to develop gastric ulcers.

The pathogenesis of peptic ulcer disease clearly is primarily related to the action of acid-peptic digestion. Many other factors have been suggested, such as stress (the mechanism proposed to be an increase in circulating corticosteroids, which are known to be ulcerogenic). The disease is presumed to be one of "civilization," and a positive correlation has been found with income level and socioeconomic status (Yodfat, 1972). This concept ignores the stress under which the members of less-developed societies exist.

The intestinal mucosa normally protects itself from autodigestion by mucus secretion, and if this capacity is lost, as in chronic gastritis, ulcer disease is more likely. Patients with hyperacidity are likewise more prone to ulceration. In general, imbalances between digestive and protective factors result in autodigestion of the intestinal mucosa, peptic ulcer disease.

The ulcer itself usually appears as a punched-out lesion in the wall of the stomach or duodenum. Microscopically the mucosa is replaced by an acutely inflamed mass of granulation tissue with an underlying scar. Within this scar are large, thick-walled arterioles. These vessels can also be digested by the ulcer process, causing one of the complications requiring surgical therapy, bleeding. Other complications involving surgical intervention are perforation, into the peritoneal cavity or another organ, obstruction by scar formation, or intractable pain. Duodenal ulcers are invariably benign and most are managed medically. Gastric ulcers are usually excised if they do not heal promptly with medical treatment, on the presumption that a nonhealing gastric ulcer is likely to be malignant.

Cancer.   The incidence of **gastric carcinoma** has dropped considerably in the United States in the 20th century, now ranking in males as the third leading cause of cancer death in the US behind cancer of the lung and colon. The tumor is much more common in other countries, such as Japan, Finland, Iceland, the People's Republic of China and Taiwan. It has been suggested that this difference is due to dietary factors, such as the ingestion of smoked fish in Iceland (Bjorksten, 1972), or asbestos-containing polished rice in Japan (Merliss, 1971).

The tumors tend to arise over a large area of the mucosa, suggesting that whatever carcinogen(s) is operating has a diffuse effect. There is also an association with blood group A. Several different gross and microscopic morphologic patterns are recognized, but the course of all tends to be insidious and the prognosis poor, with widespread metastatic disease and low survival.

Small Intestine

Infection.   Normally the upper small intestine is relatively sterile. Infection of this area has been implicated in the serious malabsorption and malnutritional states seen commonly in the aboriginal children of Australia (Gracey and Stone, 1972) and other underdeveloped areas of the world.

Certain organisms specifically infect the small intestine, causing clinical disease. Among the most serious of these is *Salmonella typhosa*, the causative agent of typhoid fever. This disease is confined to humans and transmitted by contamination of ingested food or drink. A particular hazard is that posed by typhoid carriers, who recover from the disease but continue to harbor the organism, primarily in the biliary tract. Such individuals become public health problems when they are employed as food handlers, as in the famous case of "Typhoid Mary." This cook, a known typhoid carrier, chose to become a ward of the state rather than undergo a curative removal of the gallbladder (**cholecystectomy**).

The antiquity of typhoid fever is attested to by the demonstration by Sawicki et al. (1976) of *Salmonella sp.* antigens in fecal material from a pre-Columbian mummy.

Typhoid fever played a major role in the near-disappearance of the Maoris of New Zealand in the 19th century. Before the arrival of the Europeans, the Maoris lived on hilltops, for defense. These locations also provided for natural drainage. The hilltops were found to be useless against European firearms, and the Europeans also brought wheat and corn, which grew on the flat lands. The Maoris abandoned their hilltops and moved down onto the flat, where typhoid flourished. To compound the problem, distant tribes would gather to mourn for the dead in a typhoid-infected village, and the disease would spread.

Typhoid and other infectious diseases brought the Maori population down to about 20 per cent of its pre-European level by 1896, but the population has developed immunity and now exceeds the pre-European level. This process, covering less than two centuries, shows how rapidly it is possible to adapt to infectious disease (Wright-St Clair, 1974).

Another serious infectious disease of the small intestine is **cholera,** caused by infection by bacteria of *Vibrio spp*. This was a worldwide epidemic diarrheal disease in the past, but improved sanitation in the western world now limits cholera to an endemic status in Southwest Asia and the Western Pacific. Occasional epidemics still occur in these areas, as well as in Africa and the Middle East.

The effect of the infection is due to a toxin elaborated by the *Vibrio* organism which causes an outpouring of fluid from the blood vessels of the small intestine, resulting in the characteristic watery, mucus-flecked "rice-water" stools. Death is due to dehydration, and modern intravenous fluid replacement and antibiotic therapy have considerably reduced the mortality rate.

Nalin and Haque (1977) have studied the rituals surrounding cholera in Bangladesh. The religious ceremonies amount to a brief quarantine which is ineffective in controlling the disease. The persistence of the ritual is explained by the sporadic nature of cholera. Waning of epidemics make it appear that the measures taken had some effect.

In an Afghanistan village, people with high fever were placed in the local irrigation canal, which also provided drinking water to the downstream villages. This mode of treatment facilitated the spread of an epidemic of cholera in 1965 (Dupree, 1970).

In China it was noted (Hsu, 1976) that a rural cholera epidemic was treated by traditional methods, based on moral and supernatural considerations. Readily available western medical facilities were ignored. Hsu feels that the Chinese did not distinguish in this case between "magical" and "scientific," and makes the point that attempts to introduce new techniques will be successful only if placed into indigenous cultural traditions.

This problem is seen in a broader scope by Foster (1976), who states that concepts of disease etiology are the key to cross-cultural comparison of non-western medical systems. He notes that these systems are based on a personalistic belief that disease, religion and magic are intertwined. This view contrasts with the scientific western orientation which assigns specific etiology for disease. Non-western curers have supernatural or magical powers and function as diagnosticians, in rectifying imbalances, whereas western curers deal in corrective therapeutics. Cultural conservatism explains in part the reluctance of non-western societies to adopt western medical techniques in dealing with problems such as cholera epidemics.

Infestation.   Many worms **(helminths)** involve the intestinal tract (Fig. 6–1). These include the roundworms **(nemathelminths),** flatworms (tapeworms, **cestodes**), and flukes **(trematodes).**

NEMATODES.   The roundworms are of interest in that they probably represent a relatively recent adaptation to the parasitic mode of life. These organisms have complete intestinal tracts, are heterosexual, and many are capable of a free-living existence. As parasites become better adapted to their host, they dispense with such superfluous mechanisms as an intestinal tract, simply absorbing predigested food from the intestine of the host.

Another indication of the recent adaptation of these organisms to man is the seriousness of the diseases they cause. It is counter to the interests of the parasite to cause severe damage to the host. If the host dies, the parasite at the least needs a new home, and at worst also dies.

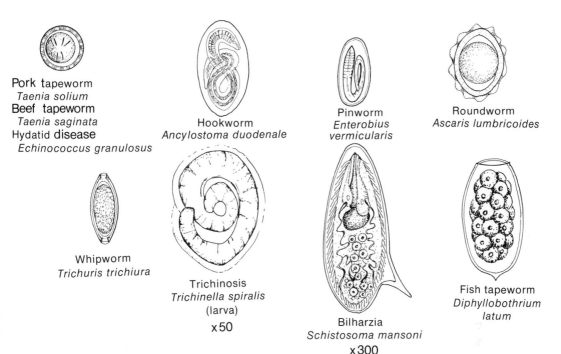

Pork tapeworm
Taenia solium
Beef tapeworm
Taenia saginata
Hydatid disease
Echinococcus granulosus

Hookworm
Ancylostoma duodenale

Pinworm
*Enterobius
vermicularis*

Roundworm
Ascaris lumbricoides

Whipworm
Trichuris trichiura

Trichinosis
Trichinella spiralis
(larva)
x50

Bilharzia
Schistosoma mansoni
x300

Fish tapeworm
*Diphyllobothrium
latum*

Infective forms of some of the common human parasitic worms. All are ova except as noted. Magnifications are × 400 except as noted.

Figure 6.1

One of these serious roundworm infestations is **trichinosis,** caused by ingestion of meat containing encysted larvae, which are released in the intestine. The larvae mature, copulate, and deposit larvae in the wall of the intestine, where they enter the lymphatics, pass into the blood stream via the thoracic duct, and encyst in skeletal muscle. If the host is a food animal the cycle starts again with ingestion of its flesh. Man represents a dead end for the parasite. The disease is a serious one, with symptoms of pain and weakness, depending on the muscles involved. Mortality varies, but can be as high as thirty per cent.

Humans acquire the disease primarily by eating undercooked pork. Those with religious proscriptions against pork are relatively safe from the disease (although unknowing ingestion of pork can occur). Freezing of pork or irradiation kills the larvae, but the best safeguard is adequate cooking of pork or of garbage fed to pigs. Ethnic preferences in food preparation can play a role in the distribution of the disease.

Many other roundworms infest the intestinal tract. Hookworm disease has been discussed in Chapter 3. The pinworm **(enterobiasis),** whipworm **(trichuriasis)** and *Ascaris lumbricoides* **(ascariasis)** are common but do not cause serious symptomatology, suggesting a longer association between parasite and host. Indeed, ascariasis has been described in the mummy of an Egyptian gentleman of 170 B.C. (Cockburn et al., 1975). It is possible that the human disease originated from the ascarids of pigs, which were domesticated in dynastic Egypt.

CESTODES.   The tapeworms are superbly adapted intestinal parasites. They have dispensed with their own intestinal tracts and vascular systems and simply consist of ribbons of hermaphroditic segments called **proglottids,** the most anterior one of which attaches to the host intestine. Several are infectious for man, and the *Taenia spp.* will be considered in some detail.

An Egyptian mummy again supplies us with evidence of the antiquity of the disease (Reyman et al., 1977). The *Taenia* affecting man are *T. saginata,* the beef tapeworm, and *T. solium,* the pork tapeworm, both acquired by eating meat containing encysted larvae. The cysts are digested in the stomach of the definitive host, and the liberated larvae attach to the intestinal wall and develop into the mature form. The ova are passed *per rectum,* sometimes in intact proglottids, and the life cycle is perpetuated when the ova are ingested by the intermediate host and infect the muscle via the blood stream. There is a high degree of specificity for the intermediate host, but man can be an intermediate host for *T. solium.* The encysted larvae can cause clinical disease, **cysticercosis,** if they lodge in the heart or brain, but this accidental disease represents a dead end for the parasite, as man is rarely eaten by hogs.

Symptoms of tapeworm are rather nonspecific, with gastrointestinal irregularities, anemia and malnutrition. As with other parasites, ethnic factors in relation to sanitation, feeding of animals and food processing are important in prevention of the disease.

TREMATODES.   The third class of intestinal parasites are the flukes. These worms have become so highly specialized that some, the **schistosomes,** actually live within the blood stream of the host. Other flukes live in the intestinal lumen, and some inhabit the liver or lung. Fluke eggs have been identified in human coprolites from the prehistoric American Southwest (Moore et al., 1974).

As is evident from the high degree of specialization of the parasite, schistosomiasis is an ancient disease. As discussed in Chapter 3, the presence of this disease is well documented in ancient and modern Egypt, and the associated debility remains a major economic problem.

Inflammation.

REGIONAL ENTERITIS.   This is a "new" disease, having been first reported by Crohn in 1932. Since his original description of regional "ileitis" the disease has been found to involve any part of the digestive tract, producing histologically identical lesions throughout. The disease appears to be increasing in incidence, and was well publicized by President Eisenhower's attacks in the 1950s.

Regional enteritis, or **granulomatous enteritis,** is more common in Jews, rare in blacks, and appears to be limited to the United States and Europe. The etiology is unknown. No microorganism has been associated with the disease, even though the identifying pathologic lesion is a granuloma somewhat similar to those seen in diseases such as tuberculosis. The disease is worsened by emotional stress, but the role of a psychosomatic mechanism in pathogenesis remains speculative.

Clinically, granulomatous enteritis is characterized by an erratic course of diarrhea and constipation persisting for many years. The pathologic picture is one of focal areas of inflammation and scarring of the affected segment of the intestinal tract. Complications of hemorrhage, perforation or obstruction may require surgery, but there is no specific medical therapy.

TUMORS.   Neoplasms of the small intestine are rare. Occasional **adenocarcinomas** arise from the mucosa. As the contents of the small intestine are liquid, obstruction is a late phenomenon, and these tumors usually are clinically silent until well advanced. **Lymphomas,** either primary or as part of a generalized malignancy, involve the small intestine more frequently.

The **carcinoid tumor** is a biochemically active neoplasm which can produce the "carcinoid syndrome." Patients with large masses of tumor develop facial flushing, diarrhea, hypotension and bronchospasm due to biologically active chemicals elaborated by the tumor and its metastases.

Obstruction.   There are a number of causes of intestinal obstruction, all of which must be dealt with surgically, as untreated obstruction usually leads to perforation, peritonitis and death. **Hernias,** weaknesses in the wall of the peritoneal cavity, can trap segments of bowel and cause obstruction. Those who perform heavy manual labor, with consequent increased intra-abdominal pressure, are most likely to develop hernias. Fibrous **adhesions** between loops of bowel, usually in patients who have had previous abdominal surgery, can entrap bowel segments. The bowel can telescope upon itself, **intussusception,** cutting off its own blood supply and becoming infarcted and obstructed. Twisting of the bowel on the mesentery, **volvulus,** likewise obstructs by cutting off the blood supply. Finally, **thrombosis** of the **mesenteric vessels** also produces obstruction secondary to infarction.

Malabsorption (sprue).   There are many causes of failure of absorption of foodstuffs, but in clinical practice the term malabsorption refers to impaired absorption of fats. **Nontropical sprue (celiac disease)** occurs in patients allergic to gluten, a component of wheat. The clinical picture and the anatomic changes (atrophy of the small intestinal villi) are reversed by a gluten-free diet. In contrast, **tropical sprue,** which presents a similar clinical and pathologic picture but is confined to tropical and semitropical areas, responds not to a gluten-free diet but to antibiotics, suggesting a microbial etiology.

Colon

Congenital Lesions. Diverticulosis is a disease due to weak points in the colonic wall at vessel entry and exit points. The mucosa herniates through these openings, and saccular dilatations filled with fecal material form. They are usually multiple and become clinically symptomatic when inflamed **(diverticulitis),** causing pain, constipation and diarrhea. Perforation and obstruction due to scarring are potential complications. Although the weak points are congenital, the disease is one of the elderly in the western world. Accumulating evidence links it to a low fiber diet, with infrequent bowel movements and straining at stool, **tenesmus.** The disease is rare in African natives, who have a high fiber diet and several loose bowel movements each day.

Imperforate anus occurs in one of 5,000 births, as a failure of perforation of the membrane separating the endodermal intestine from the ectodermal anal dimple. In western societies a simple surgical procedure is curative. Some of these cases have associated fistulous connections to the genitourinary tract.

Inflammatory Lesions.   A variety of bacteria and parasites can infect the colon. The colon is normally adapted to its microbiologic flora, but travel to a foreign country can import new types of bacteria. These are not necessarily pathogenic and are usually those which inhabit the colons of the indigenous population. The result is "traveler's diarrhea."

Amebae cause a more serious colonic infection. *Entamoeba histolytica* causes ulceration of the intestinal mucosa, and can spread to the liver and other organs to form metastatic abscesses. Involvement of the lung or brain can cause death.

Typhoid fever and **cholera** can also affect the colon, as can organisms of the *Shigella* group, causing **bacillary dysentery.** All of these infections are hazards faced by travelers to areas with rudimentary sanitation.

Tumors.   Benign and malignant tumors of the colon are very common, and evidence is accumulating that the benign **polyps** are precursors of colon **carcinoma.** Several different histologic subtypes of colonic polyps are known, and it is important to find and excise these lesions before they become malignant. Individuals with **familial polyposis** have hundreds of polyps and inevitably develop colon cancer if the colon is not resected.

Almost all colon cancer is **adenocarcinoma,** derived from the epithelium. Epidemiologic, geographic and experimental evidence implicates a high level of dietary fat in the pathogenesis of the disease (Weisburger et al., 1977).

Colonic carcinoma is primarily a disease of the elderly, but is becoming more frequent in the young (von Langenberg and Ong, 1972). It is usually manifested by blood in the stool, and if treated promptly has a relatively good prognosis. If allowed to progress, the tumor spreads directly through the colonic wall to seed the peritoneum and retroperitoneum, and metastasizes via the portal venous system and lymphatics to the liver, lymph nodes, lung, bone or elsewhere.

It is unfortunate that many patients delay seeking medical aid after they note rectal bleeding. Psychologic factors are clearly at work here, including denial of symptomatology and "cancerophobia."

Appendix

To sufferers of **acute appendicitis,** the sole function of this organ would appear to be as a site for inflammation. This is a very common disease that must be treated surgically. It is most common in young adults, and one wonders why there has not been selection for individuals less liable to the disease, as the mortality if untreated is considerable.

It is probable that obstruction by fecal material impacted within the lumen initiates the inflammatory process, with subsequent infection by colonic bacteria. An acute inflammatory infiltrate spreads through the wall, and can lead to necrosis, perforation, peritonitis and death. It is ironic that one of the first surgeons to recommend appendectomy in this disease, Dr. James Bell of McGill University, died of an unoperated ruptured appendix (Murphy, 1972).

The only other appendiceal lesion of any significance is the **carcinoid tumor.** Most of these are found incidentally at appendectomy, but they possess the same metastatic potential as those found elsewhere in the digestive tract.

Liver

Congenital Lesions. The liver may contain congenital cysts, but these rarely affect function. Various enzymatic deficiencies may cause jaundice, which must be distinguished from obstructive jaundice, which is treated surgically.

Fatty Change. One of the most common pathologic processes seen in the liver is **fatty change,** the accumulation of fat in the liver cells. This is caused by many different chemicals, of which by far the most common is alcohol. Fat is also seen in the liver in a variety of disease states, including diabetes, over- and undernutrition, chronic infection and chronic circulatory failure. Fatty change is reversible, but continued injury to the liver can lead to more serious damage.

Cirrhosis. Diffuse disruption of the normal architecture of the liver by fibrous bands, with nodular regeneration of damaged liver cells, constitutes **cirrhosis.** Many classificatory schemes have been proposed for cirrhosis in the past, most based on a combination of morphologic patterns and presumed etiology. It is currently considered that morphology does not usually correspond to specific etiologic factors, and the classification in use is simply a morphologic one. Livers with large nodules are said to have **macronodular cirrhosis,** and those with small nodules are examples of **micronodular cirrhosis.** There are also several forms of cirrhosis associated with specific etiologic factors.

The main cause of cirrhosis in the western world is alcoholism, although the role played by associated undernutrition is probably important. Cirrhosis has been increasing in frequency, affecting up to 20 per cent of certain ethnic groups in large city hospitals in the United States.

The natural history of the disease is a progressive one, unless the patient avoids alcohol and adopts a proper diet, which arrests the disease. Most patients continue their pattern of dietary indiscretion and there is progressive impairment of liver function, in some to the point of liver failure, hepatic coma and death. Obstruction of the portal veins in the liver leads to the expansion of collaterals through the splenic and esophageal veins. A significant number of these patients develop **esophageal varices,** which are liable to fatal hemorrhage. Cirrhotics also fall prey to infections and peptic ulcer disease, and the mortality rate within *one year* after the appearance of either of these major manifestations, gastrointestinal bleeding or hepatic coma, is on the order of 50 per cent.

Other forms of cirrhosis arise from biliary obstruction (usually by a stone), as a sequel of viral hepatitis (the most common cause of the disease in Africa and Asia) or from parasitic disorders such as schistosomiasis. In all of these the clinical manifestations of the disease are similar, although there may be marked morphologic variations.

Inflammation. Several infectious agents involve the liver in a diffuse fashion, **hepatitis**. Bacterial infection is extremely rare. **Leptospirosis** is caused by species of the spirochetal *Leptospira*, and is a rodent-transmitted disease of worldwide distribution. It is found in those who are occupationally exposed to rodents, primarily agricultural workers. The disease involves the kidneys and brain as well as the liver, and infection by *L. icterohaemorrhagiae* causes a serious form of the disease with a high mortality, Weil's disease. Most cases of leptospirosis, which is rare in the United States, are of a mild nature.

Yellow fever is a systemic viral disease, transmitted by *Aedes aegypti,* a domestic mosquito which readily breeds in man-made collections of water. The disease is therefore found in urban situations, being transmitted directly from man to man. In jungle settings, non-human primates serve as a reservoir. The disease affects liver, kidney, intestinal tract and brain. A very effective vaccination program has virtually eliminated the disease as a human infection, although some human foci remain in Africa and the sylvatic reservoirs will probably continue to exist.

Yellow fever appears to have originated in Africa, being brought to the New World by slaves imported by the Spaniards (Carter, 1931). Innumerable epidemics played a large role in the decimation of the indigenes, the Maya referring to the disease as *xekik*, "blood vomit" (Roys, 1931). In more modern times, yellow fever was a major factor in the delay in the construction of the Panama Canal.

Wood (1976) has suggested a role for yellow fever in the maintenance of the ABO blood group polymorphisms. The *Aedes* mosquitos have blood group-like antigens in their intestinal tracts and thus preferentially take their blood meals from type O hosts. The resultant higher yellow fever rate in type O individuals is postulated to have favored the survival of polymorphic families and balanced the intrauterine loss of the type A and B offspring of type O mothers.

The major liver infection in modern populations is **viral hepatitis**, a destructive inflammatory disease believed at present to be due to any one of at least three agents, two of which are known to be, and the other(s) believed to be, viral. There has long been a clinical distinction between forms of hepatitis with short and long incubation periods. These forms were thought to correspond to the routes of infections and were labeled "infectious" and "serum" hepatitis, respectively. New evidence has changed this scheme.

Viral hepatitis A (VHA, formerly infectious hepatitis) is caused by the hepatitis A virus (HAV), and is usually acquired by ingestion but rarely by injection **(parenterally).** This is a highly infectious acute disease, by the fecal—oral route, and is an epidemic disease in children or under conditions of crowding and inadequate sanitation. The incubation period is approximately one to two months, and the disease is characterized, as in viral hepatitis B, by fatigue, malaise, gastrointestinal symptoms and jaundice. The usual course is spontaneous subsidence after four to six weeks, followed by lifelong immunity. The ease of transmission and postinfection immunity produces a tendency to epidemics as new cohorts of susceptibles reach an age at which they come into contact with older children.

Viral hepatitis B (VHB, formerly serum hepatitis) is caused by a parenterally transmitted virus, and is generally a more severe disease than VHA, with the occasional development of a chronic phase. The incubation period is up to six months, and in the United States many infections occur in users of either blood products or illicit drugs.

An antigen of the virus (HBsAg, hepatitis B surface antigen) can be detected in the peripheral blood (Blumberg et al., 1965). Screening of blood donors has considerably diminished this avenue of infection. There are population differences in the distribution of the antigen, and Blumberg (1970) has suggested that selective pressures in different environments are responsible for maintaining a high frequency of carriers in a population.

The third form of hepatitis is not well characterized, and the viral agent has not yet been identified. The disease is referred to as VH–NAB (not A or B). The clinical disease does appear to be very similar to VHB in that it has a chronic form and can be transmitted by blood transfusion.

The pathology of hepatitis is a picture of hepatic disarray, with necrosis and inflammation. These changes are reversible, but not all sufferers from hepatitis have an uneventful recovery. Some die in the acute phase of the disease ("fulminant hepatitis") and others may progress to a chronic form eventually leading to cirrhosis and/or liver cancer and death.

Prevention of hepatitis is important for several reasons. The social cost of the disease is high, in that it disables many individuals for significant periods. Those who are entering an area of high incidence (e.g., anthropologic field workers, travelers and military personnel) can be protected temporarily by inoculation with commercially available gamma globulin containing antibody to HAV. The screening program has proved effective in blood banking, and a vaccine is under development (Purcell and Gerin, 1978). The chimpanzee is the only animal suitable for vaccine testing, an unfortunate fact which has led to fears for the survival of this endangered species (Wade, 1978).

Parasites.   Several parasites may involve the liver, secondary to intestinal infestations, as has been discussed in preceding pages (amebae, schistosomiasis), or as a primary infection, the **liver flukes**. These Oriental parasites live in the bile ducts and are responsible for an increased incidence of biliary cancer in these areas. The **dog tapeworm**, *Echinococcus granulosus*, occasionally infects man, producing **echinococcal cysts** in the liver, lung, brain or bone. These cysts cause symptoms by pressure on adjacent structures, and occasionally rupture, evoking a potentially fatal allergic reaction.

Tumors.   Most liver tumors are metastatic, usually secondary to intestinal, breast or lung cancers, although many others spread to the liver. So much of the liver may be replaced by tumor as to cause death by liver dysfunction, but generally the liver continues to function even with massive tumor replacement.

Primary tumors show a considerable epidemiologic variation. There is increasing evidence that the use of oral contraceptives is associated with an increased incidence of nodular hyperplasia and benign tumors, **adenomas**, in the livers of young women (Edmondson et al., 1976). Primary cancer of the liver arises from liver cells, **hepatoma** or **hepatocarcinoma**, or from the bile ducts, **cholangiocarcinoma**. Development of hepatoma has been linked to industrial exposure to vinyl chloride, but the tumor also occurs *de novo*. The incidence is increasing in the United States, and is relatively high in Africa, probably because of an association with cirrhosis secondary to viral hepatitis, which is more common in Africa and increasing in the United States.

Microscopically, hepatoma presents a parody of normal hepatic cells and architecture, and the tumor spreads to other organs via the blood stream. The prognosis is extremely poor, most patients dying within six months of diagnosis.

Jaundice. One of the most characteristic symptoms of liver disease is **jaundice**, the accumulation in excess in the blood stream and tissues of blood pigments normally metabolized by the liver. **Bilirubin** is a conversion product of a component of hemoglobin, the blood pigment released in the breakdown of senescent erythrocytes. The liver converts bilirubin into a water-soluble form for excretion in the biliary system. Jaundice can result if there is excessive breakdown of blood, as in the hemolytic anemias, with the liver being overwhelmed by the excess amount of unconjugated bilirubin presented to it. In hepatitis, conversion is depressed. In obstruction of the biliary ducts, usually by stone or tumor, conjugated bilirubin "backs up" into the blood. In theory, the ratio of soluble (conjugated) to insoluble (unconjugated) bilirubin should tell which factors are operating (Fig. 6.2). In practice, multiple factors, such as intrahepatic obstruction due to edema, are often involved, confusing the clinicopathologic picture.

Gallbladder

The function of the gallbladder is the storage and concentration of the bile, making for more efficient digestion of fats. There are two major diseases of the gallbladder and associated ducts to be considered: inflammation, **cholecystitis,** usually associated with stone formation, **lithiasis;** and carcinoma.

Cholecystitis and Cholelithiasis. Cholecystitis may be acute or chronic and is almost invariably associated with cholelithiasis, but it is

ANATOMIC	ELEVATED BILIRUBIN	MECHANISM
Prehepatic	Unconjugated	Hemolysis
Hepatic	Unconjugated and conjugated	Hepatocellular damage
Posthepatic	Conjugated	Obstruction

Figure 6.2   The classification of jaundice.

unclear whether the stones cause the inflammation or are secondary to it. It is probable that bacterial infection does *not* play a primary role in the disorder, and obstruction of the cystic duct by stones may be important in its causation. Stones appear to form by precipitation of bile, cholesterol and/or calcium from a supersaturated biliary solution. Current research efforts are directed at finding chemical means of dissolving stones instead of the traditional surgical approach.

Cholecystitis is a disease of middle age, and is much more common in females, particularly the obese and fecund. For unexplained reasons the disease is also very common in certain Indian tribes of the southwest United States (Porvaznik, 1972; Quilliam, 1972). Paleopathologic evidence suggests a high incidence in pre-Columbian Chile, particularly in contrast to coeval Peruvians, suggesting an environmental etiologic factor (Munizaga et al., 1978).

Stones can form anywhere in the biliary tract, most commonly in the gallbladder. Although they may remain asymptomatic, most are associated with clinical disease. Irritation of the gallbladder may be the cause of cholecystitis. The stones may pass through the cystic and common bile ducts, causing severe abdominal pain, **biliary colic**. Impaction may occur, causing jaundice. Perforation of the gallbladder leads to the formation of fistulous connection with the intestinal tract. Large stones may obstruct the small intestine, **gallstone ileus**. Finally, stones are associated with an increased incidence of gallbladder **carcinoma**. The question of whether the increased incidence is high enough to balance the known morbidity and mortality of elective cholecystectomy remains a point of controversy in modern surgical practice. This is an important point, as gallbladder carcinoma is essentially an incurable and rapidly fatal disease, with a pattern of widespread metastasis, usually present by the time the diagnosis is made.

Pancreas

Three major diseases are associated with the pancreas: **diabetes mellitus; pancreatitis;** and **carcinoma**. Of these, the most common is diabetes mellitus (as distinguished from diabetes insipidus, a disorder of the pituitary gland to be discussed in Chapter 8).

Diabetes mellitus.   Insulin is produced by the pancreatic islets of Langerhans, and its function is to facilitate the entry of glucose into the cells for energy-producing metabolism. Diabetics have an absolute or relative deficiency of insulin. As a result, glucose accumulates in the blood and is passed in the urine. For energy, the cells must metabolize proteins and fats, leading to the accumulation of their breakdown products, **ketone bodies**. Thus, the chemical triad of diabetic manifestations is **hyperglycemia, glycosuria** and **ketosis**.

The ancient Chinese recognized the clinical characteristics of diabetes as a triad still in use: **polyphagia; polydipsia;** and **polyuria** (excessive eating, drinking and urination respectively). The disease was named by Areteus c. 70 A.D., the name meaning "siphon" in Greek, and was described as a melting down of the flesh into urine, as a recognition of the chronic wasting nature of the untreated disease. The elucidation of the role of insulin in diabetes mellitus occurred in the late 19th century. Specific treatment has been available for long enough for most people, including physicians, no longer to be aware that this was a fatal disease. With treatment, the diabetic patient's life span should be close to normal.

The disease is seen throughout the world, and is currently estimated to afflict 2 per cent of the population of the United States, half of those being undetected. This incidence is likely to rise as the population increases and becomes older and more obese, both of which factors favor the development of diabetes. The prolongation of life by treatment also means that an increased percentage of the population will be diabetic, and these survivors will be more likely to pass on the hereditary predisposition to the disease. It is clear that diabetes mellitus has a genetic component, based on studies demonstrating abnormal glucose metabolism in blood-relatives of diabetics, but the mode of inheritance is still a subject for discussion. It has been suggested that the disease has evolved as a means of efficient utilization of scarce food resources, maintaining a normal blood sugar in the face of dietary inadequacy, but this concept too is a point of controversy.

Most diabetes is the **maturity onset** type, which is thought to be due to the failure of the islets to manufacture sufficient insulin. These patients can be treated with diet, insulin injections, or oral agents that lower the blood sugar (**oral hypoglycemics**). **Juvenile diabetes** appears to be a different disease, with failure of insulin production and pathologic features suggesting an autoimmune reaction. The juvenile disease is more severe and must be controlled by insulin injection.

Disease of the small blood vessels throughout the body, particularly affecting the eyes and kidneys, is associated with diabetes mellitus. Atherosclerosis is greatly advanced, damaging many other organs. It appears that careful control of the diabetic patient's blood sugar level prevents many of the complications of the disease. The accelerated atherosclerosis does lead to an increased incidence of myocardial infarction, cerebrovascular accident ("stroke") and gangrene of the extremities, the last often following trivial trauma. Indeed, the development of one of these complications is occasionally the first clinical manifestation of the diabetic state.

The small vessel disease causes blindness and a specific form of renal failure, Kimmelstiel-Wilson disease. Diabetes ranks as one of the most common causes of blindness and renal failure in the United States.

Pancreatitis.   Pancreatitis is due to the destructive effects of pancreatic enzymes on the pancreas itself. The mechanism by which this occurs is unclear. Bile reflux into the pancreatic ducts, duct obstruction, infection and allergy have all been proposed and each may play a role.

Clinically, acute pancreatitis is a catastrophic illness, presenting as an **acute abdomen** which must be distinguished from surgical emergencies such as acute appendicitis, perforated ulcer or gallbladder, and many other conditions. Pancreatitis is associated with alcoholism, but so is ulcer disease. A laboratory determination of the serum level of amylase, one of the pancreatic enzymes, usually shows an elevated level in pancreatitis, but the amylase level can be elevated in other disorders. Differential diagnosis is important, as patients with pancreatitis are poor operative risks. Occasionally exploration is necessary to rule out surgically treatable conditions.

Pancreatitis tends to be a recurrent disease, with the continual necrosis eventually resulting in fibrosis and the development of pseudocysts, areas of destruction that may simulate tumors. As pancreatic tissue is eliminated, symptoms such as failure of fat digestion and diabetes mellitus may appear. The digestive enzymes released convert the fatty tissue normally found in the pancreas to a soap, which eventually calcifies and may be visible on x-ray examination. However, the diagnosis of chronic pancreatitis is generally an elusive one.

Tumors.   Pancreatic **carcinoma** arises from the ducts. The prognosis is poor, as the retroperitoneal position of the organ means that growth is usually extensive before symptoms develop. Occasionally, carcinomas involve the common bile duct early and cause jaundice while still surgically resectable. Generally, however, the tumor kills by widespread dissemination.

The incidence of pancreatic cancer is highest in the United States, New Zealand and Canada, and is rare in Africa. This picture probably reflects diagnostic facilities rather than real differences in incidence. The increase in incidence in recent years probably is also based on improved diagnosis.

Islet cell tumors are of interest because these endocrine tumors may be functional, causing hypoglycemia (by excess insulin secretion) or persistent ulcer disease (due to gastrin secretion). These conditions are curable by surgical excision of the pancreatic lesions, but the tumors may be small or multiple.

NUTRITIONAL DISORDERS

Nutritional disorders consist of two broad groups: excess and deficiency. The major health problem of the western world today is one of excessive dietary intake and resultant obesity. Weiner (1971) suggests that modern man continues to follow the "gorging" pattern of hunter–gatherer groups, but that this mechanism is inappropriate in the absence of the periodic scarcities such groups face. The result is an overweight population with accelerated cardiovascular disease, increased diabetes, gallbladder disease, and perhaps an excess of such diseases as colon cancer.

Vitamins are organic catalysts needed for maintenance of normal cell structure and function. Most vitamin-related disorders are deficiency diseases, but vitamins A and D can be ingested in excess. This phenomenon is one of western society, usually seen in situations of non-medically supervised self-medication or misinformed overenthusiasm for vitamins by the parents of infants.

Hypervitaminosis A is characterized by hyperexcitability, bone pain, and headache with increased cerebrospinal fluid pressure. Discontinuation of intake relieves the symptoms. Interestingly, polar bear liver is extremely high in vitamin A, and early arctic explorers, shortly after its ingestion, developed the symptoms of acute vitamin A intoxication (headache, nausea, vomiting and diarrhea). The Eskimos are aware of this effect and will not eat polar bear liver.

Hypervitaminosis D causes mobilization of calcium from the bones with deposition in other tissues. The symptoms are nausea, vomiting and diarrhea, and the formation of renal stones.

Outside the western world, deficiency diseases are much more common than those of excess ingestion. Multiple deficiencies are common, not only of vitamins but also of proteins and all other essential nutrients. It is likely that there has been selection for genetically determined resistance to starvation (Motulsky, 1971), but two frequently fatal starvation type diseases of infancy are still seen. **Marasmus** is total calorie and protein deficiency, and **kwashiorkor** is a condition of protein deficiency in children with a carbohydrate-based diet adequate in calories. Children weaned prematurely are particularly liable to kwashiorkor, the syndrome of the "displaced child;" marasmus is seen in children under 1 year old. The deaths of these infants (along with female deaths in the 15 to 30 age-group associated with childbirth) largely account for the lower life spans seen in ancient populations (Clarke, 1977).

The pathology of these two diseases is essentially that of starvation. There is fatty change of the liver, and those who survive are liable to cirrhosis and possibly liver cancer. Atrophy of the pancreas is also seen and there is growth failure, edema and behavioral disturbances. The skin flakes off, and pigmented races show a red color of the hair (kwashiorkor means "red boy" in Swahili).

Adults also need an adequate protein supply, particularly during periods of stress or increased physical activity. The customs of the Tsembaga of New Guinea are of interest in this regard. Pigs are kept but rarely eaten, except during periods of stress. In the face of impending warfare, protracted illness, injuries or death, pigs are sacrificed to the ancestors, and the meat is consumed by those participating in the event. Rappaport (1974) suggests that this ritual mechanism maintains an adequate health status in the population during such stress situations.

Vitamin Deficiencies

Vitamin A.   Vitamin A functions to maintain certain specialized epithelia, to form retinal pigments, in skeletal growth, and in cell membrane structure and function. Important natural sources are fish liver oils and carotenes of vegetable origin.

Deficiency of vitamin A has very widespread effects. Retarded growth is seen in children, and atrophy of muscles and emaciation at all ages. Scaly lesions of the conjunctiva and cornea, **xerophthalmia,** are characteristic and often diagnostic. Night blindness is due to failure of formation of **visual purple**, a pigment derived from vitamin A. Multiple small skin nodules are caused by plugging of follicles, and squamous metaplasia of various ducts throughout the body may be obstructive.

Death from pneumonia is common in severe cases, as these changes predispose to bacterial infections. Therapy, as with the other deficiency diseases, consists of replacement and care of the complications of the disease.

Vitamin D.   Deficiency of vitamin D causes rickets, a bone disease discussed in Chapter 11.

The B Vitamins.   Several vitamins fall into the B vitamin group, each being associated with a specific deficiency disease. Two vitamins will be considered in this discussion: **thiamine** and **niacin**.

Thiamine is necessary for carbohydrate metabolism, and deficiency primarily affects the nervous system, which is dependent on carbohydrates for energy. Several disorders are seen, including **beri-beri, Wernicke's encephalopathy** and **Korsakoff's psychosis**. Diets high in carbohydrates can precipitate the disease, by increasing the thiamine requirement above the dietary intake. In western society these diseases are seen most frequently in malnourished alcoholics. Otherwise, vitamin B deficiencies are tropical diseases, as the vitamin requirement is temperature-related and the supply in meat from animals raised in the tropics is lower (Stewart, 1970).

Beri-beri is manifested by degeneration of the heart and subsequent circulatory failure. Resultant edema leads to the description of so-called "wet" beri-beri. The "dry" form of the disease is primarily a neurologic degenerative disorder, resulting in Wernicke's and Korsakoff's syndromes. Briefly, Wernicke's encephalopathy is characterized by degeneration of nerves supplying the eye muscles and extremities, and of the cranial nerves. Degeneration and hemorrhage in the brain progresses to coma. Korsakoff's psychosis is manifested by confabulation, the invention of stories by the individual to cover gaps in his knowledge, memory or perceptions. The syndrome appears to be a more or less permanent sequel to the brain damage of Wernicke's encephalopathy. If treatment is inadequate, mortality in beri-beri may be as high as 50 per cent.

Niacin deficiency results in **pellagra**, although some feel that multiple deficiencies are involved in this disease. Certainly other factors, including alcoholism, sunlight exposure and coexisting diseases, are important.

Pellagra is the "three-D disease": **dermatitis, diarrhea** and **dementia**. The skin is scaly, rough and pigmented. There is an enteritis and late degeneration of the nervous system, causing neurologic and psychiatric manifestations. Response to niacin therapy is prompt.

Vitamin C.   **Scurvy** is due to deficiency of ascorbic acid, a material which is widely distributed in nature in citrus fruits. Primates and guinea pigs are the only animals that require dietary vitamin C, all other animals being able to synthesize the vitamin from glucose. Man lacks the final enzyme necessary for this conversion.

The vitamin is necessary for the production and maintenance of intercellular substances such as collagen, osseomucin, chondromucin, dentin, and the substances that hold endothelial cells together. The outstanding manifestation of the disease is hemorrhage, along with skeletal lesions (Chapter 11). The areas of hemorrhage are liable to infection, and secondary infection is the most frequent cause of death. Tuberculosis, unrestricted by the usual scar formation, is especially common.

Therapy is by vitamin C replacement. The current vogue for massive prophylactic doses in the early treatment of **upper respiratory infections** (URIs, the common cold) has not been evaluated in an adequate scientific fashion.

Essential Elements

A number of elements are essential to life, including calcium, potassium, sodium, zinc, iodine, iron and many others. Most of these function for either electrolyte balance or as parts of enzyme systems. Deficiencies have been correlated with certain disease processes, usually secondary to environmental scarcity. Occasionally, drinking water becomes contaminated with excess amounts of minerals, either from natural sources or by industrial pollution, causing large-scale outbreaks of poisoning. **Minamata disease** in Japan has been shown to be due to mercury pollution of sea water, with severe neurologic damage in those who ingest contaminated fish.

On a more general level, an inverse relationship has been demonstrated between the hardness of drinking water and mortality from cardiovascular disease. It is extraordinarily difficult to provide proper controls for such studies, and conclusions must be viewed with caution.

REFERENCES

Bjorksten, J. (1972): Diet and stomach cancer. Science 175:474.

Blumberg, B. S. (1970): Adaptations to infectious disease: Australia antigen and hepatitis. Am. J. Phys. Anthropol. 32:305–308.

Blumberg, B. S., Alter, H. J. and S. Visnick (1965): "New" antigen in leukemic sera. J.A.M.A. 191:541–546.

Brothwell, D. R. (1965): Digging up Bones. British Museum, London.

Carter, H. R. (1931): Yellow Fever: An epidemiological and Historical Survey of its Place of Origin. Williams and Wilkins, Baltimore.

Clarke, S. (1977): Mortality trends in prehistoric populations. Hum. Biol. 49:181–186.

Cockburn, T. A., Barraco, R. A., Reyman, T. A. et al. (1975): Autopsy of an Egyptian mummy. Science 187:1155–1160.

Crohn, B. B. (1932): Regional ileitis: a pathologic clinical entity. J.A.M.A. 99:1323.

Dubos, R. (1971): Man Adapting. Yale University Press, New Haven.

Dupree, L. (1970): Aq Kupruk: a town in north Afghanistan. In Peoples and Cultures of the Middle East, Vol. 2: Life in the Cities, Towns, and Countryside. L. E. Sweet, ed. Natural History Press, Garden City, New York, pp. 344–387.

Edmondson, H. A., Henderson, P. and B. Benton (1976); Liver cell adenomas associated with the use of oral contraceptives. N. Engl. J. Med. 294:470–472.

Elzay, R. P., Allison, M. J. and A. Pezzia (1977): A comparative study on the dental health status of five preColumbian Peruvian cultures. Am. J. Phys. Anthropol. 46:135–140.

Foster, G. M. (1976): Disease etiologies in non-Western medical systems. Am. Anthropol. 78:773–782.

Garn, S. M., Nagy, J. M., Sandusky, S. T. et al. (1973): Economic impact on tooth emergence. Am. J. Phys. Anthropol. 39:233–238.

Gemmill, C. L. (1972): The Greek concept of diabetes. Bull. N. Y. Acad. Med. 48:1033–1036.

Gerszten, E., Munizaga, J., Allison, M. J. et al. (1976): Diaphragmatic hernia of the stomach in a Peruvian mummy. Bull. N. Y. Acad. Med. *52*:601–604.

Gracey, M. and D. E. Stone (1972): Small intestinal microflora in Australian aboriginal children with chronic diarrhea. Aust. N. Z. J. Med. *3*:215–219.

Harris, J. E. and K. Weeks (1973): X-Raying the Pharaohs. Scribner's, New York.

Heizer, R. F. and L. K. Napton (1969): Biological and cultural evidence from prehistoric human coprolites. Science *165*:653–658.

Hsu, F. L. K. (1976): A cholera epidemic in a Chinese town. *In* Health, Culture and Community. B. D. Paul, ed. Russel Sage Foundation, New York, pp. 135–154.

Kmet, J. and E. Mahboubi (1972): Esophageal cancer in the Caspian littoral of Iran: initial studies. Science *175*:846–853.

Lechin, F., Van der Dys, P., Pena, C. et al. (1973): A study of some immunological and clinical characteristics of gastritis, gastric ulcer and duodenal ulcer in three racial groups of the Venezuelan population. Am. J. Phys. Anthropol. *39*:369–374.

Leek, F. F. (1972): Teeth and bread in ancient Egypt. J. Egypt Archeol. *58*:126–132.

McKusick, V. A. (1969): Human Genetics, 2nd ed. Prentice-Hall, Engelwood Cliffs, New Jersey.

Merliss, R. R. (1971): Talc-treated rice and Japanese stomach cancer. Science *173*:1141–1142.

Molnar, S. (1971): Human tooth wear, tooth function and cultural variability. Am. J. Phys. Anthropol. *34*:175–190.

Moore, J. G., Grundmann, A. W., Hall, H. J. et al. (1974): Human fluke infection in Glen Canyon at A. D. 1250. Am. J. Phys. Anthropol. *41*:115–118.

Motulsky, A. B. (1971): Metabolic polymorphisms and the role of infectious diseases in human evolution. *In*: Human Populations, Genetic Variation, and Evolution. L. N. Morris, ed. Chandler, San Francisco, pp. 222–252.

Munizaga, J., Allison, M. J. and E. Aspillaga (1978): Diaphragmatic hernia associated with strangulation of the small bowel in an Atacamena mummy. Am. J. Phys. Anthropol. *48*:17–20.

Munizaga, J., Allison, M. J. and C. Paredes (1978): Cholelithiasis and cholecystitis in preColumbian Chileans. Am. J. Phys. Anthropol. *48*:209–212.

Murphy, J. A. (1972): James Bell's appendicitis. Can. J. Surg. *15*:1–4.

Murphy, J. M. (1964): Psychotherapeutic aspects of shamanism on St. Lawrence Island, Alaska. *In* Magic, Faith and Healing. A. Kiev, ed. Macmillan, New York, pp. 53–83.

Nalin, D. R. and Z. Haque (1977): Folk beliefs about cholera among Bengali Muslims and Mogh Buddhists in Chittagong, Bangladesh. Med. Anthropol. *1*, 3:55–68.

Perzigian, A. J. (1977): Teeth as tools for prehistoric studies. Am. J. Phys. Anthropol. *46*:101–114.

Porvaznik, J. (1972): Surgical problems of the Navaho and Hopi Indians. Am. J. Surg. *123*:545–548.

Purcell, R. H. and J. L. Gerin (1978): Hepatitis B vaccines: on the threshold. Am. J. Clin. Pathol. *70*:159–169.

Pycraft, W. B., Smith, G. E., Yearsley, M. et al. (1928): Rhodesian Man and Associated Remains. Trustees British Museum. London.

Quilliam, T. A. (1972): A pictorial archive of a vanishing culture. Med. Biol. Illus. *22*:85–93.

Rappaport, R. A. (1974): Pigs for the Ancestors: Ritual in the Ecology of a New Guinea People. Yale University Press, New Haven.

Reyman, T. A., Zimmerman, M. R. and P. K. Lewin (1977): Autopsy of an Egyptian mummy (Nakht-ROM 1): histopathologic investigation. Can. Med. Assoc. J. *117*:470–472.

Romero, J. (1970): Dental mutilation, trephination and cranial deformation. *In* Handbook of Middle American Indians, Vol. 9: Physical Anthropology. T. D. Stewart, vol. ed. University of Texas Press, Austin, pp. 50–67.

Roys, R. L. (1931): The Ethno-Botany of the Maya. Tulane University, New Orleans.

St. Hoyme, L. E. and R. T. Koritzer (1976): Ecology of dental disease. Am. J. Phys. Anthropol. *45*:673–686.

Sawicki, V. A., Allison, M. J., Dalton, H. P. et al. (1976): Presence of *Salmonella* antigens in feces from a Peruvian mummy. Bull. N. Y. Acad. Med. *52*:805–813.

Smith, P. (1978): Regional variation in tooth size and pathology in fossil hominids. Am. J. Phys. Anthropol. *47*:459–466.

Stewart, T. D. (1970): Physical plasticity and adaptation. *In* Handbook of Middle American Indians, Vol. 9: Physical Anthropology. T. D. Stewart, vol. ed. University of Texas Press, Austin, pp. 192–202.

von Langenberg, A. and G. B. Ong (1972): Carcinoma of large bowel in the young. Br. Med. J. *2*:374–376.

Wade, N. (1978): New vaccine may bring man and chimpanzee into tragic conflict. Science 200:1027–1030.

Wapnick, S., Zanamwe, L. N. D., Chitiyo, M. et al. (1972): Cancer of the esophagus in central Africa. Chest 61:649–654.

Weiner, J. S. (1971): The Natural History of Man. Universe Books, New York.

Weisburger, J. H., Reddy, B. S. and E. L. Wynder (1977): Colon cancer: its epidemiology and experimental production. Cancer 40:Suppl.: 2414–2420.

Wood, C. S. (1976): ABO blood groups related to selection of human hosts by yellow fever vector. Hum. Biol. 48:337–341.

Wright-St Clair, R. E. (1974): The impact of infection on a Polynesian community. Can. Med. Assoc. J. 110:953–956.

Yodfat, Y. (1972): A population study of peptic ulcer: its relation to various ethnic and socio-economic factors. Isr. J. Med. Sci. 8:1680–1684.

seven

The Urinary System

ANATOMY AND PHYSIOLOGY

The waste products of metabolism, particularly urea, from protein catabolism, are brought to the **kidney** for disposal by the renal arteries, branching off the abdominal aorta. Urine is elaborated by the **glomeruli**, minute convoluted vascular structures in the cortex of the kidney. Certain compounds, salts and water are selectively added to or removed from the urine by the **tubules**, which are in continuity with the capsules surrounding the glomeruli. Each glomerulus and its attendant tubule forms a unit called a **nephron** (Fig. 7.1). The urine drains from the tubules into the **pelvis** (meaning "basin") of each kidney, and on into the **ureters,** two long tubes connecting to the **urinary bladder**, a distensible muscular organ situated anterior to the rectum in the male and the vagina in the female. The outlet of the bladder, the **urethra**, is a short tube in the female, but in the male it is partially surrounded by the prostate gland and traverses the penis. These anatomic differences bear upon the pathologic changes seen in the bladder, as will be discussed below.

PATHOLOGY

Kidney

Congenital Anomalies.   Bilateral absence of the kidneys is a rare occurrence incompatible with life and found only in stillborn infants. Occasionally one kidney fails to develop, or both kidneys are hypoplastic. Usually other anomalies, often neurologic, are associated. Since much of the amniotic fluid is made up of fetal urine, little amniotic fluid is found in such pregnancies, **oligohydramnios**. The obstetrician may

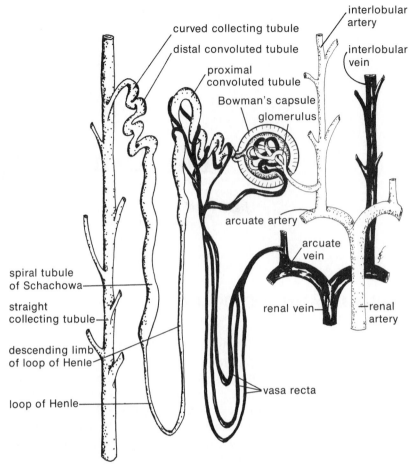

Figure 7.1   The nephron.

be alerted to the potential of this anomaly if the mother's uterus does not enlarge as much as it would in a normal pregnancy.

The kidney may be fused across the midline of the retroperitoneum, a **horseshoe kidney** (Fig. 7.2). There is no functional disturbance, but, as with multiple ureters or renal arteries, a surgeon working in this area must be aware of the variation.

Many kidneys have a few small cysts, but occasionally there is an abnormality of fetal development causing **polycystic kidneys** (Fig. 7.3). The progress of the disease is variable, most patients eventually dying of renal failure or the effects of an associated hypertension.

Glomerulonephritis.   Inflammation of the glomeruli is referred to as **glomerulonephritis**, a disease that may have a variety of manifestations.

Acute glomerulonephritis usually follows a streptococcal upper respiratory infection, and is manifested by blood in the urine, **hematuria**. Most patients (usually children) recover rapidly and completely. A few go on to develop chronic disease and renal insufficiency. The disease appears to be due to the formation of antibodies against the streptococci which can react with the patient's glomeruli.

The insidious form of the disease, **membranous glomerulone-**

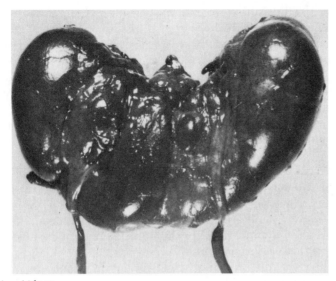

A horseshoe kidney.   Figure 7.2

phritis, is of unknown etiology, although allergic phenomena are prominent in these patients, and progression to chronic disease is common, particularly in adults. The differences among individuals that determine who acquires the disease, and the prognosis, are entirely unknown.

In both forms of the disease, damage to the glomeruli results in leakage of protein into the urine, **proteinuria,** with resultant lowering of serum osmotic pressure, leakage of fluid into the tissues, and edema. In the insidious form, this clinical picture is known as the **nephrotic**

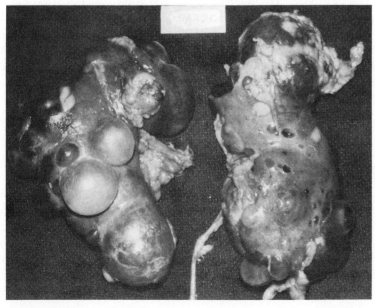

Polycystic kidneys.   Figure 7.3

syndrome. In the acute form patients become hypertensive, in addition to the hematuria described above.

The diagnosis in modern practice is based on renal biopsy, the significant changes being at an ultrastructural level, i.e., seen with the electron microscope. Treatment by steroids has greatly improved the prognosis of the disease, which in the past frequently evolved into chronic glomerulonephritis with death in renal failure.

Pyelonephritis.   Acute inflammation of the pelvis, tubules and interstitium of the kidney is a common disease almost always due to bacterial infection. The highest incidence is in young women and patients with urinary obstruction, usually elderly men with enlarged prostates. Edema of the urethra, secondary to trauma, causes partial obstruction in young women, with inflammation of the bladder ("honeymoon cystitis") and ascending infection of the kidneys.

The clinical symptoms of pyelonephritis are cloudy urine, due to pus cells, **pyuria,** fever, pain in the area of the kidneys, and symptoms of bladder infection (burning, urgency and frequency of urination). Vigorous treatment of the infection and any predisposing conditions are in order, to prevent evolution to chronic disease.

Infection can also be carried to the kidney by the blood stream. Renal tuberculosis can develop in this fashion, and must be treated surgically, with medical treatment of the primary focus, usually in the lung.

Diseases of the Renal Blood Vessels, Hypertension.   Sclerosis of the renal blood vessels is associated with hypertension, defined in Chapter 4 as a systolic pressure over 140 or a diastolic over 90. However, it is unclear whether the changes seen in the renal vessels are the cause of or are secondary to hypertension, as much of the evidence bearing on the situation is contradictory. Many patients with documented hypertension have no renal disease at autopsy, and occasional cases show renal disease with no history of hypertension.

The pathologic change consists of narrowing of the arterioles with atrophy of the kidney on a macroscopic and microscopic level. This picture is seen in most elderly individuals, in whom it is usually but not invariably associated with hypertension. A similar but more severe picture is seen in a rapidly progressive form, **malignant hypertension.** This condition is seen in younger individuals and is more common in blacks.

Occlusion of the larger vessels produces renal **infarcts.** Occlusion may be due to thrombosis or embolism, and because so much of the circulation passes through the kidneys these organs are frequently the site of infarcts. Renal infarcts usually are relatively small and heal as scars, without significantly affecting renal function.

Obstruction and Stones.   Obstruction to the outflow of urine causes a progressive dilatation of the collecting system and atrophy of the kidney, **hydronephrosis.** The cause may be congenital, due to deformities of the ureter, or acquired. There are many acquired causes, including prostatic hypertrophy or cancer, stones, pressure from an enlarged uterus, or invasion of the ureter by cancer originating in the bladder or the uterus. Hydronephrosis may be unilateral or bilateral, and tends to remain silent for long periods. In the early stages relief of obstruction will reverse the process, but if it is prolonged there is irreversible destruction of renal tissue.

Stones, **calculi**, are frequently seen within the urinary system and are usually composed of varying mixtures of calcium, phosphates and uric acid. The cause is not well understood, but basically seems to be a combination of increased ions in the urine, lesions in the walls of the urinary collecting system, and urinary stasis. One certainty is that the passage of stones through the ureter causes excruciating pain, **renal colic**. Larger stones usually remain in the kidney and manifest themselves by hematuria. Calculi also predispose to infection.

Tumors. Benign tumors, **adenomas**, are common findings at autopsy but are rarely of clinical significance. **Renal cell carcinomas** (formerly **hypernephromas**), which occasionally are histologically indistinguishable from the smaller benign tumors, are in their behavior among the most unusual tumors of man. They may remain localized, presenting with hematuria, or they may appear as metastases masquerading as primary tumors of bone, brain, lung, skin or any other site. The tumor may invade the renal vein and grow up into the heart. There is a tendency to solitary metastases, and patients have been cured by surgical removal of primary and metastatic tumor. On the other hand, metastases have appeared in patients 20 years post removal of a cancerous kidney (**nephrectomy**). The tumor may grow slowly or explosively, and is a most bewildering lesion.

Dialysis and Renal Transplantation. Patients in chronic renal failure can now be treated quite successfully by these recently developed techniques. This text has focused on etiology, pathogenesis and description, but the social aspects of the treatment of renal failure are almost as important as the medical ones. For this reason a discussion of therapy is included.

For long-term care hemodialysis with an artificial kidney is an established technique. Blood is taken from an artery in an arm or leg, circulated through an artificial kidney, and returned to a vein in the same extremity (Fig. 7.4). Several machines are available, using the same basic principle of removing impurities by filtering the blood with sheets of cellophane and other plastic.

Placement of permanent arteriovenous "shunts" has made attachment of patients to the artificial kidney simple and painless. The dialysis can even be done at home, which has the advantages of lower cost and more flexibility in regard to the patient's time schedule.

Dialysis units have been established in most major medical centers in the United States and Europe. Patients are treated two or three times a week and generally are restored to a functional level in society. However, there are complications, not the least of which is a significant incidence of hepatitis in the patients and staff. Other complications include infection and clotting of the shunt, osteoporosis, anemia and difficulties of fluid balance. Six-year survival rates are approximately

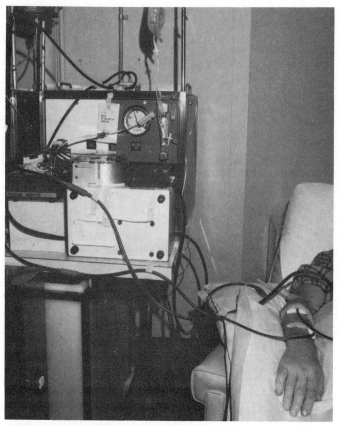

Figure 7.4 A renal dialysis machine in operation.

50 per cent for hospital dialysis and 70 per cent for home dialysis (Curtis and Williams, 1975).

In view of these problems with dialysis, **renal transplantation** would appear to be the ideal solution for the patient in renal failure. The procedure has a success rate of up to 80 per cent when sibling kidneys are used (Merrill, 1970). However, in any match other than identical twins, it is necessary to treat the recipient with immunosuppressive drugs, including corticosteroids. Many complications result from this treatment, including infection, transplantation of unsuspected tumors along with the kidney, and the development of malignant lymphomas in these long-term immunosuppressed patients. In addition the transplanted kidney may be rejected on an immunologic basis, or may develop glomerulonephritis or vascular disease. Overall survival is approximately the same as for hospital dialysis. However, the limiting factor is the social problem of finding suitable donors, in particular overcoming taboos against autopsies and the use of cadaver kidneys.

The major social aspect of the renal failure problem is related to the costs of dialysis and transplantation. The current operating costs of renal dialysis centers are over $20,000 per patient per year, excluding initial equipment costs. Home dialysis is less expensive, about $10,000 per year. Renal transplantation costs from $5,000 to $10,000 the first year, but after that entails only a few hundred dollars for immunosuppressive drugs. If a suitable donor can be found, and the patient's age and health and psychiatric status are appropriate, transplantation is the more satisfactory approach, from both the medical and economic standpoint.

These costs had reached a point in the early 1970s when patients were dying simply because they could no longer afford the expense of staying alive. In 1973 the United States government assumed the cost of all renal dialysis and transplantation programs. The cost of this service has far exceeded initial estimates, and now reaches $1 billion per year (Culliton, 1978), having been shifted from the individual to society as a whole.

Ureters

The ureters are liable to a variety of congenital variations ranging from agenesis to multiplicity. As long as there is no obstruction these variations are rarely of clinical significance (except in renal transplantation surgery).

Infection and tumors of the ureter are rare. Obstruction by stone or extrinsic tumor is fairly common, as discussed in the above section on hydronephrosis.

Urinary Bladder

The major pathologic conditions of the bladder are infection, stone formation and neoplasia. Congenital anomalies are of many different types, but are rare.

Infection.   Cystitis is the most common disorder of the bladder. The normal bladder is remarkably resistant to infection. Conversely, urinary stones, heavy bacterial contamination and obstruction predispose to cystitis. In western society most cases are iatrogenic, i.e., secondary to medical intervention such as catheterization. Infection is usually via the urethra, and is more common in females, with their short urethras, than in males. Infection occasionally descends from the kidney.

The symptoms of cystitis are frequency, lower abdominal pain and painful urination, **dysuria**. Treatment is aimed both at relieving these symptoms, by antibacterial drugs and urinary anesthetics, and at correcting any predisposing cause.

Bladder infections are often associated with stone formation. These **calculi** occur more often in males, usually associated with prostatic hypertrophy, suggesting a mechanism based in part on stasis. Geographic evidence suggests that environmental factors operate here, as there are wide differences in incidence in different populations. Urinary calculi are very common in Indochina, but extremely rare in Africa. This phenomenon is also seen in ancient populations, with wide variance in incidence in different groups of ancient Egyptians (Brothwell, 1967; Rowling, 1967).

Tumors.   Specific tumors of the bladder are derived from the epithelium, **transitional cell carcinomas,** and for practical purposes are all malignant. Even low histologic grade tumors tend to recur and become worse with each recurrence. Almost all of these carcinomas occur in those over 50, and almost all can be attributed to the effects of chemical carcinogens concentrated by the kidneys and excreted in the urine. Exposure to aniline dyes and cigarettes have clearly been associated with abnormally high rates of bladder cancer (Maklyoun, 1974).

In southern Iran the risk of cancer of the bladder has been noted to be nine times higher for males than for females. Opium addiction, which is eight times more common among Iranian males than among females, has been proposed as the cause of the differential incidence (Sadeghi and Behmard, 1978). The suggested mechanism is the urinary retention seen in addicts, prolonging exposure to carcinogens in the urine, and/or a direct carcinogenic effect of opium or opium smoke.

Other forms of chronic irritation such as schistosomiasis have also been implicated in bladder cancer.

These tumors tend to be locally invasive, if at all, and metastases are infrequent. Death is usually due to ureteral obstruction with secondary renal disease.

REFERENCES

Brothwell, D. R. (1967): Evidence of endemic calculi in an early community. *In* Diseases in Antiquity. D. R. Brothwell and A. T. Sandison, eds. Charles C Thomas, Springfield, Ill., pp. 349–351.

Culliton, B. J. (1978): Health care economics: the high cost of getting well. Science *200*:883–885.

Curtis, J. R. and G. B. Williams (1975): Clinical Management of Chronic Renal Failure. Blackwell Scientific Publications, London.

Maklyoun, N. A. (1974): Smoking and bladder cancer in Egypt. Br. J. Cancer *30*:572–581.

Merrill, J. (1970): Transplantation. *In* Harrison's Principles of Internal Medicine, 6th ed. M. M. Wintrobe, G. W. Thorn, R. D. Adams et al., eds. McGraw-Hill, New York, pp. 357–363.

Rowling, J. T. (1967): Urology in Egypt. *In* Diseases in Antiquity. D. R. Brothwell and A. T. Sandison, eds. Charles C Thomas, Springfield, Ill., pp. 532–537.

Sadeghi, A. and S. Behmard (1978): Cancer of the bladder in southern Iran. Cancer *42*:353–356.

eight

The Endocrine System

INTRODUCTION

As noted in Chapter 2, the control mechanisms of the body are neural and endocrinologic. These systems in fact are intimately inter-related. The central nervous system, in particular the hypothalamus, is a major factor in the control of hormonal secretion, and hormones directly affect the function of the nervous system.

The endocrine system provides for long-term control of many bodily functions, by the action of hormones. A **hormone** is defined by Vander et al. (1970) as a "chemical substance synthesized by a specific organ or tissue and secreted into the blood, which carries it to other sites in the body, where its actions are exerted."

Reproduction, metabolism and energy balance are hormonally regulated. Reproduction is absolutely dependent on hormonal control, and hormones function in the other systems in adaptation to environmental change and to stress.

Hormones generally are highly specific, affecting only certain **target-organ** cells. The target may be limited to one organ, as in the effect of thyroid stimulating hormone (TSH) on the thyroid, or may be more generalized, as in the case of growth hormone (GH). The circulating levels of hormones are determined by the rate of synthesis and secretion, and by removal by inactivation, usually by the target or **end organ** or by the excretory mechanisms of the liver or kidney. Hormones operate by altering the rates of reactions, usually by increasing enzyme activity or by changing the rate of transport of substances into cells.

Hormones are produced by many glands, including the anterior and posterior pituitary, thyroid, parathyroids, adrenal cortex and medulla, pancreas, kidney, gastrointestinal tract and gonads.

THE PITUITARY GLAND

Anatomy and Physiology

The pituitary gland, or **hypophysis**, is a small structure lying in a bony pocket at the base of the skull. The gland, connected by a stalk to the **hypothalamus** of the overlying brain, consists of an anterior endocrine portion and a posterior neural portion. The anterior pituitary secretes six hormones. The posterior pituitary, even though it is histologically neural tissue, secretes two hormones.

Four of the six secretions of the anterior pituitary are **trophic** hormones; they stimulate the hormonal secretion of other glands. **Thyroid stimulating hormone** (TSH) causes the release of **thyroid hormone** (TH) from the thyroid gland, and **adrenocorticotropic hormone** (ACTH) stimulates the adrenal cortex to release **cortisol.** Two **gonadotropins** are concerned with reproduction, along with a fifth hormone, **prolactin.**

The gonadotropins are identical in males and females, although they are referred to by the names originally given them for their actions in females. **Follicle stimulating hormone** (FSH) stimulates the growth of follicles in the ovary; **luteinizing hormone** (LH) stimulates the production of the ovarian hormones **estrogen** and **progesterone**. In males, FSH and LH are necessary for the production of testosterone and spermatozoa.

Prolactin affects the breasts, but is probably of little importance in females, and has no apparent reproductive function in males.

The sixth anterior pituitary hormone is **growth hormone** (GH), which stimulates the growth of tissues by a diffuse metabolic effect. All tissues, including the skeleton and viscera, are affected..

The anterior pituitary is in turn controlled by "releasing factors," in actuality hormones, elaborated in minute amounts by the hypothalamus. These hormones set the level of pituitary secretion, which is then maintained by feedback mechanisms based on the blood concentration of the target organ secretions.

The **posterior pituitary**, or **neurohypophysis**, is an extension of the hypothalamus and produces two hormones: **oxytocin** and **antidiuretic hormone** (ADH). Oxytocin stimulates the uterus to contract at the time of delivery, **parturition,** and has a role in the delivery of milk to the nipple. Nursing in turn stimulates the release of oxytocin, through the mediation of higher brain centers. Nursing also inhibits the release of FSH and LH by the anterior pituitary, with blockage of ovulation. The phenomenon of lactational amenorrhea (cessation of menses) has been demonstrated in baboons (Altmann et al., 1978), and humans. The mechanism is thought to be inhibition of the appropriate releasing factors of the hypothalamus. There are marked ethnic and individual differences in amenorrhea during nursing (Winikoff, 1978). Maternal nutritional status also appears to play a role, but frequency of breast-feeding is probably the most important factor in prolonging amenorrhea (Huffman et al., 1978). Although breast-feeding is significant as a population control measure, it is of limited reliability for individuals (Knodel, 1977).

ADH is a small molecule, consisting of only eight amino acids, which operates by increasing the permeability of the renal tubules to water. The tubule is the site of active resorption of sodium from the glomerular filtrate, with chloride and water following passively. Under normal circumstances the tubules are relatively impermeable to water, which is excreted in the urine in high volume, **diuresis**. ADH allows water to be resorbed with sodium, resulting in a low urine volume. In stress ADH secretion promotes retention of sodium and water, an adaptive mechanism in the face of potential losses by sweating or hemorrhage. On the other hand, destruction of the posterior pituitary causes massive loss of water in the urine, **diabetes insipidus**.

Pathology

Diseases of the pituitary produce their effects by two mechanisms: mechanical expansion and hyper- or hyposecretion of hormones.

Enlarging tumors of the pituitary may exert pressure on the optic nerves, causing progressive blindness, or may erode into adjacent sinuses and the brain. As tumors enlarge they cause an increase in intracranial pressure, manifested by headache, nausea and vomiting.

Destructive lesions cause a decrease in hormone production, the degree and effect of which are dependent on the amount of destruction. Most commonly the destructive process is infarction, secondary to a rapid drop in blood pressure, as in obstetric hemorrhage (Sheehan's postpartum pituitary necrosis). Such patients gradually develop pituitary insufficiency, i.e., decreased activity of the glands regulated by the pituitary. Rarely, infection causes a similar picture.

Tumors of the pituitary may be destructive or hyperfunctional. Most tumors are considered to be benign, **adenomas**, but there are no reliable histologic criteria for assessing the potential malignancy of these lesions and their behavior must be evaluated clinically.

Excessive production of GH causes excessive growth, as would be expected. In children, or in experimental animals, the result is **giantism,** involving not only stature but also the viscera. If the disease has its onset in adults the viscera are similarly enlarged, but increase in the length of the long bones is impossible, as the growth areas, **metaphyses,** of the bones are closed. Instead, bone is deposited around the surfaces of the bones, particularly at the extremities of the body, the **acral** areas, such as the hands, feet, chin, etc. This condition is known as **acromegaly.**

Children deficient in GH become well-proportioned dwarfs (Fig. 8.1), in contrast to the disproportionate anomalies seen in achondroplastic dwarfs (Chapter 11). If treated early enough in life with GH extracted from cadaver pituitaries, such GH-deficient dwarfs can be brought to a normal height. African Pigmies, on the other hand, have normal GH levels, but show end-organ unresponsiveness to the hormone (Rimion et al., 1969).

The posterior pituitary is rarely involved by disease. As mentioned above, destructive lesions can cause diabetes insipidus, with the excretion of as much as 20 liters of dilute urine per day.

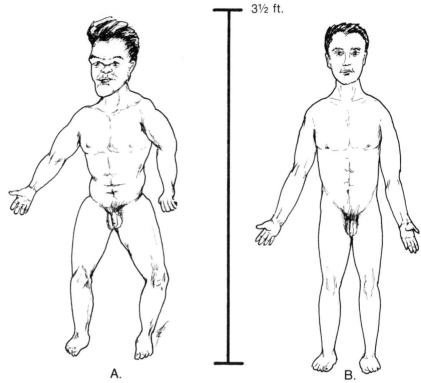

3½ ft.

A.

B.

Figure 8.1   *A,* Achondroplastic dwarf. *B,* GH-deficient dwarf.

THE THYROID GLAND

Anatomy and Physiology

The thyroid gland is a bilobate organ in the neck which secretes a number of hormones, the most significant of which is **thyroxine**. This iodine-containing hormone increases the metabolism of most of the tissues of the body. The effect is dramatic and long-term, raising the oxygen consumption and heat production of tissues, often by the catabolism of tissue fat and protein. The effects of thyroxine are perhaps best illustrated by the changes seen in states of deficiency or excessive production of the hormone.

Pathology

Deficiency of thyroxine production may be due to one of several mechanisms, all of which result in enlargement of the thyroid gland, **goiter**. The most common cause of goiter is a deficiency of iodine in the food and drinking water, usually in mountain or inland areas. This geographic distribution was known to the Chinese 5,000 years ago, and to the ancient Egyptians and Romans. Julius Caesar was impressed by the large necks of the Gauls, considering it a national characteristic. Incidentally, the word goiter derives from the Latin *guttur*, "throat."

The Romans also noted that the thyroid enlarged in periods of physiologic stress, and developed a ritual of measuring the circumference of a new bride's neck before and a week after marriage. The thyroid swells with the physiologic and emotional changes of the initiation of sexual activity, and an increase in the neck circumference was confirmation of the consummation of the marriage.

Cultural attitudes toward goiter have varied from considering it an affliction, or punishment for some transgression, to regarding it in Renaissance Europe as an adornment, to be emphasized with a "choker."

The addition of iodine to the diet has essentially eliminated the disease in the United States and Europe, but it remains a serious problem in underdeveloped areas, particularly Latin America. The introduction of iodized salt in Guatemala reduced the incidence of goiter from about 50 to 5 per cent in eight years (Scrimshaw and Tejada, 1970), but the disease remains endemic in the mountains of South America.

Goitrogenic substances can block thyroid hormone production. These agents contain sulfhydryl groups (SH^-) which compete with and block the uptake of iodide (I^-), especially if the dietary intake of iodine is low. Goitrogens are produced by some strains of intestinal bacteria and are found in turnips, cabbage, rutabaga, kale and other vegetables.

The effect of these agents was demonstrated in the 1950s in Tasmania. The Australian government began a program in 1949 to combat endemic goiter in the area by giving iodine tablets to schoolchildren. Over the next several years the incidence of goiter actually increased. It developed that this paradox was related to a free milk program begun in the schools at about the same time. To satisfy the increased demand for milk, local dairymen kept their cows at pasture over the winter. As grass was not available, the cows grazed on frost-resistant kale, which contains a goitrogen, as noted above. This compound was secreted unchanged in the milk and blocked utilization of the iodine in the tablets.

A possible link to a human polymorphism has been the discovery that the ability to taste phenylthiocarbamide (PTC), an artificially produced bitter-tasting goitrogen, may function to protect the individual against the goitrogenic action of these vegetables. It has long been known (Fox, 1932) that the crystals of PTC were bitter to some and tasteless to others. Greene (1973) studied an Andean community in which not only were goiter and **cretinism** (congenital hypothyroidism) endemic, but an entire range of delay of neurologic maturation on the basis of subclinical hypothyroidism was noted. A significant correlation was found between visual-motor maturation and PTC tasting ability, suggesting (Greene, 1974) that PTC tasters had an adaptive advantage in detecting a bitter taste in, and therefore not consuming, foodstuffs containing goitrogenic compounds.

Other studies have been contradictory. An earlier report by Paolucci et al. (1971) failed to show any relationship between PTC tasting and goiter. Bryce et al. (1976) did find a positive association between PTC non-tasting and goiter in an area of goiter endemicity in Papua-New Guinea. The details of selection for this polymorphism certainly remain to be studied, and the correlations observed may hold in some populations and not in others. The fact that the calcium content of bones from cretins is higher than normal (DeVasto, 1976) may allow identification of hypothyroidism in archeologic populations and lead to a study lending a historical perspective to this problem.

A third mechanism for goiter is a hereditary defect in the synthesis or transport of TH. Several different such deficiencies are known.

Whatever the mechanism, the effect is the same. The serum TH level is low, the pituitary TSH production goes up, and the thyroid is stimulated to enlarge, usually in an asymmetric or nodular configuration, but with subnormal TH production.

Clinically, hypothyroidism is either a congenital disorder, **cretinism**, or acquired in childhood or adulthood, **myxedema**. Myxedema can result from a variety of conditions, including the goitrogens discussed above, iatrogenic obliteration of the thyroid, inflammation, or pituitary insufficiency. The myxedematous individual is **hypometabolic**, with slow movements and mentation. The face is puffy, the tongue thick, and there is intolerance to cold. Degenerative changes are seen in many of the organs, particularly the heart and other muscles.

Cretinism is expressed primarily by retardation of physical and mental development, in addition to the clinical signs seen in myxedema. The disease is endemic in areas of iodine deficiency.

A goiter may also be hyperactive, resulting in the condition known variously as **hyperthyroidism, exophthalmic goiter, Graves' disease,** or **diffuse primary hyperplasia**. Clinically the condition is manifested by **hypermetabolism** (increased metabolic rate, rapid pulse, intolerance to heat, weight loss and increased sweating), **exophthalmos** (protrusion of the eyes) and **goiter** (Fig. 8.2). It appears that the condition is due to

Figure 8.2   Exophthalmic goiter.

excessive stimulation by a recently discovered material, **long-acting thyroid stimulator** (LATS), which circulates in the blood and is thought to be an antibody to an as yet unidentified component of the thyroid. Thus, Graves' disease is considered an immunologic disorder. Many questions remain unanswered, including the site of production of LATS and its mechanism of action.

Treatment of hypothyroidism is by administration of iodine or TH, appropriate to the underlying condition. Hyperthyroidism is treated medically, by drugs that interfere with TH production, or by partial ablation of the thyroid, surgically or by radiation. The thyroid is extraordinarily efficient at trapping iodine, so that the administration of radioactive iodine (RAI) can be used to ablate the gland partially with no risk of damage to other organs.

Tumors. Benign tumors are rarely of clinical significance but must be distinguished from cancers. Carcinoma of the thyroid is not rare, and occurs twice as often in females as in males. There is a significant correlation with a past history of radiation to the neck. A variety of subtypes is based on microscopic architecture. The peak incidence is seen in middle age, but the **papillary** type of carcinoma occurs most commonly in young females. Tumors are treated surgically, and most papillary carcinomas have a slowly progressive pattern of behavior. Even the presence of bone and lung metastases is not inconsistent with survival for many years. Other types may be more rapidly progressive, however.

THE ADRENAL GLANDS

Anatomy and Physiology

The two adrenal glands, situated just above the kidneys, have a distinct cortex and medulla. Both are hormonally active, although the medulla is actually a large sympathetic ganglion, part of the autonomic nervous system. The two portions are physiologically independent, and anatomically separate in many lower species.

The cortex produces hormones which are based on the steroid nucleus. Side chains determine the action of the various hormones, which fall into three groups. The **mineralocorticoids** play a role in salt and water metabolism; the **glucocorticoids** deal with carbohydrate, fat and protein metabolism; and the **androgens** and **estrogens** deal with sexual features. A feedback mechanism operates based on ACTH production by the anterior pituitary, and a deficiency in any one of the corticosteroids may provoke an increase in ACTH production. As with the thyroid, the function of these hormones is best illustrated in pathologic states of excessive or decreased production.

The secretion of the adrenal medulla, principally epinephrine, is controlled by the hypothalamus. Epinephrine acts by increasing the activity of the sympathetic nervous system, and is therefore important in the classic "fight or flight" reaction.

Pathology

There are three major clinical expressions of **hyperadrenalism**: hyperaldosteronism; Cushing's syndrome; and the adrenogenital syndrome.

Hyperaldosteronism (Conn's Syndrome). This is characterized by hypertension, polyuria and polydipsia, decreased serum potassium and periodic paralysis. Aldosterone is produced in excess by a benign tumor of the cortex, and removal of the tumor is curative. This condition is of clinical importance as a treatable cause of hypertension.

Cushing's Syndrome. This is usually due to hyperplasia of the adrenal cortex, apparently caused by excess amounts of ACTH in the circulation. It is becoming increasingly common as an iatrogenic disorder in patients being treated with steroids for a variety of diseases. The clinical picture (Fig. 8.3) is unmistakable, with a characteristic truncal obesity ("buffalo hump"), moon face, abdominal striae (stretch marks), weakness, hypertension, osteoporosis and potential diabetes mellitus. Mental disturbances are also common.

The excessive ACTH can be from a pituitary tumor or from some

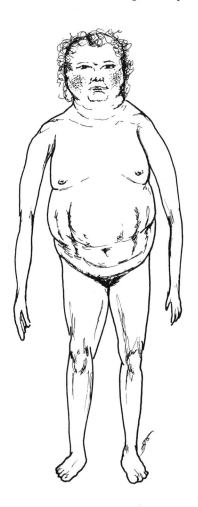

Figure 8.3　Cushing's syndrome.

other ACTH-producing neoplasm, such as certain lung or pancreatic carcinomas. Such conditions are potentially reversible, by adrenalectomy or removal of a tumor, but some cases of Cushing's syndrome remain unexplained.

Adrenogenital Syndrome.   In this syndrome, individuals lacking certain enzymes needed for steroid synthesis suffer disruption of the adrenal-pituitary feedback mechanism, and the pituitary then produces excess ACTH. Production of androgens, which occurs in males and females, is not blocked, and the excess androgen formation causes virilization of the individual. The enzyme deficiency is congenital and the disorder is often manifested in infancy, but it may develop later in life.

Hypofunction of the adrenal is classically due to destruction of the cortex by tuberculosis. With the decline in incidence of tuberculosis of recent years, most cases of Addison's disease are now of unknown etiology, **idiopathic.** The clinical picture is one of weakness, pigmentation of the skin and mouth, hypotension, hypoglycemia, dehydration, and periods of shock after trauma or infection.

Tumors.   Benign and malignant tumors of the adrenal cortex occur and may or may not be functional. Adenomas are rarely of clinical importance, unless hyperfunctional. Adrenocortical carcinomas are highly malignant, metastasizing widely throughout the body and causing death.

Adrenal Medulla.   The hormones of the medulla, epinephrine and norepinephrine, are not essential for life. Tumors of the medulla, **pheochromocytoma,** may secrete enough of these hormones to cause hypertension. Again, this is a potentially reversible form of the disease.

The remaining hormones to be covered are not under the control of the hypothalamus-pituitary system. These include the secretions of the pancreas which regulate blood glucose (Chapter 6), the parathyroids which regulate blood calcium, the kidney for red blood cells, aldosterone which regulates urine flow (discussed above), and the gastrointestinal tract (Chapter 6, the digestive enzymes). Simple control mechanisms operate on these hormones, based on feedback systems responsive to the levels of the material to be controlled.

THE PARATHYROID GLANDS

Anatomy and Physiology

The four parathyroid glands are minute, bean-shaped structures, usually located on the posterior surface of the thyroid gland. Occasionally they can be found in other sites, lower in the neck or in the chest. The secretion, **parathormone** or **parathyroid hormone** (PTH), regulates the level of calcium in the blood. This is a most important function, as calcium must be maintained within narrow limits. High levels of parathormone result in **hypercalcemia** and abnormal calcification of body tissues, as well as the formation of stones, particularly in the urinary system. Low hormone levels cause **hypocalcemia**, associated with irregular muscular twitching, weakness and possible convulsions, a condition referred to as **tetany**. Severe neuroses and psychoses (Chapter 12) can also be seen in hypocalcemia.

Many factors affect the serum level of calcium, including dietary intake, vitamin D, and the individual's respiratory status. It has been suggested that behavioral disorders in at least two populations are actually due to abnormalities of calcium metabolism. **Piblokto**, an acute dissociative hysterical state seen in Eskimos, has been linked to low dietary calcium intake, decreased vitamin D levels due to the dark Arctic winter, and hyperventilation (Katz and Foulks, 1970). **Ghost sickness** in Comanches similarly has been linked to hyperventilation, which alone lowers the serum calcium (Jones, 1972).

Parathormone regulates the calcium level by operating at three sites. Virtually all the calcium in the body is stored in the bones, and parathormone releases calcium from bone by stimulating cells that break down bone, the **osteoclasts**. Secondly, parathormone increases the intestinal absorption of calcium, and finally it decreases the renal excretion of calcium. The action of parathormone is regulated directly in a simple feedback system based on serum calcium level and by a secondary control system based on **thyrocalcitonin**, a thyroid hormone that opposes the action of parathormone on bone.

Pathology

Disease of the parathyroid glands is manifested clinically by either hyper- or hypofunction. A decrease or absence of parathormone causes hypocalcemia and tetany, as discussed above. Most commonly this condition is due to unintentional removal of the parathyroid glands during thyroid surgery.

Hyperparathyroidism is manifested by hypercalcemia and often initially presents as urinary stones. Other signs and symptoms, such as bone pain, pathologic fractures, peptic ulcer disease and mental changes, may dominate the clinical picture. It is of interest that hyperparathyroidism is being diagnosed more frequently in modern practice than in the past. Blood chemistries are currently being performed on a multiple test machine, and cases of asymptomatic hypercalcemia are being "picked up," diagnosed and treated properly, usually by surgical exploration of the parathyroid glands. This approach prevents damage to tissues liable to abnormal calcification.

There are many causes of hypercalcemia, but those relating most directly to the parathyroids are chronic renal failure and parathyroid hyperplasia or tumor. The loss of calcium in renal failure can stimulate the parathyroids to a **secondary hyperplasia**, or the hyperplasia may be spontaneous. Benign (**adenoma**) or malignant (**carcinoma**) tumors are often hormonally active.

The lesions seen in hyperparathyroidism include abnormal calcification in the soft tissues, such as the eye, kidney, lung, stomach, heart and blood vessels. Resorptive lesions in the bones are referred to as **brown tumors**, or **osteitis fibrosa cystica**. These are not true tumors, but areas of replacement of the bone with fibrous tissue showing hemorrhage and abortive bone formation. Such lesions must be distinguished from true bone tumors. Damage to the kidneys in hyperparathyroidism can be severe and life-threatening.

ERYTHROPOIETIN

Red blood cells are in a sense degenerate cells, in that they have lost their nucleus and most of their synthetic metabolic mechanisms. They have become so highly specialized for the function of carrying oxygen that they have become short-lived (120 days) bags of hemoglobin. The constantly dying red cells are replaced by new cells produced in the bone marrow, and the level is regulated by erythropoietin, a hormone currently thought to originate in the kidneys. A small amount of the hormone is in the circulation. Decreased oxygen in the tissues stimulates a rise in the erythropoietin level and an increase in erythrocyte production. This is probably the mechanism of high altitude polycythemia (Chapter 4), but little more than this outline is known.

REFERENCES

Altmann, J., Altmann, S. A. and G. Hausfater (1978): Primate infant's effects on mother's future reproduction. Science 201:1028–1030.

Bryce, A. J., Harrison, G. A., Platt, C. M. et al. (1976): Association between PTC taster status and goiter in a Papua New Guinea population. Hum. Biol. 48:769–777.

DeVasto, M. A. (1976): The percentage of calcium and phosphorus in human bone as diagnostic of severe hypothyroidism. Yearbook Phys. Anthropol. 20:338–346.

Fox, A. L. (1932): The relationship between chemical constitution and taste. Proc. Natl. Acad. Sci. USA 18:115–120.

Greene, L. S. (1973): Physical growth and development, neurological maturation and behavioral functioning in two Ecuadorian Andean communities in which goiter is endemic. Pt. I. Am. J. Phys. Anthropol. 38:119–134.

Greene, L. S. (1974): Physical growth and development, neurological maturation and behavioral functioning in two Ecuadorian Andean communities in which goiter is endemic. Pt. II. Am. J. Phys. Anthropol. 41:139–152.

Huffman, S. L., Chowdhury, A.K.M.A. and W. H. Mosley (1978): Postpartum amenorrhea: how is it affected by maternal nutritional status? Science 200:1155–1157.

Jones, D. E. (1972): Sanapia: Comanche Medicine Woman. Holt, Rinehart and Winston, New York.

Katz, S. H. and E. F. Foulks (1970): Mineral metabolism and behavior: abnormalities of calcium homeostasis. Am. J. Phys. Anthropol. 32:299–304.

Knodel, J. (1977): Breast feeding and population growth. Science 198:1111–1115.

Paulucci, A. M., Ferro-Luzzi, A., Modiano, G. et al. (1971): Taste sensitivity to phenylthiocarbamide (PTC) and endemic goiter in the Indian natives of Peruvian Highlands. Am. J. Phys. Anthropol. 34:427–430.

Rimion, D. L., Merimee, T. J., Rabinowitz, D. et al. (1969): Peripheral subresponsiveness to human growth hormone in the African Pygmies. N. Engl. J. Med. 281:1383–1388.

Scrimshaw, N. S. and C. Tejada (1970): Pathology of living Indians as seen in Guatemala. In Handbook of Middle American Indians, Vol. 9: Physical Anthropology. T. D. Stewart, vol. ed. University of Texas Press, Austin, pp. 203–225.

Vander, A. J., Sherman, J. H. and D. S. Luciano (1970): Human Physiology: The Mechanisms of Body Function. McGraw-Hill, New York, p. 193.

Winikoff, B. (1978): Nutrition, population and health: some implications for policy. Science 200:895–902.

nine

The Reproductive System

Reproductive *(germ)* cells are produced in the gonads, spermatozoa in the testis and ova in the ovary. In the course of formation of these germ cells, one division step is *meiotic* rather than *mitotic* (Fig. 2–5). In meiosis the DNA is not reduplicated but is simply split in half. Thus, each human daughter cell has 23 rather than 46 chromosomes, and union of the germ cells, *fertilization*, restores the full complement of chromosomes, 23 coming from each parent.

THE MALE REPRODUCTIVE SYSTEM

Anatomy and Physiology

Spermatozoa leave the testis through a ductal system, the *epididymis* and *vas deferens*, the proximal part of which serves as a storage area. The vas deferens receives secretions from the *seminal vesicles* and *prostate* before emptying into the prostatic portion of the urethra. The bulk of the ejaculate consists of these secretions, which provide the fructose used by the sperm for energy.

Erection, caused by vascular engorgement of the penis, is an automatic reflex triggered by highly sensitive mechanical receptors in the tip *(glans)* of the penis. Higher brain centers also have considerable control over erection. Thoughts or emotions can cause erection in the absence of mechanical stimulation, and failure of erection *(impotence)* is frequently due to psychologic factors.

Ejaculation is a reflex mediated by the spinal cord. The ejaculate

128

contains about 300 million sperm, which must be of adequate numbers and quality, particularly motility, for successful fertilization. Only one sperm unites with the ovum.

The male reproductive functions are under hormonal control, responding to the gonadotropins of the anterior pituitary, FSH and LH, and to *testosterone*, produced by the testis. FSH stimulates spermatogenesis directly; LH (in the male, often called *interstitial cell stimulating hormone*, or ICSH) stimulates the interstitial cells of the testis to produce testosterone. ICSH indirectly stimulates spermatogenesis, as testosterone is required for this process.

Testosterone is a general anabolic hormone, stimulating growth of all tissues. It is the determinant of the male secondary sexual characteristics: beard growth; muscularity and general male body configuration; deep voice; hair pattern; and sex drive *(libido)*. A small amount of testosterone is secreted by the adrenal cortex in both sexes. A pathologic increase in production can cause virilization in the female.

In normal males hormonal control is constant and does not change over the reproductive span. This pattern is in contrast to the cyclic nature of the female reproductive hormones. Although most elderly men do become impotent, there is no direct counterpart of the female menopause.

Pathology

PENIS

Diseases of the penis consist of a variety of congenital anomalies, infections and tumors. A few of the most common conditions will be discussed in some detail.

The urethral opening may be located on the ventral surface of the penis, *hypospadias*, or the dorsal surface, *epispadias.* Such conditions may be associated with urinary obstruction or more serious anomalies in the genitourinary tract. Certain groups of Australian aborigines practice *subincision*, an artificially induced hypospadias. The asexual transmission of venereal diseases such as gonorrhea has been documented in the rituals associated with subincision. Ceremonies related to maturation rites and the transmission of tribal myths involve considerable direct genital contact between subincised males, allowing incidental transmission of gonococci (White, 1977).

The penile infections of importance are primarily the venereal diseases, including syphilis (Chapter 3).

Tumors of the penis are rare, mostly being carcinomas of the overlying skin. This cancer is rare in circumcized males, presumably because circumcision prevents the accumulation of secretions and allows for better hygiene and fewer infections. It is of interest that penile cancer is rare in Mohammedans, in whom circumcision is practiced before the age of ten, and is essentially unknown in Jews, who are circumcized shortly after birth. African tribes vary in age of circumcision, and those with the lowest incidence of penile cancer practice ritual circumcision at the lowest ages.

TESTIS AND EPIDIDYMIS

The testis develops in the abdominal cavity and descends into the scrotum just before birth. In about 1 per cent of males the testis fails to descend *(cryptorchidism)*. If not placed in the scrotum surgically, the cryptorchid testis becomes atrophic after puberty, and such a testis is more likely than a descended testis to develop a cancer.

Inflammation of the testis, *orchitis*, may develop as a complication of mumps, gonorrhea, syphilis and many other infections. The testis becomes painfully swollen, and may form abscesses in gonorrhea. Acute inflammation may resolve or proceed to a chronic inflammatory state, with the possibility of atrophy and sterility. Occasionally tuberculosis may involve the testis and epididymis.

A variety of tumors arise in the testis, from the germ cells, the hormonally active interstitial cells, and the stromal components. Usually the testis is enlarged, with or without pain, most often in men under 45. The cause is unknown, but familial occurrence suggests a genetic component, and there is often a past history of orchitis.

The classification of testicular tumors is on a histologic basis, and many of these tumors have counterparts in ovarian tumors, as seen in Figure 9.1. An oddity is that one type, choriocarcinoma, is resistant to chemotherapy and uniformly fatal in males and in females when of ovarian origin. The same tumor, arising in the placenta, is curable by the administration of methotrexate. These tumors must be biochemically different even if histologically identical.

PROSTATE GLAND

Anatomy and Physiology.   The prostate is a multilobar glandular and muscular organ in males, situated in the pelvis at the origin of the urethra. It is easily palpable through the rectal wall, particularly if enlarged. The prostate receives the vas deferens and passes the spermatozoa into the urethra via the ejaculatory ducts, adding prostatic fluid to the ejaculate.

Pathology.   The prostate is liable to acute and chronic inflammation and most of the infections that can occur elsewhere in the genitourinary tract.

The major clinical problem regarding the prostate is the distinction between benign *hyperplasia* and *carcinoma.* Hyperplasia, referred to clinically as *benign prostatic hypertrophy* (BPH), is found in almost all elderly men, and is a frequent cause of urinary obstruction. The patho-

MALE	FEMALE
Seminoma	Dysgerminoma
Embryonal carcinoma	Embryonal carcinoma
Teratocarcinoma	Teratocarcinoma
Choriocarcinoma	Choriocarcinoma

Figure 9.1   Malignant tumors of germ cell origin, male and female.

genesis of the lesion is believed to be related to the hormonal changes of aging, but whether these changes are due to sensitivity to androgen, decreased androgen, or relatively increased estrogen is unclear at present. Both the glandular and muscular elements of the gland take part in the hyperplasia, and surgical resection may be necessary to relieve obstruction.

Carcinoma of the prostate is responsible for up to 8 per cent of cancer deaths in men over 50, but many more elderly males have microscopic evidence of prostatic cancer in prostates removed for hyperplasia or examined at autopsy. It is not known what prevents the dissemination of these "latent" cancers.

The etiology of prostatic cancer is unknown, but endocrine factors are suspect. There is much contradictory evidence in this regard. Marked racial and geographic differences in incidence are known, clinical disease being much less common in mongoloids than in whites or blacks. The incidence of latent cancers seems to be about the same in all races.

The interpretation of these statistics is difficult. For example, clinical prostatic disease was said to be rare in Indonesia, but when systematic studies were done, it was found that the symptoms of urinary obstruction were simply being accepted as a matter of course by elderly Indonesians (Tannenbaum, 1977).

Adenocarcinoma of the prostate usually arises in the peripheral portions, causing symptoms of obstruction late in the course. The location does allow transrectal needle biopsy. The tumor spreads locally and widely, especially to the skeleton.

Treatment is by excision and hormones. The cancer is thought to be androgen-dependent, so these elderly patients are treated by castration and estrogens, usually with dramatic temporary destruction of tumor, relief of symptoms and prolongation of life. Eventually, most of these tumors recur, to be treated with chemotherapy and radiation.

When hormonal therapy was first attempted, it was found that the cancers were controlled but that patients were dying of excessive cardiovascular disease. An extensive nationwide study was necessary to establish an optimum estrogen dose, low enough to avoid the cardiovascular complications but high enough to maintain antitumor activity (Tannenbaum, 1977).

THE FEMALE REPRODUCTIVE SYSTEM

Anatomy and Physiology

The reproductive organs of the female consist of the ovaries, fallopian tubes or oviducts, the uterus and the vagina. Reproduction requires the production of an ovum by the ovary and passage into the fallopian tube, where fertilization takes place. The fertilized ovum passes on into the uterus where it implants and develops in the uterine wall.

The ovary has two functions, the production of ova and the elaboration of the hormones **estrogen** and **progesterone.** In contrast to the testis, which continually produces new germinal cells, the ovary at birth has a full complement of *primordial follicles,* consisting of an ovum and a surrounding cell layer. No new follicles are formed after birth. The two ovaries contain approximately 400,000 such follicles, only some 400 of which reach maturity. The remainder degenerate, and the mechanism that determines which follicles mature and which degenerate is unknown. Those that mature late in a woman's reproductive years are 30 to 35 years older than those released just after puberty, and it has been suggested that certain defects observed in the offspring of older women are related to aging changes in the ovum.

The process of ovulation consists of growth of the ovum and follicle, with the formation of a cystic fluid-filled space which eventually ruptures to the surface of the ovary, releasing the ovum into the pelvic cavity. The end of the fallopian tube waves over the ovary, and cilia in the tube sweep the ovum in. It takes several days for the ovum to traverse the tube, and if unfertilized the ovum is eventually passed out of the uterus, usually in the menstrual discharge. If fertilization occurs the embryo implants in the wall of the uterus, which has been prepared by a series of hormonal actions.

Ovulation is thought to be controlled by the release of LH from the anterior pituitary, but the mechanism involved is not understood. The effect of estrogen and progesterone on the *endometrium,* the lining of the uterus, is much clearer. Estrogen, secreted by the follicle cells and the *corpus luteum* (the residual structure after rupture of the follicle), stimulates the growth of the endometrium and the muscle wall of the uterus, the *myometrium.* These changes occur in the first 14 days of the menstrual cycle (counting from the beginning of the menstrual flow). Ovulation takes place on day 14, and progesterone secreted by the corpus luteum causes the endometrial glands to become tortuous and filled with glycogen. These changes and the increased vascularity of the endometrium create an optimal environment for the implantation of a fertilized ovum. If fertilization has not occurred, the corpus luteum degenerates about day 25, and the fall in the estrogen and progesterone levels triggers destruction of the secretory endometrium, initiating menstruation. In most women the cycle is approximately 28 days in length, although there are many variations between women and in the same woman from cycle to cycle.

PREGNANCY

The fertilized ovum implants about day 21 of the cycle, having developed by this time into a multicellular ball of cells with a central fluid-filled cavity. The inner mass of cells develops into the *fetus* proper, and specialized cells, the *trophoblast,* are formed by the outer layer, which burrow into the uterus and form the *placenta.* The endometrium undergoes a progesterone-stimulated change, decidualization, which prepares it to accept the trophoblast. The placenta develops an intimate contact with the maternal blood supply and serves the functions of lungs, digestive tract and kidneys for the fetus.

The placenta also functions as an endocrine gland, secreting *chorionic gonadotropins* that stimulate the corpus luteum to produce progesterone in high levels, which is essential to prevent menstruation. Secretion by the trophoblast begins shortly after implantation, and thus may play a role in the continuing viability of the corpus luteum. Again, the exact mechanism is unknown. Chorionic gonadotropin levels drop by the end of the third month and, although the corpus luteum of pregnancy remains, the production of progesterone and estrogen is accomplished almost entirely by the placenta.

Pregnancy is terminated either by delivery of a live child, *parturition*, or interruption with delivery of a dead fetus, *abortion*. For therapeutic or social reasons, abortion can be produced mechanically by scraping of the endometrium *(curettage)*, vacuum, or instillation of saline. *Spontaneous abortion* is usually in response to a dead or nonviable fetus. Occasionally such fetuses are retained and become calcified *(lithopedion)*, sometimes not being found until many years later (Korenyi-Both et al., 1978).

The initiating factor in parturition is unknown. Oxytocin is a stimulant of uterine smooth muscle, but this hormone is reflexively released by the action of receptors in the uterus. Progesterone is an inhibitor of uterine contraction and usually drops just before delivery, but not in all women. A biologic clock may be in operation here. Experimental animals enter labor at the appropriate time even if the fetus has been removed weeks earlier. The human fetus, particularly the brain, grows to a maximum size consistent with passage through the pelvic canal (Montague, 1968), but experimental evidence indicates that the size of the fetus is not an initiating factor in parturition.

Delivery is accomplished by rhythmic contractions of the uterus which expel the fetus through the cervix and vagina. The placenta and membranes follow shortly afterward. Most deliveries are head first (Fig. 9.2A), an arrangement that makes for maximum dilation of the cervix and, usually, an uncomplicated delivery. On occasion, other parts of the fetus may present for delivery first (Fig. 9.2 B,C), posing some potential

A	B	C
left occiput anterior	left mentum anterior	left sacrum posterior (breech)

Fetal presentations.

Figure 9.2

difficulties, such as entanglement in the umbilical cord. Fortunately even most of these deliveries are uncomplicated.

The Kaguru of East Africa consider children presenting other than head first to be abnormal creatures dangerous to their families. These unfortunate infants are strangled at birth (Beidelman, 1971).

LACTATION

The high levels of estrogen and progesterone during pregnancy cause the breasts to enlarge, by proliferation of the secretory glands and the ductal system. After birth prolactin and cortisol secretion both increase, stimulating the production of milk. Production of these hormones is maintained by reflexes from the nipples to the hypothalamus initiated by suckling. Milk production ceases shortly after nursing stops, but continues as long as nursing continues.

CONTRACEPTION

Techniques of birth control in western society have been based on mechanical prevention of fertilization, as by condom or vaginal diaphragm, or by the use of spermicidal jellies and foams. An alternative is the use of the "rhythm method," abstinence around the time of ovulation. In preliterate societies, population control is accomplished by several other mechanisms: social control of mating; abortion; infanticide; prolonged lactation (which lowers fertility by inhibiting ovulation); and taboos against postpartum intercourse (Swedlund and Armelagos, 1976). For a variety of reasons, all these techniques are only moderately effective.

More recently the "pill" has been developed as a simple oral contraceptive for women. There are several varieties, most being combinations of estrogen and progesterone that inhibit the secretion of pituitary gonadotropins, thus preventing ovulation. In addition, the general endocrine environment and the status of the endometrium is inimical to implantation. A number of side-effects, some serious, have been reported in women taking oral contraceptives. Statistically, these complications are rare in comparison to the morbidity and mortality expected in pregnancies, but this is of little consolation to the woman who develops a stroke or suffers a hemorrhage into a benign liver tumor.

Another highly effective contraceptive is the intrauterine device (IUD), which is a small plastic device placed in the cervix. The mechanism is thought to work by interference with the preparation of the endometrium for implantation.

A study by Stycos (1976) of a birth control clinic in Puerto Rico has revealed the importance of the consideration of cultural factors in population control programs. Reduction in mortality without a concomitant drop in fertility leads to severe economic problems. In underdeveloped areas cultural patterns insuring high fertility have traditionally balanced high mortality. When western medicine leads to a rapid reduction of mortality, culturally determined fertility rates decrease too slowly to achieve a new balance. For a population control program to be successful, Stycos concludes that cultural factors must be considered, particularly in terms of making the small family an attractive proposition.

Almost totally effective techniques are severing of the fallopian tube (tubal ligation) and vas deferens (vasectomy). Even these operations can fail, and they are essentially irreversible, although newly developed reconstructive surgical procedures have had some success.

Pathology

SEXUAL DIFFERENTIATION

The gonadal tissues of male and female are initially identical and begin to differentiate in the second month after fertilization. Regulation of this process is by testosterone in males, produced by the fetal testes, and by maternal estrogen in females. A bewildering variety of anomalies can develop in this scheme, which can be broken down into intersex states and localized developmental abnormalities. Chromosomal abnormalities account for some intersex states, such as XO (Turner's syndrome) and XXY (Klinefelter's syndrome), individuals resembling females and males respectively (Fig. 9.3). In the testicular feminization syndrome, the individual is XY with normal androgen production, but the sexual development is female, with a shallow vagina ending blindly and normal female breast development. The defect appears to be unresponsiveness of the tissues to androgen. In these conditions the guiding factor should be the individual's social and psychologic status; surgical correction should be aimed at maintaining the person in the sex in which he or she has been raised and is accustomed to, rather than producing the "correct" genotypic sex.

Localized deformities are much less complex in the social sense, presenting as mechanical problems. Associated anomalies of the urinary tract are frequent and potentially serious. The various organs may be absent, atrophic, duplicated or connected by fistulous tracts. Almost all these anomalies are amenable to plastic and reconstructive surgery.

Vulva. The external genitalia are liable to a variety of infections, including the venereal diseases. *Herpes simplex,* the virus of the cold sore or fever blister, has been found to be increasing in incidence as a genital infection, and one strain has been suggested to be involved in the etiology of vulvar and cervical cancer.

Many chronic conditions affect older women, with atrophy or thickening of the skin and the possibility of the eventual development of cancer. Other lesions worthy of note are the so-called venereal wart, *condyloma acuminatum*, of viral etiology, and the occasional presence of breast tissue in the vulva.

Vagina. Vaginal infections are common, including gonorrhea, *trichomoniasis* (a protozoan infection which is sexually transmissible), *candidiasis* (a fungus) and *herpes simplex.*

Vaginal adenosis has been discussed in Chapter 1. In general,

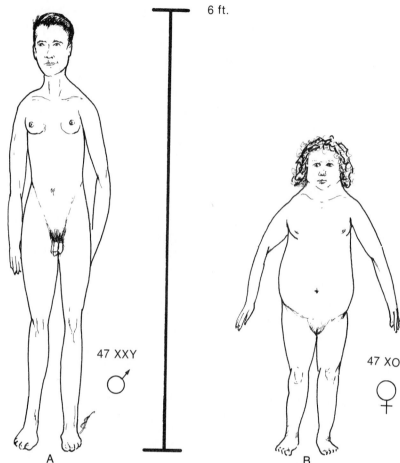

6 ft.

47 XXY

47 XO

A

B

Figure 9.3   *A,* Klinefelter's syndrome. *B,* Turner's syndrome.

tumors of the vagina are rare. A primary tumor, *sarcoma botryoides*, arises from pluripotential mesodermal cells and consists of multiple soft tissue types. This lesion occurs at any age, even in childhood, and carries a very poor prognosis.

Cervix.   Inflammation of the cervix, *cervicitis,* is extremely common and usually chronic and nonspecific, i.e., not associated with any particular organism. Most cases are asymptomatic or present with a discharge. The danger of cervicitis is a possible progression to cervical cancer.

Squamous carcinoma of the cervix is the third most common cancer in American women. Several factors have been positively associated with the development of cervical cancer. One such is parity, but this association disappears when controlled for age at marriage. The real factor appears to be age at first intercourse. Frequency of intercourse, number of partners and hygiene of the partner(s), particularly circumcision, all seem to play a role. These factors can be reduced to two elements, trauma and infection. *Herpes simplex* virus has come to be implicated in the disease, and the likelihood of infection rises with the number of partners and amount of intercourse. The epidemiology of the disease also suggests an infectious origin (Beral, 1974).

Cervical cancer is unique in that it arises in an area open to medical observation, and it is not surprising that this is the area in which the concept of carcinoma in situ was developed. The inflamed cervix can follow a course of change in type, *(squamous metaplasia)*, followed by atypical changes in the epithelium *(dysplasia)*, followed by the development of the histologic cellular changes of malignancy in the epithelial cells *(carcinoma in situ)*, followed by infiltration of the underlying tissue *(invasive carcinoma)*. Serial studies and statistical evidence indicate that this progression is not inevitable, but can stop and (rarely) regress at any stage, and that the evolution of cancer takes years, or of course may never develop.

The superficial cells of the cervix can be removed and studied (the Pap smear, Fig. 9.4, Papanicolaou and Traut, 1943) and therapy directed accordingly. Dysplastic lesions can be observed and, if severe, biopsied, with evaluation for more extensive surgery. Routine use of pap smears allows early diagnosis of potentially malignant lesions and definitive treatment of such lesions at an early stage. Socioeconomic factors are of importance, in that those of lower status are more liable to the disease and present the most difficulties in terms of follow-up of abnormal smears. In spite of the availability of this diagnostic technique, cervical cancer still accounts for many deaths. If allowed to pro-

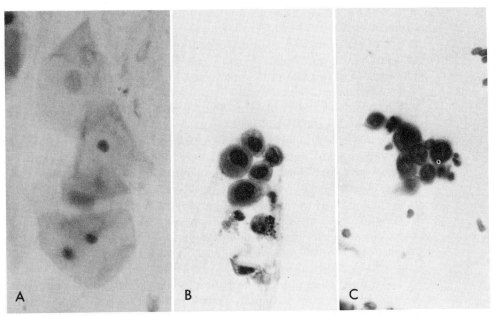

Pap smears. *A*, Normal squamous cells. The nuclei are small with a low nuclear/cytoplasmic ratio. *B*, Abnormal (dysplastic) cells. The nuclei are larger with more irregular borders. The cells are smaller, further increasing the nuclear/cytoplasmic ratio. *C*, Carcinoma. The nuclei are larger still, with irregular staining and borders, and make up the bulk of the cells. Pap stain, × 400.

Figure 9.4

gress, the lesion infiltrates through the wall of the uterus and kills either by distant metastasis or by direct involvement of the ureters. Death is most frequently due to urinary obstruction.

Corpus of the Uterus.   Infection of the endometrium, *endometritis,* is rare and usually linked to abortion, coexisting tubal infection or the presence of an IUD. Tuberculous endometritis is now a rare entity.

ABNORMAL UTERINE BLEEDING.   Abnormal bleeding is associated with a wide variety of pathologic conditions, and the correct diagnosis is dependent on a careful evaluation of the clinical and pathologic findings. The patient's age is of prime importance, in that bleeding in the reproductive years is usually related to a pregnancy, whereas postmenopausal bleeding is often due to hyperplasia or neoplasia of the endometrium, or to a tumor of the myometrium.

A normal pregnancy is manifested by cessation of menses, but, in cases of threatening or actual abortion, a variable degree of vaginal bleeding will be present. If fetal or placental tissue has already been expelled *(incomplete abortion),* the uterine contents must be curretted out. An empty uterine cavity stimulates the organ to contract, thus limiting bleeding. It is incumbent upon the pathologist to identify the tissue products of conception in the currettings, in order to exclude an ectopic pregnancy (see below).

Irregular uterine bleeding, in the absence of any clear cause, is said to be *dysfunctional.* Most of these patients are in the perimenopausal period and have a variable nonspecific histologic endometrial pattern. In many a definitive diagnosis is never established.

In postmenopausal women bleeding is a more serious phenomenon, as it is often associated with pathologic overgrowth of the endometrium, *hyperplasia.* This lesion appears to be due to the continued action of estrogen, no longer opposed by progesterone. The progression of hyperplasia to cancer in some cases has been documented, and hyperplasia is considered an indication for hysterectomy, especially in a postmenopausal woman.

In contrast to cervical carcinoma, *adenocarcinoma* of the endometrium is a disease of higher frequency in the upper socioeconomic group. It affects peri- and postmenopausal women, continuing estrogen stimulation again being implied. Obese women are more liable to the disease, as other hormones are converted into estrogen by adipose tissue. The tumor forms a mass in the endometrial cavity and the prognosis is good, as long as penetration into the myometrium is limited.

Two major conditions affect the myometrium. *Adenomyosis* is the appearance of islands of endometrial glands and stroma in the myometrium. These lesions are histologically benign, but may cause painful menstrual periods as they react to hormonal stimuli.

The most common lesion of the myometrium is the *leiomyoma,* a benign smooth muscle tumor known to the lay public as "fibroids." These tumors (Fig. 9.5) are frequently large, may be multiple, and may cause bleeding, pain or a pelvic mass. They can calcify, and have been found in ancient human remains. Rarely, malignant tumors of this type, *leiomyosarcomas,* develop.

Fallopian Tube *(salpinx).*   The most common disorder of the tube

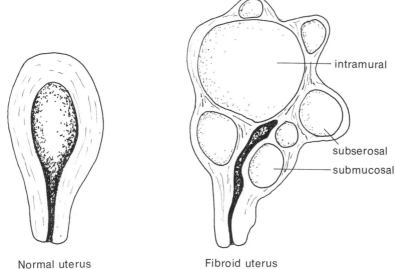

Normal uterus   Fibroid uterus

A normal uterus and one with multiple leiomyomata ("fibroid" uterus).   **Figure 9.5**

is inflammation, usually complicating venereal infection. The initial infecting organism is most frequently the gonococcus, but as the disease progresses to *chronic salpingitis (pelvic inflammatory disease*, or PID*)*, other superinfecting organisms become more prominent. These organisms may include anaerobes, difficult to culture and to treat.

Chronic salpingitis is almost always bilateral, and can lead to a variety of complications. The tube may become closed by scarring and filled with the clear fluid secreted by the lining cells, *hydrosalpinx* or with pus, *pyosalpinx.* The infection can expand to involve the ovary, producing an abscess cavity, a *tubo-ovarian abscess* (TOA). If fertilization occurs in a damaged tube, the passage of the ovum can be retarded, causing implantation in the tube, *ectopic pregnancy.* Invasion of the wall of the tube by trophoblast results in hemorrhage and perforation, a life-threatening surgical emergency, requiring salpingectomy.

The tube can be the site of ectopic islands of endometrium, *endometriosis.* These growths are benign, even though they can occur in other areas of the body. Scarring in endometriosis may lead to infertility, and may be part of a more generalized pelvic endometrisosis.

Tumors of the tube are rare but highly malignant.

Ovary.   The various anatomic and functional components of the ovary are each liable to their own specific forms of pathology. Only a sample of these lesions can be covered in this survey.

Infections are rare except as extensions from salpingitis, as noted above. *Atrophy* occurs at menopause, leaving an ovary composed of stroma, which produces androgen.

A variety of benign *cysts* develop in the ovary. Cysts of the follicles or corpus luteum are usually small and asymptomatic. Occasionally, hemorrhage into a corpus luteum cyst causes pain and a palpable mass, indications for surgery. Endometriosis may also result in large blood-filled cysts, causing pain and infertility. Such lesions have been suspected to be due to reflux of menstrual blood with implantation of viable endometrium, or to metaplasia of the epithelium covering the ovary.

The major pathologic change occurring in the ovary is the development of a variety of tumors, both benign and malignant. These tumors arise from any of the components of the ovary and present a number of clinical problems. Because of the location of the ovaries, tumors tend to remain silent for long periods and may be quite advanced by the time of their discovery. The benign tumors may gradually develop to very large size, and malignant tumors have often spread beyond the ovary before discovery. These tumors may present as masses, as fluid accumulations in the abdomen *(ascites)* due to peritoneal seeding by tumor, or with abdominal pain due to torsion.

The benign tumors are predominantly cystic tumors originating from the surface epithelium. These tumors can be very bulky, and the histologic picture may shade over into malignancy. Tumors also arise from the stromal components responsible for hormone production, and the tumors may produce any of the sex hormones, male or female, or even adrenal steroids. These include the *granulosa-theca cell tumors* and *arrhenoblastoma*, and, if androgen-producing, may result in virilization. Most of these hormonally active tumors are benign.

A group of tumors arises from the germ cells, mostly in children and young women. *Dsygerminoma* is identical in histologic appearance to testicular seminoma, and, as in males, is extremely radiosensitive and even curable by radiation after dissemination has occurred.

Choriocarcinoma is a rare primary ovarian tumor, more often developing in the placenta.

Teratomas of the ovary are composed of tissues of ectodermal, mesodermal and endodermal origin. *Benign cystic teratoma (dermoid cyst)* is a cyst lined by skin-like epithelium and composed of mature tissues, filled with desquamated keratin debris and hair. Almost any tissue may be found: bronchus, fat, muscle, bone, teeth, brain, thyroid, etc. Chromosomal analysis indicates that teratomas are parthenogenetic tumors developing from a single germ cell after its first meiotic division.

Rarely a component of a cystic teratoma may become malignant, but *malignant teratomas (teratocarcinomas)* are usually solid tumors with the same mixture of cells and tissue types as seen in dermoids. Any of these tissues may become malignant. Some of the tissues of a teratoma may also be hormonally active, causing, for example, the carcinoid syndrome (Chapter 6) or hyperthyroidism (Chapter 8). Finally, germ cell tumors may be a mixture of any of the cell types described.

Tumors may also be *metastatic* to the ovary. Most of these are adenocarcinomas arising in the stomach, colon or breast. There is diffuse infiltration of the ovary, producing a large firm mass known as a *Krukenberg tumor.* An oddity is that resection of the primary tumor and the involved ovaries may be followed by a prolonged symptom-free period.

Diseases Related to Pregnancy.   The placenta and its accompanying membranes can display many variations in form and implantation in the uterus. Occasionally the placenta implants directly into the myometrium rather than into the decidualized endometrium, resulting in postpartum hemorrhage requiring hysterectomy. Implantation may occur outside the uterus, in the tube, as discussed above, or in the cervix, ovary or elsewhere in the abdomen. Such pregnancies are associated with high fetal mortality. Implantation may also occur low in the uterus, with the placenta lying over the cervical opening or *os*, leading to bleeding at labor.

Six per cent of pregnant women develop *toxemia of pregnancy* or *preeclampsia*, characterized by salt retention, protein in the urine, edema and hypertension. In the severe form, *eclampsia*, there are convulsions with coagulation abnormalities and necrosis of liver, kidney and brain. Constrictive lesions in the arteries of the uterus, probably due to an immunologic reaction, appear to be the basic pathology in the condition.

Infections may develop in the membranes and placenta, and transplacental infection of the fetus by viruses accounts for many congenital malformations. Prolonged labor after rupture of the fetal membranes may allow bacterial infection and pneumonia in the infant.

The placenta is markedly enlarged in *erythroblastosis fetalis*, a condition in which there is an incompatibility between the fetal and maternal blood types, maternal antibodies crossing the placenta and destroying fetal red cells. Most of these incompatibilities are of Rh genotypes. There is evidence that Rh-negative mothers have more offspring than Rh-positives, which offsets to some extent the loss of their children (Johnston, 1973).

Current therapy is aimed at destroying fetal red cells as they enter the maternal circulation at birth, thus preventing the development of maternal antibodies and allowing future pregnancies to progress without difficulty.

Occasionally the trophoblast, physiologically an invasive tissue, becomes overly aggressive. *Hydatidiform mole* is a trophoblastic disease that occurs in about one of 2,000 pregnancies in the United States, but about ten times more frequently in Asia and Mexico. Nutritional factors have been proposed to account for this difference, but the pathogenesis is unclear. The mole is a large placenta composed entirely of grape-like swollen villi (Fig. 9.6). Most moles are benign, but the covering trophoblast may appear malignant histologically. The mole may invade deeply into the wall of the uterus, or even spread to the lungs. In both sites, the invasive character of the trophoblast may lead to serious hemorrhage, requiring surgery or chemotherapy. Such lesions usually regress with conservative therapy, but the true malignancy of the trophoblast, *choriocarcinoma*, is an extraordinarily malignant tumor, which metastasizes early and widely. In the past almost always fatal, this tumor has been found to be curable by chemotherapy with methotrexate and actinomycin D. As the trophoblast manufactures human chorionic gonadotropin, HCG levels can be monitored to evaluate the efficacy of therapy.

Pseudocyesis is a state of false pregnancy, usually seen in infertile

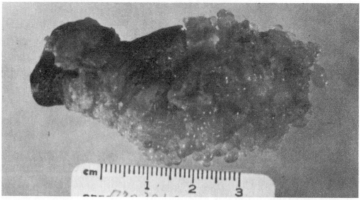

Figure 9.6   Hydatidiform mole. This abnormal development of the placenta consists of many grape-like vesicles.

women with a strong desire for children. These patients develop all the external signs of pregnancy, including amenorrhea, abdominal enlargement and lactation, but pregnancy tests are negative. The condition is frequently resolved by evaluation for causes of infertility.

The Breast.   The breast is liable to all the diseases seen in other organs, but almost all of these present in the breast as a lump. The emphasis is on excluding or diagnosing breast cancer, the most common cancer in the American female.

Supernumerary breast tissue may develop anywhere along the embryologic milk line, extending from the axilla to the groin. Such ectopic breast tissue can develop all the disease of the normally positioned breast.

Breast tissue may develop in the male, *gynecomastia.* This is due to a hormonal imbalance, either an increase in the normally low levels of estrogen in the male or abnormal sensitivity of the tissues to estrogen. Patients with cirrhosis cannot detoxify estrogen, and gynecomastia and male breast cancer are considerable problems in Egypt, where schistosomal cirrhosis is a common disorder.

Inflammatory disorders include acute bacterial infections associated with nursing, tuberculosis and fat necrosis. The last may be associated with trauma or other diseases, and may simulate breast cancer.

Fibrous tissue may proliferate in the breast, causing a mass. When associated with ductal dilatation, the condition is referred to as *fibrocystic disease.* This benign disorder occurs in the 30s and 40s and is associated with an increased risk of developing breast cancer.

Several types of benign tumors develop in the breast. These lesions present as masses which must be distinguished from carcinoma by biopsy. Fortunately, the histologic patterns are usually distinctive enough to allow diagnosis by frozen section while the patient is under anesthesia. Occasionally, diagnostic problems make it impossible to render a rapid diagnosis, but statistics have shown that the breast cancer patient's prognosis is unaffected by a delay of up to several weeks in diagnosis and definitive therapy. The merits of the frozen section are that it shortens the patient's period of anxiety and avoids a second anesthesia.

Carcinoma of the breast is one of the greatest clinical problems with which physicians have to deal. The disease currently accounts for 30,000 deaths per year in the United States, and the risk of breast cancer for American women is one in 15. Despite efforts at earlier diagnosis and surgery and the use of chemotherapy, hormonal therapy and radiation, the prognosis has changed little in the past 50 years.

The etiology of breast cancer is unknown, but research efforts are focused on hormonal stimulation (principally estrogen), viruses, and immunologic and genetic mechanisms. Radiation appears to be carcinogenic in the breast. Evidence of an increased incidence of breast cancer in women subjected to multiple x-rays for diagnosis of pulmonary disease (Myrden and Hilty, 1969) suggests that current radiologic breast-screening projects *(mammography)* may lead to an increase in breast cancer, although dosage is said to be very low. Breast-feeding was once thought to be protective against the development of cancer, but apparently is not so. The marked decrease in breast-feeding over the past several decades has not led to a significant rise in breast cancer incidence.

Marked geographic differences in the distribution of the disease are known, with a relatively low rate in Japanese women. Japanese immigrants to the United States show an increased rate of the disease over Japanese women in Japan, but less than that of American women. This suggests an environmental influence. The increase is even higher in the second generation, suggesting that early exposure to the new culture and environment is a factor (Buell, 1973).

The incidence of breast cancer is positively associated with socioeconomic status. In this respect the disease is similar to endometrial cancer, and contrasts with cancer of the cervix.

Breast cancer patients and their mothers have similar patterns of altered estrogen metabolism. Patients with cancer of the breast have usually had their first child at a later age than controls, usually past 30, and menopause is also delayed compared to controls (Henderson et al., 1974).

There are several clinical and histologic types of breast cancer, but almost all are adenocarcinomas arising from the ductal and occasionally the lobular epithelium. These lesions present as painless masses which generally are treated by excisional biopsy, frozen section diagnosis and, if indicated, *mastectomy*, removal of the affected breast and contiguous lymph nodes. The value of the more extensive **radical** mastectomy, including removal of the underlying muscle, has come under question, and this procedure is performed less frequently than in the past. Chemotherapy has come to be an important adjuvant therapy. If the lesion remains localized to the breast the prognosis is good. Spread to axillary lymph nodes worsens the prognosis. Unfortunately, it is often impossible to determine clinically if the axillary nodes are involved.

Breast cancer has a high potential for metastasis, involving the lungs, liver, bone, brain, ovaries and adrenal glands. Chemotherapy of disseminated disease has a palliative effective. Some of the tumors are hormonally dependent, allowing palliation by a variety of hormonal techniques, including ablative surgery of ovaries, adrenals and pituitary.

Carcinoma of the male breast is rare but generally similar to the disease in females.

REFERENCES

Beidelman, T. O. (1971): The Kaguru: A Matrilineal People of East Africa. Holt, Rinehart and Winston, New York.

Beral, V. (1974): Cancer of the cervix: a sexually transmitted infection? Lancet 1:1037–1040.

Buell, P. (1973): Changing incidence of breast cancer in Japanese-American women. J. Natl. Cancer Inst. 51:1479–1483.

Henderson, B. E., Powell, B., Rosario, I. et al. (1974): An epidemiologic study of breast cancer. J. Natl. Cancer Inst. 43:609–614.

Johnston, F. E. (1973): Microevolution of Human Populations. Prentice-Hall, Englewood Cliffs, New Jersey.

Korenyi-Both, A., Pragaz, D. A., Alker, G. J. et al. (1978): Lithopedion: case report and ultrastructural study of the skeletal muscle. Hum. Pathol. 9:358–363.

Montague, M. F. A. (1968): Brains, genes, culture, immaturity, and gestation. In Culture: Man's Adaptive Dimension. M. F. A. Montague, ed. Oxford University Press, New York, pp. 102–113.

Myrden, J. K. and J. E. Hilty (1969): Breast cancer following multiple fluoroscopies during artificial pneumothorax treatment of pulmonary tuberculosis. Can. Med. Assoc. J. 100:1032–1034.

Papanicolaou, G. and H. F. Traut (1943): Diagnosis of Uterine Cancer by the Vaginal Smear. Commonwealth Fund, New York.

Stycos, J. M. (1976): Birth control clinics in crowded Puerto Rico. In Health, Culture and Community, B. D. Paul, ed. Russel Sage Foundation, New York, pp. 189–210.

Swedlund, A. C. and G. J. Armelagos (1976): Demographic Anthropology. Wm. C. Brown, Dubuque, Iowa.

Tannenbaum, M. (1977): Urologic Pathology: The Prostate. Lea and Febiger, Philadelphia.

White, G. (1977): Culture, community medicine, and venereal disease. Med. J. Aust. 1:17–18.

ten

The Skin

ANATOMY AND PHYSIOLOGY

The skin covers the surface of the body and serves three functions: a barrier between the body and the environment; a sense organ for monitoring the environment; and a means of temperature regulation. The structure of the skin **(cutis)** is specialized for these tasks, and differs from epithelium elsewhere in that it has a superficial devitalized layer and that it contains sense organs and other skin appendages.

Skin is composed of **epidermis** and **dermis,** overlying a subcutaneous layer of fat. The epidermis has four microscopic layers (Fig. 10.1). The **basal** layer rests on the **basement membrane,** which separates it from the dermis. Melanin pigment, which determines the color of the skin, is formed in the basal layer and scattered throughout the more superficial layers. The basal layer gives rise to the **prickle cell layer,** so-called because these cells exhibit minute interconnecting projections or "bridges." These cells synthesize keratin, a tough protein relatively impermeable to water. The nuclei of the cells are lost in the **granular** layer, and the **cornified** layer consists of devitalized masses of keratin. This layer prevents the underlying tissues from dying out.

Within the connective tissue of the dermis are the skin appendages, including the hair follicles and sweat and sebaceous glands. Hair is found over the entire body except for the palms and soles, glans penis, terminal phalanges (and in most individuals the middle phalanges, as a genetic variant) and the eardrum. Hairs are keratinized cells derived from the skin, and the follicles surrounding the base are invaginations of the epidermis. Attached to the sides of the follicles are small muscles, called **arrectores pilorum,** which contract and erect the hairs in response to cold or emotional stress ("goose flesh"). In animals this acts as an insulating mechanism, but human hair is not thick enough to provide significant insulation, even when erect.

145

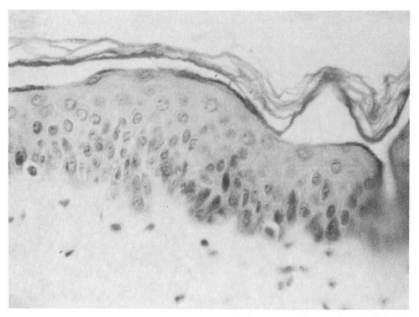

Figure 10.1   The layers of the skin. A basement membrane, not well seen with this stain, separates the epidermis from the subjacent dermis. The four layers of the skin, from deep to superficial, are the basal layer, prickle cell layer (stratum spinosum, malpighian layer), granular layer and cornified layer (stratum corneum). Nuclei are absent in the stratum corneum. Hematoxylin and eosin stain, × 400.

The skin contains sense organs for touch, heat, cold, pain, tickle and itch. These organs serve to protect from mechanical and chemical trauma. The epidermis heals rapidly after damage, but wounds deep enough to involve the dermis heal by scarring, with loss of the appendages.

Much of the heat of the body is produced by the large skeletal muscles, their metabolic activity increasing in cold and decreasing in heat. The skin regulates temperature by a relatively precise mechanism involving water loss. A certain amount of water evaporates passively from the skin and the lining of the respiratory tract under normal circumstances. This **insensible** water loss is on the order of 600 cc. per day. Under heat stress, **sweat,** a dilute salt solution, is actively pumped to the skin surface, where its evaporation produces a cooling effect. Up to 4 liters per hour can be produced (9 pounds of water)! Any factor that prevents evaporation, such as high humidity, will eliminate the cooling effect, despite the best efforts of the sweat glands.

The sebaceous glands release **sebum** over the surface of the body. This oily material has some antibacterial activity and, when irradiated, as by the sun, produces vitamin D.

The dermis is composed of fibrous tissue with a rich blood supply. Anastomoses between arterioles and venules are present in large numbers and are well innervated. When these are open, blood bypasses the capillary network as a heat conservation mechanism. When they are closed, blood enters the skin for heat loss.

PATHOLOGY

Only a representative few of the great number of skin diseases can be considered here. It should be noted at this point that many systemic or visceral diseases are associated with cutaneous lesions.

Infection

Infections of the skin are very common, as are systemic infections with cutaneous manifestations. The common childhood disorders are mostly viral in origin. These include measles **(rubeola),** German measles **(rubella),** chickenpox **(varicella)** and mumps **(epidemic parotitis).** Other viral diseases include smallpox **(variola),** yellow fever, the common cold sore **(herpes simplex)** and shingles **(herpes zoster).**

These viruses require a certain minimum population to remain endemic. As man entered the New World in relatively small numbers, the endemic viruses were not able to tag along (St. Hoyme, 1969). It remained for the Spaniards to introduce diseases such as smallpox, measles and yellow fever to the New World, with results catastrophic to the American Indians (Wolf, 1959).

Rickettsial diseases also involve the skin, through diffuse involvement of blood vessels. These include such insect-borne diseases as Rocky Mountain spotted fever and typhus.

Staphylococci produce localized skin abscesses **(furuncles, boils),** and streptococci cause scarlet fever and erysipelas. Streptococcal infections may be complicated by immunologic reactions to the organisms, with myocarditis, endocarditis or glomerulonephritis.

By far the most common skin infections are those caused by the fungi. These superficial infections by a variety of organisms are particularly severe and common in the tropics, but even in the United States over half the population is afflicted by athlete's foot **(tinea pedis)** at one time or another. Patterns of fungal infection are often determined by occupational exposure.

Inflammatory Disorders

There are many inflammatory diseases of the skin of uncertain etiology. One general group consists of the **vesicular** diseases, characterized by raised fluid-filled areas of cleavage in the skin. Some of these are common and only annoying, such as **eczema,** which is often due to an allergic reaction to some external chemical or to food. In contrast, **pemphigus** is a vesicular disease that may be so extensive as to cause death by loss of proteins and electrolytes. This disease is thought to be due to an immunologic attack on the intercellular bridges **(desmosomes)** of the epidermis, but the inciting factor(s) of this reaction are unknown. Steroid therapy usually produces prolonged remissions.

Lupus Erythematosus (LE).   LE is another disorder that appears to be autoimmune in nature. Discoid LE is a variant, fortunately the more common, confined to the skin and characterized by well-defined plaques, often in a butterfly shape over the cheeks and bridge of the nose.

Systemic lupus (SLE) is a much more severe disease, both in the skin and elsewhere. Blood vessels are involved diffusely, particularly in the spleen and kidney. Skin ulcers may lead to fatal sepsis, or death may be due to renal failure. Acute attacks are often precipitated by exposure to sunlight, and young women are most often affected. Although the disease has been recognized as a clinical entity only in recent years (Harvey et al., 1954), a case has been diagnosed in an ancient Peruvian mummy (Allison et al., 1977), dating to 890 A.D.

The intriguing features of the disorder are the demonstration of antibodies in the skin and the discovery of the diagnostic "LE cell," actually a rosette of acute inflammatory cells surrounding a histiocyte with ingested nuclear material (Fig. 10.2), suggesting an immunologic antinuclear reaction. As in other immunologic disorders, steroids and ACTH therapy induce remissions.

Psoriasis. This chronic disease shows diffuse scaliness of the skin, with a peculiar predilection for symmetric distribution, especially on the elbows and knees. An occasional complication is a severe arthritis.

A plant-derived folk medicine has been used for psoriasis in Egypt for many years, and has recently been found effective. Egyptian sufferers take the medicine and then expose themselves to sunlight, and it has been discovered that ultraviolet light is necessary for the drug to be effective.

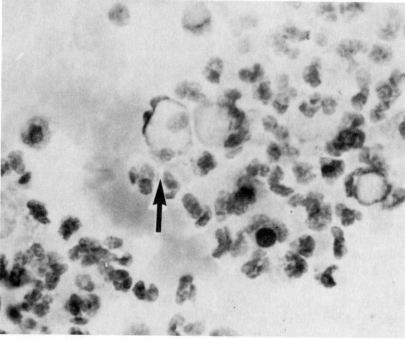

Figure 10.2   A "lupus prep." A rosette of leukocytes surrounds a histiocyte containing altered nuclear material (*arrow*). Wright's stain, × 400.

Keloids. Wounds of the skin heal by scar formation. In some, particularly blacks, the scar is composed of dense acellular hypertrophic collagen, a **keloid.** Such healing may produce a severe cosmetic deformity, requiring surgical excision. It has been suggested by Polednak (1974) that this fibroblastic overgrowth is the result of natural selection for a wound-healing mechanism protective against infection, a greater danger in tropical Africa than in temperate zones.

Pigments. A variety of pigments may be deposited in the skin. Arsenic, silver, gold, carotene, bismuth and mercury may be deposited when injected or ingested. Tattoos are deposits of metal or vegetable pigments. Mercuric sulfide is a commonly used red pigment, and it is of interest that syphilitic lesions may spare the red components of tattoos, as mercury kills the spirochetes. Tattoos may also be useful as population markers. A frozen Eskimo mummy dated by C^{14} to c. 400 A.D. (Zimmerman and Smith, 1975) was tattooed in motifs characteristic of the Old Bering Sea phase of Alaskan prehistory, dated to the same period (Smith and Zimmerman, 1975), providing a useful confirmation.

Other pigments found in the skin are blood pigments **(hemosiderin)** in old bruises, and melanin. Melanin may be absent locally **(vitiligo)** or totally **(albinism).** Albinism is due to a recessive gene, and the trait has been found to be useful as an index of inbreeding, as in a 1959 study (Woolf and Dukepoo) of Hopi Indians.

Diseases of the Skin Appendages

There are many disorders of the appendages of the skin. The sweat glands may secrete excessively or insufficiently, or become infected. In **acne,** the sebaceous glands become obstructed and infected. **Alopecia** is the medical term for baldness, and hair and nails are liable to fungal infections. Spoon-shaped nails **(koilonychia)** are seen in iron deficiency anemia, and a Roman age votive statuette exhibiting the condition has been found in an iron-rich area of England, probably an offering from a sufferer cured by local water (Hart, 1973).

Tumors

Both benign and malignant tumors of all components of the skin are known. These tumors generally are grouped on the basis of their origin from epidermis, dermis and the skin appendages.

Epidermis. Benign tumors of the epidermis are extraordinarily common. The common wart, **verruca vulgaris,** probably is not a true neoplasm but rather a florid reaction to a viral infection. Somewhat similar cauliflower-shaped masses are seen in the genital area, the **condylomata acuminata.** The common name for these lesions, **venereal wart,** reflects an ancient understanding of the relationship of these lesions to promiscuity, as depicted in epigrams by Martial.

Squamous carcinoma of the skin is positively associated with exposure to sunlight. There is a complex relationship involving skin pigmentation, vitamin D metabolism, and the carcinogenic effects of the ultraviolet light present in solar radiation. A certain amount of ultraviolet light is necessary for the synthesis of vitamin D and the prevention of rickets. However, overexposure to sunlight is hazardous, in terms of potential overproduction of vitamin D (Loomis, 1967), potential breakdown of nutrients such as folate (Branda and Eaton, 1978), and degenerative and neoplastic changes in the skin (Freeman, 1968). Protection is afforded against overexposure by the formation of a melanin pigment screen in the skin, both on a genetic and a facultative ("tanning") basis (Quevado et al., 1975). It is probable that evolutionary changes in pigmentation adaptive to ultraviolet light levels account for the present-day distribution of skin color (Neer, 1975), progressive depigmentation being seen in more northerly latitudes.

The adaptation of depigmentation is an efficient one, for the daily exposure of the nearly transparent pink cheeks of a European infant is adequate for the prevention of rickets. However, a liability to skin cancer is the price paid for allowing more ultraviolet light to penetrate the skin. Modern technology has become a negative microevolutionary force, upsetting adaptations achieved over millennia by flying emigrant Englishmen to sunny Australia and South Africa, where the highest rates of skin cancer are recorded. In contrast, skin cancer is rare in the deeply pigmented races indigenous to these areas (Uhrbach, 1969). The few skin cancers seen in Africans are usually secondary to infected long-standing tropical ulcers, arising from trauma or poor nutrition.

The other side of the coin is that the air pollution engendered by the Industrial Revolution prevented passage of ultraviolet radiation, causing a virtual epidemic of rickets until the use of dietary vitamin D in cod liver oil eliminated the disease (Loomis, 1970).

White skin exposed to the sun, as among outdoor workers or the English emigrés, develops an increased incidence of both precancerous and cancerous lesions. The skin early shows some of the histologic features of malignancy without involvement of the full thickness or invasion of the underlying dermis. This condition is referred to as **solar keratosis.** Such a picture may progress to frank malignancy, **squamous carcinoma,** with invasion of the dermis and distant metastases. The microscopic picture is a caricature of normal skin, with the formation of diagnostic irregular nests of keratin. These tumors tend to be locally invasive, but they have a definite metastatic potential.

The simplest prevention of solar degenerative changes would be the most effective — avoidance of exposure. However, most cannot or will not follow this course, and the aim of researchers in this field is to develop an effective topically applied sunscreen combined with an artificial tanning agent, thus achieving a medically effective result and satisfying the dictates of fashion (Ippen, 1969).

A historic note of interest is that squamous carcinoma of the scrotum in chimney sweeps was described by Sir Percival Pott in 1775. As mentioned in Chapter 3, this was the first example of an industrial cancer, being due to failure of the sweeps to wash off the carcinogenic hydrocarbons in the soot that permeated their clothes.

In contrast to squamous carcinoma, another common malignancy of the skin, **basal cell carcinoma** (or **basal cell epithelioma**), is a locally aggressive tumor with little metastatic potential. The tumor derives from and resembles the cells of the basal layer of the epidermis. It arises primarily in exposed areas, especially the faces of fair-skinned individuals. In an early stage such lesions are easily excised, but if neglected they can produce remarkable destruction of soft tissue, cartilage and bone. Occasionally they can cause death by extension through the meninges, with subsequent infection.

The third major malignancy of the epidermis is the **malignant melanoma. Nevus cells** are pigmented cells of neuroectodermal origin in the basal layer of the epidermis. For unknown reasons these cells tend to aggregate at the dermal-epidermal border and/or in the dermis, as junctional, dermal or compound **nevi.** Every person has a few of these benign tumors, but in some the nevus cells become malignant **(melanocarcinoma** or **malignant melanoma).** These tumors almost always continue to produce melanin and as a result are almost always pigmented. Melanomas are extemely aggressive, killing by widespread metastases.

Dermis. The dermis consists of fibroadipose tissue containing muscle, blood vessels and the specific appendages of the skin. Most of these structures may give rise to benign and malignant tumors. One lesion of paleopathologic interest is the **trichoepithelioma,** a benign tumor derived from the hair follicles. Such lesions can be familial and multiple, and an example of the syndrome (Fig. 10.3) is seen in a series of coins depicting Roman emperors (Hart, 1973).

Perhaps the most common tumor of the skin is not a true tumor at all, but rather a cystic inclusion of epithelium in the dermis, the **epidermoid cyst.** Known commonly as **wens** or **sebaceous cysts,** these lesions are lined by stratified squamous epithelium and filled by greasy degenerating keratin. They are caused by the introduction of epidermis into the underlying tissue, and can even occur in bones. Treatment is by excision.

A coin depicting the Parthian king Orodes I (1st century B.C.) with a tumor of the forehead, a **trichoepithelioma**. Other royal coins show this tumor, derived from hair follicles, to be a hereditary condition. (Courtesy of Dr. Gerald D. Hart.)

Figure 10.3

REFERENCES

Allison, M. J., Gerszten, E., Martinez, A. J. et al. (1977): Generalized connective tissue disease in a mummy from the Huari culture (Peru). Bull. N. Y. Acad. Med. 53:292–301, 1977.

Branda, R. F. and J. W. Eaton (1978): Skin color and nutrient photolysis: an evolutionary hypothesis. Science 201:625–626.

Freeman, R. G. (1968): Carcinogenic effect of solar radiation and prevention measures. Cancer 21:1114–1120.

Hart, G. D. (1973): The diagnosis of disease from ancient coins. Archeol. 26:123–127.

Harvey, A. M., Shulman, L. E., Tumulty, P. A. et al. (1954): Systemic lupus erythematosus: review of literature and clinical analysis of 138 cases. Medicine 33:291–296, 1954.

Ippen, H. (1969): Topical agents for protection against ultraviolet radiation. In The Biological Effects of Ultraviolet Radiation (With Emphasis on the Skin). F. Uhrbach, ed. Permagon, New York, pp. 681–687.

Loomis, W. F. (1967) Skin-pigment regulation of vitamin-D synthesis in man. Science 157:501–506.

Loomis, W. F. (1970): Rickets. Sci. Am. 223, #6:76–91.

Neer, R. M. (1975): The evolutionary significance of vitamin D, skin pigment and ultraviolet light. Am. J. Phys. Anthropol. 43:409–416.

Polednak, A. P. (1974): Connective tissue responses in negroes in relation to disease. Am. J. Phys. Anthropol. 41:49–58.

Pott, P. (1775): Chirurgical Observations (Section on Cancer Scroti). Hawkes, Clark and Collins, London.

Quevado, W. C., Fitzpatrick, T. B., Pathak, M. A. et al. (1975): Role of light in human skin color and variation. Am. J. Phys. Anthropol. 43:393–408.

St. Hoyme, L. E. (1969): On the origins of new world paleopathology. Am. J. Phys. Anthropol. 31:295–302.

Smith, G. S. and M. R. Zimmerman (1975): Tattooing found on a 1600 year old frozen mummified body from St. Lawrence Island, Alaska. Am. Antiq. 40:434–437.

Uhrbach, F. (1969): Geographic pathology of skin cancer. In The Biological Effects of Ultraviolet Radiation (With Emphasis on the Skin). F. Uhrbach, ed. Pergamon, New York, pp. 625–650.

Wolf, E. R. (1959): Sons of the Shaking Earth. University of Chicago Press, Chicago.

Woolf, C. M. and F. C. Dukepoo (1959): Hopi Indians, inbreeding and albinism. Science 164:30–37.

Zimmerman, M. R. and G. S. Smith (1975): A probable case of accidental inhumation of 1600 years ago. Bull. N. Y. Acad. Med. 51:828–837.

eleven

The Musculoskeletal System

ANATOMY, PHYSIOLOGY AND BIOCHEMISTRY

The skeletal framework of the body (Fig. 11.1) consists of the **axial** and the **appendicular skeletal systems**. The axial skeleton is made up of the skull, vertebral column, ribs, shoulders and pelvis. To the latter two are attached the appendicular bones of the upper and the lower limbs, respectively.

The skull is divided into two functional components, the **neurocranium** and the **viscerocranium.** The neurocranium, a roughly spherical aggregate of the **frontal, parietal, occipital** and **temporal bones,** encases the brain, serving a protective function. The viscerocranium is composed of the various smaller bones of the face and jaws, and provides sites for the sensory organs and ingress to the respiratory and digestive systems. The orbits also serve a protective function and, in man, orient the eyes to the straight-ahead position necessary for stereoscopic vision. In the upper and lower jaws (**maxilla** and **mandible**) are the teeth, tongue and salivary glands, all needed to facilitate the initiation of digestion.

The vertebral column is divided into five regions: **cervical, thoracic, lumbar, sacral** and **coccygeal.** The spinal cord is protected within the vertebral column, and spinal nerves emerge between the individual vertebrae. During childhood the vertebral column grows at a faster rate than the spinal cord, with the result that in the adult the spinal nerves must take a downward course in the canal, and the cord terminates at the level of L1–2. The spinal nerves below this point are referred to as the **cauda equina** ("horse's tail"). The coccyx is a vestigial group of vertebrae of importance only as a source of pain when fractured.

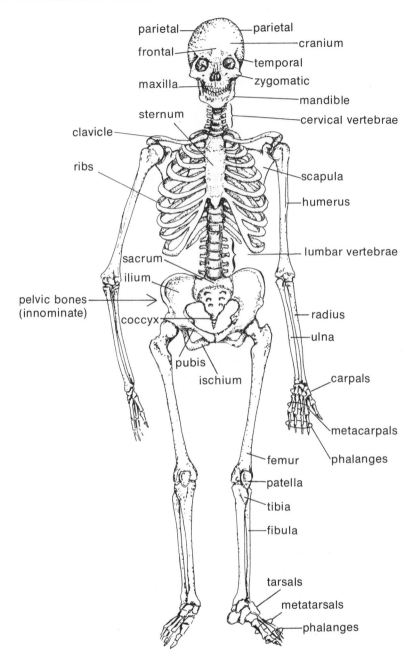

parietal
parietal
cranium
frontal
temporal
zygomatic
maxilla
mandible
sternum
cervical vertebrae
clavicle
ribs
scapula
humerus
lumbar vertebrae
sacrum
ilium
pelvic bones
(innominate)
coccyx
radius
ulna
pubis
ischium
carpals
metacarpals
phalanges
femur
patella
tibia
fibula
tarsals
metatarsals
phalanges

Figure 11.1   The human skeleton.

Attached to the vertebral column are the ribs, which together with
the breastbone (**sternum**) and collarbones (**clavicles**) make up the chest
cage. These bones serve a protective function for the heart and lungs,
and with their attendant muscles are vital for the mechanics of respiration. Attached posteriorly to the ribs are the shoulder blades (**scapulae**),
which with the clavicles make up the shoulder girdles.

The pelvic girdle is composed of the sacrum and the hip (**innomin-**

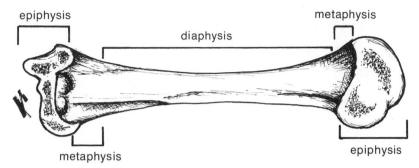

epiphysis

metaphysis

diaphysis

metaphysis

epiphysis

Zones of a long bone (immature humerus).   **Figure 11.2**

ate) bones, the latter being the result of fusion of the pubic, iliac and ischial bones. These bones protect the pelvic organs and are the point of attachment to the legs. There are marked differences in the pelvic anatomy of males and females, the latter having a broader pelvis with a wider outlet, more suitable as a birth canal than that of males, but less suitable for upright walking and running.

The appendicular skeleton consists of the bones of the arm (**humerus, ulna** and **radius**), wrist and hand; and the leg (**femur, tibia** and **fibula**), ankle and foot. The same general scheme is evident in both the upper and the lower limbs, but the specific anatomy has evolved in relation to function. The arm is adapted to tool use and load-lifting, and the leg is a mechanism for weight-bearing and locomotion.

There are two general types of bone: **membranous,** which develops directly from the soft tissues and forms flat layers of bone, as in the skull; and **enchondral,** formed by replacement of a cartilaginous anlage, as in the long bones. A typical long bone has a shaft, the **diaphysis;** two ends, the **epiphyses;** and two junctional **metaphyses,** where longitudinal growth takes place (Fig. 11.2).

In cross-section (Fig. 11.3) the bone has a dense **cortex,** the structural component, and a **cancellous** portion, or **medulla,** which contains the blood cell-producing **marrow.**

At the microscopic level a bone consists of the mass of compact cortical bone and the spicules of cancellous bone, between which are interspersed particles of marrow and fat (Fig. 11.4).

The organic matrix or **osteoid** of the bone is produced by the bone

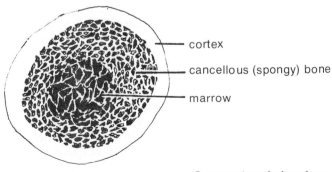

cortex

cancellous (spongy) bone

marrow

Cross-section of a long bone.   **Figure 11.3**

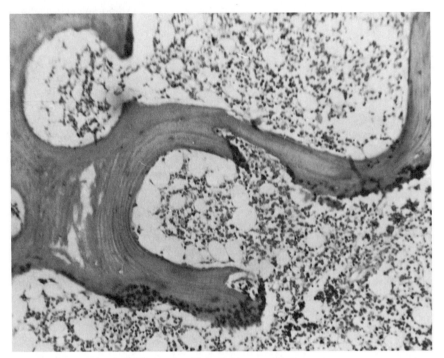

Figure 11.4   A microscopic section of bone. Between the spicules of cancellous bone is the bone marrow, hematopoietic cells admixed with adipose tissue. Hematoxylin and eosin stain,
× 100.

cells, **osteoblasts,** and consists primarily of collagen (95 per cent), with
some carbohydrates and proteins. Oxygen and exogenous carbohydrates are required for this synthesis, which is affected by age and
hormonal factors. As the matrix is synthesized the osteoblast becomes
entrapped and embedded as an **osteocyte.** Once buried, the cells cease
producing collagen (perhaps because of a lack of oxygen or substrate)
but remain viable, being nourished by fine vascular canaliculi (Volk-
mann's canals). The osteocytes may have some role in bone resorption,
but the major cell involved in this process is the **osteoclast.** This is a
multinucleated giant cell which is found in irregular indentations,
called Howship's lacunae, in bone being resorbed. Bone is continuously being formed, resorbed and re-formed by these several cells, the
process being referred to as **remodeling.**

Bone salts, essentially calcium phosphate, are deposited in the
organic matrix in two forms: innumerable tiny needle-shaped crystals
and hollow amorphous spheres. It is thought that the minerals are
precipitated initially in the amorphous form and then rapidly rearrange
into crystals. The small size of the crystals results in an enormous
surface area (about 150 acres for a 70-kilogram person), which accounts
for the active metabolism of bone.

Much work has been done on the physical chemistry of the deposition of bone salts, but for the purposes of this discussion it is sufficient
to note that the plasma concentration of calcium and phosphate ions is
in the supersaturated range, in which precipitation can be caused by

any substance that acts as a nucleus for crystallization. Pure collagen has this capacity (and makes up most of osteoid). A variety of substances can inhibit this reaction. They have been found in urine and plasma, and probably exist in normal soft tissues, which contain collagen.

Once crystallization begins, it proceeds very rapidly. The crystals contain many defects which slowly rearrange into a more stable structure. Experiments show that small amounts of fluorine result in crystals with fewer defects, and this may be the mechanism involved in the protective effect of fluorine against dental caries.

The over-all picture of bone formation is that of the osteoblasts synthesizing matrix, and some inhibitor being removed or some factor initiating crystallization of the bone salts. The crystals are precipitated rapidly and then slowly mature over several weeks. Unlike the soft tissues of the body, bone is continuously resorbed and re-formed throughout life (Enlow, 1976). Resorption actually appears to stimulate accretion, but the mechanism of this reaction is unknown. Many factors influence the rate of this remodeling process, including the anatomic site, age, hormonal status and disease. Garn et al. (1973) have clearly demonstrated an association between economic status and ossification, the former representing a complex of prenatal care, maternal education, nutrition and medical care. A delay in ossification is seen in lower status American children, but it probably still is not as severe as that seen in archeologic populations.

Environmental stresses also affect the bones. Rats exposed to cold show thinning of cortical bone. This anatomic feature is also seen in humans of the mongoloid race, along with many other features suggested to be cold-adaptive (Riesenfeld, 1976), such as a short habitus and a high proportion of body fat.

Bone resorption is intimately related to the metabolism of calcium and phosphate. The supersaturated levels appears to be maintained by the production of organic acids by bone cells, lowering the pH at the bone surfaces and increasing the solubility of the minerals. Bone is the major storehouse of calcium in the body and, should the serum calcium level drop for any reason, calcium is mobilized from the bones to increase the level. This system is regulated by the parathyroid glands, as discussed in Chapter 8. Parathormone produces changes in bone metabolism promoting resorption, and the serum calcium level rises. Phosphate follows a similar course, and in altered metabolic states the serum values of calcium, phosphorus and the enzyme alkaline phosphatase can be correlated with the radiologic, morphologic and clinical changes in arriving at the proper diagnosis and treatment (Appendix 1).

At the junctions between bones are the **joints,** which vary in structure depending on the degree of movement of the bones. The joints between the bones of the skull are immovable **synarthroses.** Slightly movable joints, as in the pelvis, are **amphiarthroses,** and the fully movable joints are **diarthroses.**

Diarthrodial or **synovial** joints are those most commonly affected by pathologic processes. These joints have an open joint space, lined by a synovial membrane and filled with a lubricating synovial fluid. The articular surfaces of the bones are capped by a cushion of cartilage.

There are no blood vessels in this cartilage, nutrition coming from the synovial fluid. Surrounding the joint is a capsule, which contains many sensory nerve fibers, accounting for the pain associated with joint injuries and disease.

Vertebral joints differ from all others in that the space between each vertebral body contains an **intervertebral disc,** an elastic cushioning structure with a jelly-like center, the **nucleus pulposus,** and an outer coat of dense connective tissue. On the opposing faces of the vertebral bodies are **end-plates** of cartilage similar to the articular cartilage of diarthrodial joints.

The **skeletal muscles** are attached to the bones by **tendons,** the anatomic arrangement of the muscles and joints determining the direction and range of motion. Muscle fibers are composed of several proteins which are aligned to give skeletal muscle its characteristic microscopic striations. In contraction these proteins slide alongside each other to come closer together. Thus, the contractility of muscle is due to shortening of its contractile proteins. As muscles contain elastic and viscous components, it is possible for them to increase in tension without a significant decrease in over-all length. Such a contraction is **isometric;** contraction against a load, with shortening of the muscle, is **isotonic.**

Skeletal muscle is under voluntary control and is excited to contract by nervous stimulation. It lacks the inherent contractility of cardiac and smooth muscle.

The energy required for muscle contraction is derived from the hydrolysis of ATP, which is derived from intermediary metabolism (Chapter 2). Glucose in the blood stream enters muscle cells and is broken down, initially by anaerobic glycolysis and, if exercise is prolonged, by the citric acid cycle. The anaerobic pathway is utilized for short violent bursts of activity, as oxygen cannot be brought to the muscles quickly enough for severe exertion. However, the production of lactic acid by the anaerobic pathway rapidly drops the pH of the muscle, depressing the enzymes needed for the reactions. Continued exercise must be at a slower pace, utilizing the aerobic pathway of the citric acid cycle. Athletic training increases the oxygen consumption of muscles and allows for greater exertion without using the less efficient anaerobic glycolysis.

Muscle is up to 50 per cent efficient in utilizing its energy stores, the remainder being liberated as heat. This heat production is an important mechanism in maintaining body temperature, both by exercise and shivering.

PATHOLOGY

Skeletal Pathology

It must be kept in mind that bone is a specialized type of connective tissue which is in an active metabolic state. Both the organic matrix and the inorganic bone salts are constantly being broken down and re-formed, although at varying rates. There is ample opportunity during these dynamic processes for the development of pathologic changes.

A condition of too little bone is called **osteoporosis.** Different specialists view this condition differently. For the clinician it is an area of weakness, usually in an elderly patient. For the radiologist, osteoporosis is an area of radiolucency, and for the pathologist it is represented by decreased osteoid and thin bone spicules. The archeologist sees the condition as a lightweight bone.

Tensile strength testing reveals the weakness of osteoporotic bone to be due not only to a quantitative decrease in the amount of bone, but also to a qualitative structural weakness (Evans, 1976).

There are three major causes of osteoporosis: (1) disuse atrophy, as in immobilization for a fracture or with bed rest; (2) a decrease in anabolic hormones, especially in postmenopausal women; and (3) an increase in catabolic hormones, such as corticosteroids in Cushing's syndrome, either spontaneous or iatrogenic.

Osteoporosis affects the weight-bearing vertebrae predominantly, and pathologic fractures can occur, causing hunchback (**kyphosis**) and loss of stature. These patients often have hypercalcemia, and the administration of calcium can precipitate the formation of renal stones.

The diagnosis of senile osteoporosis essentially consists of ruling out the other causes mentioned above, as well as metastatic carcinoma or multiple myeloma, which can produce similar clinical and radiologic pictures. Specific treatment for any of these conditions, if present, will help correct the osteoporosis. For postmenopausal women the cyclic administration of oral estrogens will help arrest the demineralization process.

Another chemical abnormality of bone is the deposition of abnormal elements, such as lead, which also concentrates in the brain and kidneys. Clinical manifestations include brain damage, anemia and the formation of a blue line along the gums, the "lead line." In western society this is a disease of children who eat peeling paint (this habit is called "pica"). It has been suggested that a factor in the decline of the Roman Empire was chronic lead poisoning, acquired from lead-contaminated cooking and eating utensils.

Rickets is a disease of vitamin D deficiency. Vitamin D regulates the rate of calcium absorption by the intestinal mucosa. Deficiency causes a lowering of the serum calcium level and mobilization of calcium from the bones by the action of parathormone. The result is **osteomalacia** (decalcification of the osteoid) and softening of the bones. Fractures, bowing of the bones and scoliosis (lateral curvature of the spine) can be seen in this condition.

Vitamin D is synthesized in the skin in the presence of ultraviolet light, as noted in Chapter 10. During the Industrial Revolution the sooty skies of Europe led to a virtual epidemic of rickets, but it was not until some 50 years ago that the role of vitamin D in the disease was appreciated.

There is a bewildering variety of developmental abnormalities of bone, some of which have been mentioned in preceding chapters. This discussion will be confined to one relatively common condition, **achondroplastic dwarfism.**

Achondroplasia (Fig. 8.1) is a defect in the formation of enchondral bone, bone first formed as cartilage. It is hereditary, being controlled by a simple mendelian dominant gene. Achondroplastic dwarfs have a subnormal fertility, but the condition is maintained at a constant rate in the population, apparently by recurrent mutations. The bones of the extremities are short and thick, and similar changes at the base of the skull make the mandible and forehead appear prominent. This condition is of great antiquity and wide geographic distribution. Animals are also afflicted, dachshunds and basset hounds being examples (Beachley and Graham, 1973).

Bones of course are liable to trauma, and fractures constitute a significant portion of both orthopedic and pathologic practice. The orthopedist is called on to treat fractures, and the pathologist may be asked to exclude the possibility of **pathologic** fractures (usually due to metastatic carcinoma), or may have the task of distinguishing the exuberant process of repair from a primary bone tumor.

The sequence of events in fracture repair consists of an initial formation of a blood clot, a **hematoma,** at the fracture site. The area rapidly becomes inflamed and then infiltrated by reparative granulation tissue. Cartilage and osteoid are then deposited to form the **callus,** which unites the bone ends. The callus is eventually resorbed and converted to bone, which completes the healing of the fracture. If there is adequate immobilization of the bone, including the joints above and below it, healing can be almost perfect. Healing is always better and more rapid in the young. Poor immobilization can lead to imperfect union, or even nonunion, and formation of a false joint, a **pseudoarthrosis.**

Bone infection is called **osteomyelitis.** These are mostly bacterial infections, which reach the bone by any one of several potential routes. One is by the blood stream from a distant site. There can be direct extension from an infection such as a soft tissue or dental abscess or a sinus infection. Finally, bacteria can be introduced mechanically by a penetrating injury such as a laceration or a **compound** fracture, one in which the skin is broken. A number of variables affect the course of such an infection, including the nature of the causative organism, the route of the infection, and the age and health status of the patient. It must also be recognized that in the modern world the use of antibiotics has markedly altered the general course of bone infections.

Pyogenic infections are those caused by any of the common bacteria, such as staphylococci, streptococci and occasionally salmonella. For unknown reasons, those with sickle cell disease are particularly liable to salmonella osteomyelitis. Hematogenous infections occur most commonly in children and affect the metaphyses, the most vascular areas of the bone. The infected bone becomes necrotic and can become separated from the viable bone as a **sequestrum.** This fragment is surrounded by purulent exudate which drains through sinus tracts. Such infections can be very difficult to treat and may persist for years. The sinuses come to be lined by squamous epithelium and can form epidermoid cysts in the bone or, with continuing infection and drainage, squamous carcinoma.

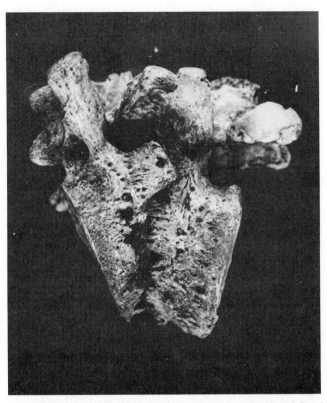

Tuberculous kyphosis. This example is from medieval Czechoslovakia.   **Figure 11.5**
(Courtesy of C. Toomey.)

Bone **tuberculosis** is an important infection, as it is still seen in the lower socioeconomic groups of the western world and in the under-developed nations. The infection is usually hematogenous, spreading from primary disease in the lungs. Joints as well as bone are destroyed, with involvement of the vertebral bodies (Fig. 11.5) causing collapse and kyphosis (Pott's disease). The microscopic picture is similar to that of tuberculosis in other sites, although giant cells may be infrequent. Treatment is by antituberculous medication. Surgery may be necessary, particularly if vertebral disease compresses the spinal cord.

The classification of bone **tumors** is at best confusing and it seems as if no two authors use the same scheme. Most are based on the tissue of origin. Figure 11.6 presents Aegerter's classification (1975). Primary bone tumors are of mesodermal origin and, more so than tumors of other tissues have specific predilections for age, site, sex and course.

Benign and malignant tumors are found in all of Aegerter's groups except the myelogenic, in which all are malignant (the leukemias, Chapter 4). The benign tumors are of many types, with varying histologic patterns, but most have some important features in common. They manifest themselves by pain, swelling, local pressure effects, or occasionally by pathologic fracture. The last occurs only if the tumor is **osteolytic**, destroying the bone. Some benign tumors are **osteoblastic** and stimulate the deposition of bone.

The important radiologic characteristic of a benign tumor (or al-

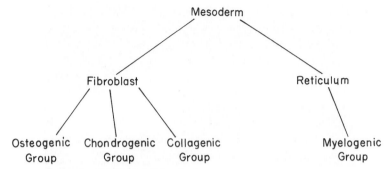

Figure 11.6   Aegerter and Kirkpatrick's classification of bone tumors.

most any other benign process, such as infection) is the presence of a dense margin of sclerotic bone surrounding the lesion. Most benign tumors grow slowly, allowing ample time for bony reaction. In contrast, malignant tumors, primary and secondary, grow rapidly, with no bony reaction, and appear as punched-out lesions in the radiograph. Of course, the major differential point lies in the behavior. Benign tumors grow only locally, whereas malignant bone tumors have an extraordinary metastatic potential.

The malignant tumors of the skeletal system fortunately are relatively rare. Of these, the most common arise in cartilage and bone. **Chondrosarcoma** is a slowly growing tumor rare in those under 30 years of age. The classic location is in the distal femur, but this is true for many bone tumors. X-ray examination reveals a destructive lesion, but the pathologic diagnosis is often difficult. The pathologist looks for cellular atypia and the presence of multiple cells within lacunae. No bone pathologist should make a diagnosis without an adequate history and x-ray examination, and this is particularly true in chondrosarcoma. If the patient is young, a proliferating cartilaginous lesion is probably benign. If the patient is older, over 30 years of age, the lesion is almost certainly malignant.

Treatment is by radical surgery, with a relatively good prognosis. The five-year survival is about 35 per cent, far better than osteogenic sarcoma.

Osteogenic sarcoma (osteosarcoma) is a disease of children and young adults, in contrast to chondrosarcoma. There is a second peak of incidence in elderly patients with Paget's disease, a hypertrophic condition of bone. The tumor in children again occurs most commonly around the knee. X-ray examination shows destruction of the bone (although some may be osteoblastic) and a characteristic elevation of the periosteum, known as Codman's triangle. There are a number of microscopic variants of the tumor, but the important diagnostic features are atypical cells and the presence of osteoid, which may not be calcified. This has been a lethal tumor, with a five-year survival rate of under 5 per cent, death usually occurring within 18 months with lung metastases. Recently it has been realized that most of these patients have lung metastases when seen initially, even if they are not seen on chest x-ray. The use of chemotherapy in conjunction with radical surgery has resulted in some improvement in these dismal statistics.

The malignant potential of radioactive materials was demonstrated by a group of deaths due to osteosarcoma in factory workers in the United States in the 1920s. These young girls were employed to paint watch dials with radium-containing luminous paint. In pointing their brushes with their lips, they swallowed small amounts of paint, and the radium was concentrated in the skeleton. Total radium amounts at autopsy ranged from 10 to 180 micrograms, but these minute amounts led to the development of osteosarcoma.

Tumors metastatic to bone are common. The chief offenders are tumors primary in the lung, breast, prostate, kidney and thyroid. Metastatic carcinoma must be differentiated from **multiple myeloma,** a primary tumor of plasma cells that arises in the marrow and spreads widely throughout the skeletal system.

Pathology of the Joints

Joint pathology is determined to a great extent by the peculiar anatomy and physiology of these areas. Traumatic injuries, **strains, sprain** and **dislocations,** are common. Infectious arthritis is rarely seen since the advent of antibiotics, but two conditions occasionally encountered are tuberculous and gonococcal arthritis.

There are several forms of chronic arthritis, the most common of which are **rheumatoid arthritis** (RA) and **degenerative joint disease** (DJD, **osteoarthritis).** RA is a systemic disorder with symptoms primarily relating to the joints, tending to produce crippling deformities. The etiology in man is unknown but a bacterial infection has been shown to cause a condition similar to RA in animals (Sikes et al., 1956). Hudson et al. (1975) have suggested a causal relationship between the high incidence of RA-like changes in the skeletons of southeastern American Indians and their subsistence on white-tailed deer, carriers of the pathogenic bacterium. The Cherokees noted this association and incorporated it into their world view, labeling it as magical.

The clinical picture in a classic case of RA is one of weight loss; migratory polyarthritis, often symmetric; ulnar deviation of the hands; and subcutaneous nodules, usually around the elbow.

The pathology is fairly specific, after an initial phase of edema, acute inflammation and granulation tissue. In the more advanced stages there is infiltration by lymphocytes and plasma cells, with areas of fibrinoid (pink staining, or eosinophilic, material) deposition in the synovium. The end result is destruction of the joint by hypertrophied synovium and granulation tissue, referred to as **pannus,** which actually invades and destroys the articular cartilage and underlying bone.

RA is often complicated by a secondary DJD, producing a complex pathologic picture. The predilection of RA for the knees, hands and feet may be a useful diagnostic feature.

DJD or osteoarthritis is a senescent arthritis that primarily affects the larger weight-bearing joints and is essentially a degenerative process of the articular cartilage. Comparative studies of skeletal samples from several different populations (Jurmain, 1977a, b) indicate that the etiologic agent is severe functional stress. Different populations show varying incidence and degree of severity of the condition, proportional to the stress experienced in life.

The pathologic picture is one of proliferation and ossification of the cartilage at the margins of the joint, producing a characteristic "lipping" appearance, readily seen in vertebral columns grossly and on x-ray examination. Unlike RA, the synovial membrane usually remains normal until an advanced stage of the disease. In addition, DJD is not complicated by the systemic manifestations seen in RA.

Still another form of arthritis is **gout.** This is an important condition because it is fairly common, painful and disabling, and treatable. The disease is due to an excess of uric acid in the circulation, **hyperuricemia.** Urates are deposited in the affected joint and occasionally in other organs such as the kidney and heart. The treatment is with drugs that facilitate the urinary excretion of urates, **uricosuric** agents, and patients must be advised to avoid such precipitating agents as exposure, exhaustion, trauma and alcoholic overindulgence.

Muscle Disorders

Most disorders of muscle are part of a more generalized disease process. Infections are usually attributable to extension from soft tissue abscesses. One diagnostic infectious lesion is the **psoas abscess** seen in

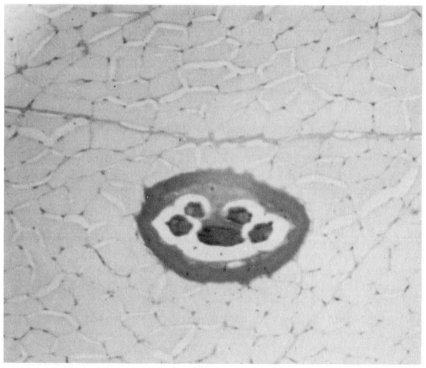

Figure 11.7   *Trichinella spiralis* larva encysted in the muscle of Elmer McCurdy, a train robber killed in 1911 and embalmed in arsenic. (Courtesy of Dr. T. A. Reyman.)

tuberculous involvement of that muscle as an extension of vertebral infection. A characteristic case was seen in the mummy of an Egyptian priest of the 21st Dynasty (c. 1050 B.C.), Nesperehan, as clear evidence of the existence of tuberculosis in dynastic Egypt (Morse et al., 1964).

The larvae of *Trichinella spiralis* are deposited in skeletal muscle, and a good example (Fig. 11.7) was seen in the body of an Oklahoma (or rather, Indian Territory) train robber named Elmer McCurdy, who was embalmed in arsenic in 1911 and autopsied when his body appeared as a side show attraction in 1977 (Reyman and Horne, 1978).

Disruption of the nerve supply causes **atrophy** of the affected muscles, and two ancient examples of muscle atrophy have been postulated to be due to poliomyelitis on this basis (Harris and Weeks, 1973; Mitchell, 1900). The **muscular dystrophies** are genetically determined conditions of progressive muscular weakness, often fatal early in life.

Tumors of skeletal muscle are rare. A tumor-like lesion is **myositis ossificans,** caused by calcification of repeated hemorrhages into muscle adjacent to bone. The uninitiated can be misled into considering this lesion a true bone tumor, even the microscopic appearance being deceptive. It is of interest that the original femur of *Homo erectus* discovered by Dubois has a lesion which may be this entity. True tumors of skeletal muscle, **rhabdomyosarcomas,** are rare and highly malignant.

PALEOPATHOLOGIC FINDINGS IN SKELETAL REMAINS

Bone Preservation

The preservation of bone varies with the type of soil. Acid soil decalcifies bone. For example, the "bog bodies" of northern Europe are medieval human corpses that have been preserved by the tannic acid in the bogs, but their bones often are considerably decalcified (Glob, 1969). If conditions are otherwise, bones may be preserved for thousands of years (Stout and Teitelbaum, 1976). Such specimens can be examined microscopically, permitting the diagnosis of metabolic diseases. The microscopic structure of bone also shows age-specific changes, useful in determining age at death (Bouvier and Ubelaker, 1977; Singh and Gunberg, 1970).

Careful excavation with complete clearing of soil is essential before an attempt can be made to remove buried bones. Most bones can be cleaned simply with warm water, and skulls should be examined before washing for remnants of brain and for the ossicles of the middle ear.

A variety of materials is available for the preservation of skeletal specimens. Hot paraffin wax can be damaging, and although shellac will preserve the surface it begins to peel off in a few years, taking bone with it. Soluble plastics appear to be the best choice. The bones are washed and dried, and then soaked in Alvar 1750 or polyvinyl acetate (Brothwell, 1965). This procedure is best carried out in the laboratory, and can be done under negative pressure for more thorough impregnation. Plaster of Paris can be used for support, but it is hard to remove from the bones should this become necessary.

Evidence of Disease

As the techniques and nuances of the diagnosis of disease in ancient skeletal material have been covered by Steinbock (1976), the present discussion will be confined to a survey of the diseases described in such material.

METABOLIC DISEASES

Osteoporosis in archeologic bone specimens is manifested by light weight of the bone. A more exact evaluation can be achieved by a photon absorptiometric method. One such study (Perzigian, 1973), comparing groups of prehistoric American Indians, showed that Hopewell Indians, considered on archeologic evidence to be better nourished than Indian Knoll Indians, had more osteoporosis. These data were interpreted as indicating that adequate nutrition does not prevent the development of senile osteoporosis.

There is some scattered evidence for ancient rickets, ranging from the possibility of the disease in *H. erectus* and, more likely, in Neanderthals, to clear-cut cases in Cro-Magnons and medieval Europeans. Some cases have been suggested in Egyptian remains, perhaps related to the custom of **purdah,** the shrouding of women when outdoors, preventing exposure to ultraviolet light.

Hormonal abnormalities are rare in ancient material. A case of acromegaly has been described in an Egyptian skull (Brothwell, 1965).

CONGENITAL DISEASES

Achondroplasia has been well documented in ancient Egypt from predynastic times up to the 30th Dynasty (3000 B.C.–300 B.C.) (Dawson, 1927), not only in skeletons but in wall paintings in tombs, figurines and statues. Several of the dwarf skeletons must have been persons of considerable wealth and importance, having been found in their costly tombs. Modern achondroplastics are generally of high intelligence, and some ancient dwarfs are known to have held important offices. They are also depicted in charge of jewelry or pets, or in personal attendance upon their masters. They were certainly clever enough to capitalize on their disorder, acting then, as now, as jesters.

Even the ancient Egyptian word for dwarf is known, *nemew.* The depictions are very accurate, with muscular bodies, short limbs and large heads. Some show a marked protrusion of the lower spine, **lordosis,** and bowed legs. A magical significance was attached to dwarfs, accounting for the figurines and amulets, associated with spells to facilitate birth. There are also several achondroplastic skeletons from the New World.

Other examples of congenital disease include **hydrocephaly,** from Roman Britain, Egypt and Neolithic Germany (Brothwell, 1965), and multiple osteochondromatosis. In a case described by Sjovold et al. (1974), a fetus with multiple congenital osteochondromata was found impacted in the pelvis of a medieval female skeleton. The maternal pelvis was obstructed by similar tumors, and death was probably due to a ruptured uterus.

Gray (1967) noted spina bifida in Egyptian mummies, and Hawkes and Wells (1976) reported an Anglo-Saxon burial in which the individual was congenitally missing his entire left arm and shoulder girdle. In view of several wounds indicating multiple attacks on this person, the investigators suggested that his deformity may have driven him to become literally an Anglo-Saxon one-armed bandit.

TRAUMA

Physical trauma seems to have been common throughout human evolution. Fractures are frequent in nonhuman primates; 36 per cent of the gibbons studied by Schultz (1967) had healed fractures.

The Shanidar Neanderthals show evidence of many fractures, mostly healed. One of these individuals had suffered an amputation of an arm early in life. He probably was also blind and must have been cared for by others, an early evidence of human social organization (Solecki, 1971). This case also demonstrates that prolonged survival is possible even after what was almost certainly a traumatic amputation (Majno, 1975).

The pattern of fractures seen in studies of large populations have been used in making inferences on life styles and in drawing comparisons with modern populations. For example, hand fractures are rare in ancient Nubian skeletons and very common in modern mechanized London (Bourke, 1972).

Common in Egyptian skeletons are **parry** fractures, fractures of the radius and ulna at the midpoint, suffered when an individual raises his arm to ward off a blow at the head and is struck on the arm. Parry fractures are easily distinguished from those seen at the distal ends of these bones in falls (Colle's fractures). The relative incidence of these can provide an index of strife in a population (Swedlund and Armelagos, 1976).

The Edwin Smith papyrus (Breasted, 1930) is a surgical treatise with much emphasis on physical injuries. Fractures were treated by reduction and splinting, and many well-healed fractures have been seen, as well as examples of malunion and nonunion. Examples of cranial trauma are seen in this era and going back to Neanderthals and *Homo erectus.*

Trepanation (trephination) is a special form of cranial trauma. This procedure consists of the removal of a piece, usually about 3 to 5 cm. across, of the skull cap, the **calvarium,** without damaging the underlying blood vessels, meninges or brain. The practice was worldwide, beginning in Europe 10,000 years ago, and examples are seen in Egypt dating to 1200 B.C. (Lisowski, 1967). It is probably still practiced in

Africa (Margetts, 1967). In South America the practice dates to about the 5th century B.C. and examples are also seen from Middle America (Romero, 1970; Wilkinson, 1975).

The procedure was carried out for magical or therapeutic reasons, and it is very difficult to separate these two. It may have been done for fracture or headache, or to let out "evil spirits." In 20th century Kenya it was done most often for headache. When performed post mortem, the piece of bone from the skull of a person previously trephined was a good luck charm. The African procedure involved alcohol as an anesthetic and a variety of instruments to remove the pieces of bone, by drilling, incising or scraping. Most patients seem to have survived the procedure. In evaluating crania, it must be kept in mind that spontaneous diseases can cause defects similar in appearance to trephination in the skull (Stewart, 1975).

Another form of trauma is seen in a Peruvian mummy showing the radiologic changes of frostbite, atrophy of the distal phalanges. The individual was a male but had been buried in the attitude used for females, and the authors (Post and Donner, 1972) speculated that the frostbite may have been incurred in the course of exposure as a punishment for a sexual deviation.

INFLAMMATORY CONDITIONS

An important fact is that most infections do not involve the bone directly. An indirect effect is seen in the diseases of childhood, in that there is an associated cessation of growth of the long bones during the time of illness (or starvation). A relative excess of calcium is deposited in the metaphyseal growth zone, leaving a radiopaque line after growth resumes (Harris, 1931). The number of these lines has been suggested as an index of morbidity in a given population, modern or ancient (Wells, 1964a). Some questions have been raised as to the validity of applying this technique to ancient populations (Marshall, 1968), as Harris lines have been shown to disappear later in life. They have also been seen after immunization procedures, suggesting that they could result from trivial subclinical infections.

There are some examples of pyogenic infections of bones. Cases of osteomyelitis show the course of disease in the preantibiotic era, and this distinction must be kept in mind when comparing ancient and modern material. Examples of the disease go back to a 200 million-year-old Dimetrodon (Moodie, 1923). Osteomyelitis is a nonspecific infection; i.e., it can be caused by a number of organisms, all of which produce the same pathologic picture.

Dental disease such as caries or periodontal disease can lead to infection of the middle ear and the sinuses of the mastoid bone, as Wells (1964b) so vividly dramatized in his reconstruction of the death of the Rhodesian Neanderthal afflicted with caries and mastoiditis (Pycraft et al., 1928). Pseudopathology can be a problem in the examination of this anatomic area. Rowling (1961) cautions that anthropophagic insect damage can mimic mastoiditis in mummies, and Lynn and

Benitez (1974) did indeed find a beetle larva (of the family *Staphylinidae*, genus probably *Atleta*) embedded in resin in the left external auditory canal of a 2,600 year-old Egyptian mummy. Beetles of this family are often found associated with carrion. It was most likely that the larva was entrapped in the ear during the mummification process. The perforations of the eardrums found in this mummy were probably due to antemortem disease, as determined by the size, shape and location.

Other examples of mastoiditis have been found in skeletons of Nubians, other Egyptians and prehistoric Europeans. Many of these skulls show breakdown of the mastoid bone and fistula formation (McKenzie and Brothwell, 1967).

There are good examples of bone tuberculosis from dynastic Egypt (Morse et al., 1964). The absence of evidence of the disease in predynastic remains (Smith and Jones, 1910) makes it attractive to postulate the evolution of the human disease from bovine tuberculosis at the beginning of the historic period of Egyptian history, the time of the domestication of cattle. Bone tuberculosis is noted in Europe by 2000 B.C. and in pre-Columbian America, where many kyphotic pottery figurines also are found.

There is no skeletal evidence of leprosy from Egypt or Europe until the 5th century A.D., despite statements that the •ancient Egyptians considered the disease to be a punishment for eating pork, which was sacred to Osiris (Radbill, 1976) and Biblical references to the disease; these perhaps are actually cases of syphilis (Møller-Christiansen, 1967). As noted in Chapter 3, the studies of Møller-Christiansen on skeletons from a medieval leper house cemetery have outlined the bone changes of leprosy.

The origin of syphilis has been a point of controversy since the 16th century (Oriel and Cockburn, 1974). There are a few bones showing questionable evidence of the disease from pre-Columbian America and Europe. Modern Indians are relatively immune and do not suffer from neurosyphilis (Scrimshaw and Tejada, 1970). Most likely the disease was present in both areas but became more virulent after 1492, for unknown reasons. The modern disease may be derived from yaws, another treponemal disease which is ancient in the tropics. It is theorized that yaws evolved to endemic syphilis, a skin disease acquired in childhood, when man became domesticated. With the use of clothing and better sanitary facilities, direct transmission became more difficult for the organism and it adapted to venereal transmission.

Parasites do not affect the bones directly, unless an associated anemia results in porotic hyperostosis (Chapter 4). As discussed in Chapter 4, such cases can also be seen on a nutritional basis.

TUMORS

As osteolytic tumors leave only a defect in a bone, the diagnosis of such a tumor is difficult or impossible. Osteoblastic tumors are much easier to diagnose. This differential factor must be kept in mind when discussing the incidence of tumors in ancient material.

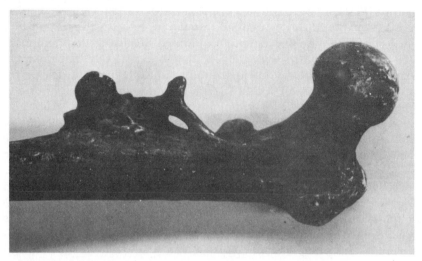

Figure 11.8   Lesion on the original *Homo erectus* femur, variously interpreted as myositis ossificans or a fluoric exostosis.

Benign **osteomas** (ivory osteomas, small, button-like tumors, usually on the skull) have been described in skeletons from several different populations, as have **osteochondromas,** which may be spontaneous or congenital, as noted earlier in this chapter (Sjovold et al., 1974).

The original *Homo erectus* femur shows an osteophytic lesion which possibly is myositis ossificans (ossification of a traumatic hematoma) as mentioned above (Fig. 11.8). A good case has been made for this lesion being a proliferative disorder due to excess ingestion during life of fluorine, which is found in high concentration in the volcanic ash of Java in which the fossil was discovered (Soriano, 1970). In either case, this lesion represents the oldest example of disease in the genus *Homo*.

Malignant tumors are extremely rare in ancient material. A case of osteosarcoma from Egypt described by Ruffer and Willmore (1914) is probably an osteochondroma. There is no periosteal reaction, and the location, in the pelvis, is atypical for osteosarcoma. A few more likely cases are reported from Europe and Peru, although these could possibly be reactive processes (Brothwell, 1967).

Bone can be directly involved by extension from adjacent soft tissue tumors. Strouhal (1978) has reported such a case in an Egyptian skull eroded by a probable nasopharyngeal carcinoma, and there is one example of an Egyptian sacrum eroded by a possible rectal cancer or a tumor peculiar to the sacrum, a **chordoma** (Brothwell, 1967).

Metastatic tumors present the problem of distinction from multiple myeloma. A number of skeletons with multiple punched-out lesions have been diagnosed as multiple myeloma (Morse et al., 1974), the number actually exceeding those diagnosed as metastatic disease. This is an unreasonable ratio, as in modern populations the overwhelming number of bone tumors are metastatic, less than 20 per cent being myeloma.

JOINT PATHOLOGY

Rheumatoid arthritis (RA) is a disease of the smaller bones of the hands and feet, and the changes at times are visible only radiographically, so the diagnosis is difficult in the usual archeologic material.

There is indeed very little paleopathologic evidence of RA, and Short (1974) has hypothesized that the disease is of recent origin, evolving out of **ankylosing spondylitis** (a special form of vertebral arthritis) early in the Christian era. Klepinger (1979) offers supportive evidence for this concept in a Hellenistic skeleton showing features suggestive of a transition between the two diseases.

Osteoarthritis is probably the most frequently diagnosed disease in paleopathology. It has been described in Neanderthals from La Chapelle Aux-Saints, in Cro-Magnons and in Paleolithic man. Many ancient Egyptian skeletons show characteristic lesions, virtually identical to those seen in modern patients (Bourke, 1972). The presence of the disease in Egypt has etiologic implications, as it was once thought to be related to cold, damp climates. In Europe this etiologic concept led to an effective therapy. The folk "theory of signs" states that signs suggesting a remedy are to be found in the area where the disease originates. An extract from the pith of the willow tree, which grows in swampy areas, was found to be an effective treatment. The willow contains salicylates, still one of the best remedies for arthritis.

An Egyptian mummy with gout has also been described in which uric acid deposits were found in the joints (Smith and Dawson, 1924).

REFERENCES

Aegerter, E. and J. A. Kirkpatrick, Jr. (1975): Orthopedic Diseases: Physiology, Pathology, and Radiology, 4th ed. Saunders, Philadelphia.

Beachley, M. C. and F. H. Graham (1973): Hypochondroplastic dwarfism (enchondral chondrodystrophy) in a dog. J. Am. Vet. Med. Assoc. *163*:283–284.

Bourke, J. B. (1972): Trauma and degenerative disease in Ancient Egypt and Nubia. J. Hum. Evol. *1*:225–232.

Bouvier, M. and D. H. Ubelaker (1977): A comparison of two methods for the microscopic determination of age at death. Am. J. Phys. Anthropol. *46*:391–394.

Breasted, J. H. (1930): The Edwin Smith Surgical Papyrus. University of Chicago Press, Chicago.

Brothwell, D. R. (1965): Digging up Bones. British Museum, London.

Brothwell, D. R. (1967): The evidence for neoplasms. *In* Brothwell, D. R. and A. T. Sandison, op. cit., pp. 320–345.

Brothwell, D. R. and A. T. Sandison (1967): Diseases in Antiquity: A Survey of the Diseases, Injuries and Surgery of Early Populations. Charles C Thomas, Springfield, Ill.

Dawson, W. R. (1927): Pigmies, dwarfs, and hunchbacks in ancient Egypt. Ann. Med. Hist. *9*:315–326, 1927.

Enlow, D. H. (1976): The remodeling of bone. Yearbook Phys. Anthropol. *20*:19–34.

Evans, F. G. (1976): Age changes in mechanical properties and histology of human compact bone. Yearbook Phys. Anthropol. *20*:57–72.

Garn, S. M., Nagy, J. M., Sandusky, S. T. et al. (1973): Economic impact on tooth emergence. Am. J. Phys. Anthropol. *39*:233–238.

Garn, S. M., Sandusky, S. T., Rosen, N. M. et al. (1973): Economic impact on postnatal ossification. Am. J. Phys. Anthropol. *38*:1–4.

Glob, P. V. (1969): The Bog People: Iron-Age Man Preserved. R. Bruce-Mitford, Trans. Cornell University Press, Ithaca, N.Y.

Gray, P. H. K. (1967): Radiography of ancient Egyptian mummies. Med. Radiogr. Photogr. 43:34–44.

Harris, H. A. (1931): Lines of arrested growth in long bones in childhood; correlation of histological and radiographic appearances in clinical and experimental conditions. Br. J. Radiol. 4:561, 622.

Harris, J. E. and K. Weeks (1973): X-Raying the Pharaohs. Scribner's, New York.

Hawkes, S. C. and C. Wells (1976): Absence of the left upper limb and pectoral girdle in a unique Anglo-Saxon burial. Bull. N.Y. Acad. Med. 52:1229–1235.

Hudson, C., Butler, R. and D. Sikes (1975): Arthritis in the prehistoric southeastern United States: biological and cultural variables. Am. J. Phys. Anthropol. 43:57–62.

Jurmain, R. D. (1977a): Paleoepidemiology of degenerative knee disease. Med. Anthropol. 1, #1:1–23.

Jurmain, R. D. (1977b): Stress and the etiology of osteoarthritis. Am. J. Phys. Anthropol. 46:353–365.

Klepinger, L. (1979). Paleopathologic evidence for the evolution of rheumatoid arthritis. Am. J. Phys. Anthropol. 50:119–122.

Lisowski, F. P. (1967): Prehistoric and early historic trepanation. In D. R. Brothwell and A. T. Sandison, op. cit., pp. 651–672.

Lynn, G. and J. T. Benitez (1974): Temporal bone preservation in a 2600 year old Egyptian mummy. Science 183:200–202.

Majno, G. (1975): The Healing Hand: Man and Wound in the Ancient World. Harvard University Press, Boston.

Margetts, E. L. (1967): Trepanation of the skull by the medicine men of primitive cultures, with particular reference to present-day native East African practice. In D. R. Brothwell and A. T. Sandison, op. cit., pp. 673–701.

Marshall, W. A. (1968): Problems in relating the presence of transverse lines in the radius to the occurrence of disease. In The Skeletal Biology of Earlier Human Populations, D. Brothwell, ed. Pergamon, London, pp. 245–261.

McKenzie, W. and D. R. Brothwell (1967): Disease in the ear region. In D. R. Brothwell and A. T. Sandison, op. cit., pp. 464–473.

Mitchell, J. K. (1900): Study of a mummy affected with anterior poliomyelitis. Trans. Assoc. Am. Physicians 15:134–136.

Møller-Christiansen, V. (1967): Evidence of leprosy in earlier peoples. In D. R. Brothwell and A. T. Sandison, op. cit., pp. 295–306.

Moodie, R. L. (1923): Paleopathology: An Introduction to the Study of Ancient Evidences of Disease. University of Illinois Press, Urbana.

Morse, D., Brothwell, D. and P. J. Ucko (1964): Tuberculosis in Ancient Egypt. Am. Rev. Resp. Dis. 90:524–541.

Morse, D., Dailey, R. C. and J. Bunn (1974): Prehistoric multiple myeloma. Bull. N.Y. Acad. Med. 50:447–458.

Oriel, J. D. and T. A. Cockburn (1974): Syphilis: where did it come from. Paleopath. Newsl. #6:9–12.

Ortner, D. J. (1976): Microscopic and molecular biology of human compact bone: an anthropological perspective. Yearbook Phys. Anthropol. 20:35–44.

Perzigian, A. J. (1973): Osteoporotic bone loss in two prehistoric Indian populations. Am. J. Phys. Anthropol. 39:87–96.

Post, P. W. and D. D. Donner (1972): Frostbite in a preColumbian mummy. Am. J. Phys. Anthropol. 37:187–192.

Pycraft, W. B., Smith, G. E., Yearsley, M. et al. (1928): Rhodesian Man and Associated Remains. Trustees British Museum, London.

Radbill, S. X. (1976): The role of animals in infant feeding. In American Folk Medicine: A Symposium. W. D. Hand, ed. University of California Press, Berkeley, pp. 21–30.

Reyman, T. A. and P. Horne (1978): Light and electron microscopic studies on tissue from Elmer McCurdy. Paleopath. Newsl. #22:T4.

Riesenfeld, A. (1976): Compact bone changes in cold-exposed rats. Am. J. Phys. Anthropol. 44:111–112.

Romero, J. (1970): Dental mutilation, trephination and cranial deformation. In Handbook of Middle American Indians, Vol. 9: Physical Anthropology. T. D. Stewart, vol. ed. University of Texas Press, Austin, pp. 50–67.

Rowling, J. T. (1961): Pathological changes in mummies. Proc. R. Soc. Med., Sed. Hist. Med. 54:409–425.

Ruffer, M. A. and J. G. Willmore (1914): Studies in paleopathology. Note on a tumor of the pelvis dating from Roman times (250 A.D.) and found in Egypt. J. Pathol. Bacteriol. 18:480–484.

Satinoff, M. I. (1972): The medical biology of the early Egyptian populations from Aswan, Assyut and Gebelen. J. Hum. Evol. *1*:247–257.

Schultz, A. H. (1967): Notes on diseases and healed fractures of wild apes. *In* D. R. Brothwell and A. T. Sandison, op. cit., pp. 47–55.

Scrimshaw, N. S. and C. Tejada (1970): Pathology of living Indians as seen in Guatemala. *In* Handbook of Middle American Indians, Vol. 9: Physical Anthropology. T. D. Stewart, vol. ed. University of Texas Press, Austin, pp. 203–225.

Short, C. L. (1974): The antiquity of rheumatoid arthritis. Arthr. Rheum. *17*:193–205.

Sikes, D., Naher, G. M. and L. P. Doyle (1956): The pathology of chronic arthritis following natural and experimental *Erysipelothrix* infection of swine. Am. J. Pathol. *32*:1241–1251.

Singh, I. J. and D. L. Gunberg (1970): Estimation of age at death in human males from quantitative histology of bone fragments. Am. J. Phys. Anthropol. *33*:373–382.

Sjovold, T., Swedborg, I. and L. Diener (1974): A pregnant woman from the middle ages with exostosis multiplex. Ossa *1*:3–23.

Smith, G. E. and W. R. Dawson (1924): Egyptian Mummies. Unwin, London.

Smith, G. E. and F. W. Jones (1910): Archeological Survey of Nubia: Report on the Human Remains. National Printing Office, Cairo.

Solecki, R. (1971): Shanidar. Knopf, New York.

Soriano, M. (1970): The fluoric origin of the bone lesion in the *Pithecanthropus erectus* femur. Am. J. Phys. Anthropol. *32*:49–58.

Steinbock, R. T. (1976): Paleopathological Diagnosis and Interpretation. Charles C Thomas, Springfield, Ill.

Stewart, T. D. (1975): Cranial dysraphism mistaken for trephination. Am. J. Phys. Anthropol. *42*:435–438.

Stout, S. D. and S. L. Teitelbaum (1976): Histological analysis of undecalcified thin sections of archeological bone. Am. J. Phys. Anthropol. *44*:263–270.

Strouhal, E. (1978): Ancient Egyptian carcinoma. Bull. N.Y. Acad. Med. *54*:290–302.

Swedlund, A. C. and G. J. Armelagos (1976): Demographic Anthropology. Wm. C. Brown, Dubuque, Iowa.

Wells, C. (1964a): Harris lines and ancient disease. Hum. Biol. *36*:72.

Wells, C. (1964b): Bones, Bodies and Disease. Thames and Hudson, London.

Wilkinson, R. G. (1975): Trephination by drilling in ancient Mexico. Bull. N.Y. Acad. Med. *51*:838–850.

twelve

The Nervous System

ANATOMY AND PHYSIOLOGY

The major control mechanism of the body is that provided by the nervous system, consisting of the **central nervous system** (CNS), the brain and spinal cord, surrounded by the membranous **meninges** and encased in the skull and vertebral column, and the **peripheral nervous system** (PNS), the nerve cells and fibers lying outside these bones.

The basic structural component of both parts of the nervous system is the **neuron,** a cell which is specialized to transmit messages along its processes by electrochemical impulses. Communication between nerves, at anatomic junctions called **synapses,** is by chemical transmitters, most commonly acetylcholine. The afferent processes of neurons, the **axons,** are coated with a fatty substance called **myelin** which is responsible for the white appearance of peripheral nerves and the white matter of the CNS, in the periphery of the spinal cord and the central area of the brain (Fig. 12.1). The cell bodies make up the gray matter of the cortex of the brain and the central areas of the spinal cord. The bulk of the NS is actually made up of supporting **glial** cells, **astrocytes** and **oligodendroglial cells.**

The brain has three major gross components, the **cerebrum, cerebellum** and **brain stem** (Fig. 12.2). Studies have failed to demonstrate any correlation between brain size and intelligence, but Van Valen (1974) has suggested that the evolutionary trend to a large brain in humans is actually due to selection against small brain size at birth. Intelligence is positively correlated with both brain and over-all weight at birth.

Looking at this problem from the other side, Epstein (1973) has noted that only a small increase in the size of the birth canal would allow passage of infants with adult-sized brains. However, the output of the infant's metabolism would be insufficient to nourish such a large

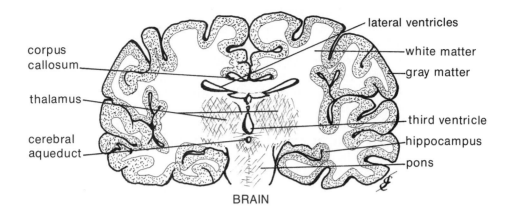

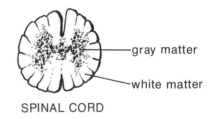

corpus callosum

thalamus

cerebral aqueduct

lateral ventricles

white matter

gray matter

third ventricle

hippocampus

pons

BRAIN

gray matter

white matter

SPINAL CORD

Cross-sections of the brain and spinal cord.   **Figure 12.1**

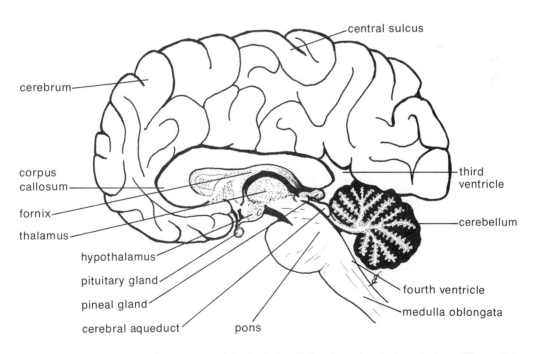

central sulcus

cerebrum

corpus callosum

fornix

thalamus

hypothalamus

pituitary gland

pineal gland

cerebral aqueduct

pons

third ventricle

cerebellum

fourth ventricle

medulla oblongata

Components of the brain (medial surface of sagittal section).   **Figure 12.2** brain. The newborn brain is in a marginal state of nourishment, and any increase in size would be limited by this metabolic constraint.

The cerebral cortex is a mass of gray matter composed of billions of neuronal cell bodies that provide the higher neurologic functions of thought, memory, emotion, etc. The underlying white matter consists of nerve fibers connecting the various areas of the cortex with each other and the remainder of the nervous system. A significant area near the base of the brain is the hypothalamus, which provides a vital linkage with the other control mechanism of the body, the endocrine system (Chapter 8).

The cerebellum provides involuntary control of muscular movements. This includes coordination of different muscle groups involved in speech, arm movements, or locomotion, and balance. The cerebellum does not initiate motion but acts as a coordinating center.

The brain stem, including the thalamus, pons and medulla oblongata, is evolutionarily the oldest and in some sense the most important part of the brain. It is necessary for life, as it controls the vital processes of respiration, circulation and consciousness. All impulses to and from the cerebrum and cerebellum must pass through the brain stem.

The CNS is dependent on a rich blood supply. It stores virtually no energy, has no anaerobic metabolic pathway and cannot utilize fats or proteins. It is thus totally dependent on the blood stream for oxygen and glucose. Brain function is decreased after cerebral blood flow is cut off for one minute, and a three-minute interruption results in irreversible damage.

The brain is also perfused by cerebrospinal fluid (CSF), a clear almost cell-free fluid that circulates in the four cavities, the **ventricles,** of the brain and over its outer surfaces. The fluid, which cushions the brain against physical forces, originates from specialized vascular tissue in the ventricles, the **choroid plexus**, and circulates over the brain to drain into the venous system. Obstruction of this circulation results in an increase in the amount and pressure of the fluid, **hydrocephalus.** The pressure can be high enough to expand the skull of a child and to cause severe brain damage at any age.

The peripheral nervous system is separated into **afferent** and **efferent** divisions. The afferents translate external stimuli into electrochemical potentials which they transmit to the CNS. The efferent system in turn is divided into the **somatic** and **autonomic nervous systems** (SNS and ANS). The SNS innervates skeletal muscle for voluntary activity, and the ANS innervates the involuntary smooth muscle of the various hollow organs of the body. Activation of part of the ANS also stimulates the adrenal medulla, as both the nervous and endocrine systems regulate involuntary functions.

PATHOLOGY

The nervous system is liable to the same range of disorders seen in the other organ systems and also to specific psychiatric disorders. The latter are usually unassociated with any detectable anatomic lesions (at least at our current level of diagnostic sophistication).

Anomalies

The embryology of the brain is extremely complex. A variety of factors operating early in pregnancy, including radiation, drugs and viral infections, can cause this process to go awry.

The brain develops from an open neural tube, and the failure of this tube to close ranges from complete lack of development of the brain and its encasing skeletal components, **anencephaly,** a condition incompatible with life, to failure of closure of the sacral bones, the extremely common and asymptomatic **spina bifida occulta.** All gradations occur between these extremes.

Spina bifida has been documented many times in archeologic skeletal material. Bennett (1972) found its incidence in Modoc Indians to be 90%, so high as to be considered a population marker. It has also been reported in dynastic Egyptians (Zimmerman, 1976), and its presence in adults suggests that social conditions in ancient Egypt were such that children with this potentially disabling disorder could survive to adulthood (Fig. 12.3).

Spina bifida, in an ancient Egyptian sacrum.   **Figure 12.3**

Trauma

The course of cranial trauma is governed by the anatomy peculiar to the region. The skull is a rigid case containing the brain, which is of pudding-like consistency, floating in a small amount of CSF within the delicate meninges and somewhat thicker dura mater. A blow to the head causes a rapid movement in the direction of the force. When musculoskeletal anatomy stops the motion of the skull, the brain continues in the same direction, striking the inside of the skull opposite the initial trauma. Such **contrecoup** injuries may result in an extremely confusing clinical and pathologic picture.

Another feature of cranial anatomy is that the room within the skull is limited. Any injury increasing the volume of the cranial contents, such as hemorrhage into or around the brain, or cerebral edema, causes an acute rise in intracranial pressure. If severe, the brain may be forced down through the foramen magnum, the opening for the spinal cord at the base of the skull, with potentially fatal compression of the vital centers in the brain stem.

The dura mater covering the brain is intimately adherent to the inside of the skull. Trauma can result in hemorrhage in the **epidural** or **subdural** space. **Epidural hematomas** are usually associated with fractures and arterial tears, and must be treated promptly by surgical evacuation. In contrast, subdural hematomas may occur without fracture, or even without direct cranial trauma. Abrupt head movements, particularly in older individuals with cerebral atrophy, may tear veins and cause hemorrhage. These hematomas tend to organize and enlarge, acting as a tumor-like mass that can cause brain stem herniation at the foramen magnum. This entire process may be insidious and unrecognized for a long period, sometimes not being diagnosed until autopsy.

Cranial trauma may also cause direct damage to the brain. **Concussion** is defined as loss of neurologic function after blunt injury, with pathologic change limited to the microscopic level. **Contusion** is bruising of the brain by severe direct trauma, and usually involves **coup** and **contrecoup** areas of hemorrhage and necrosis, eventually turning into a scar, if the victim survives. Tears in the brain, **lacerations,** are frequently associated with contusions. Hematomas may develop within the brain if intracerebral vessels are torn, or secondary to fat embolization from damage to the marrow of the long bones.

Cranial trauma has certainly been long known to man. As discussed in the preceding chapter, many examples of prehistoric trephination are clearly attempts to treat traumatic injury. The Edwin Smith papyrus deals extensively with the treatment of head wounds in ancient Egypt (Risse, 1972).

Infections

Many organisms have the potential to infect the meninges and brain, often as a complication of infection elsewhere in the body. The reasons why some individuals develop infections of the nervous system and others do not are not understood.

Multiple routes of infection are known, including direct traumatic introduction of organisms, infection via veins from the face to vascular sinuses around the brain, infected emboli from the lung via arteries to the brain, or bacteremia from some other locus of infection. Most of these infections are treatable, but the source of the infection must also be identified and treated.

The diagnosis of neurologic infection is based on the clinical picture and on microscopic and microbiologic examination of the CSF. Samples of CSF are obtained relatively easily by inserting a sterile needle through the lumbar intervertebral spaces (a **lumbar puncture,** or LP) into the spinal canal. The pressure is determined and the fluid examined for decreased glucose (used by the microorganisms for their metabolism) and the presence of pus and/or bacteria.

Many organisms can invade the meninges, the membranes covering the brain. Usually **meningitis** is caused by the pneumococcus or meningococcus, and occasionally by *Hemophilus influenzae.* If untreated, deep coma and death occur rapidly. Tuberculous and fungal meningitis are more chronic processes, but again are fatal if unsuccessfully treated. Fungal meningitis is becoming a not uncommon complication seen in compromised hosts, i.e., patients with deficient immune systems on the basis of a specific disease or treatment with agents such as steroids or immunosuppressives.

The brain can also be infected by many viruses, resulting in **encephalitis.** Several epidemics of encephalitis have occurred in the 20th century, all presumed to be viral and transmitted by an insect vector, although in most instances neither virus nor vector was identified. Clinically these infections are all similar, being characterized by high fever, stupor or coma, tremor, paralysis and other neurologic signs. No specific treatment exists and, although mortality is high in some epidemics, most patients recover spontaneously. Many do show persistent neurologic deficits.

Viruses may also affect the spinal cord, causing **myelitis.** The introduction of the polio vaccine has resulted in a spectacular reduction and potential elimination of **poliomyelitis,** but the disease is of interest as an example of the evolution of a disease as determined by cultural factors. As described in Chapter 3, the poliovirus is a normal inhabitant of the human intestinal tract, and in societies with poor sanitation the organism is acquired early in life as a harmless commensal. Those who are separated from the intestinal microorganisms of others by the virtues of modern plumbing run the risk of acquiring the infection later in life, when they are no longer protected by maternal antibodies, and can develop paralytic poliomyelitis.

Rabies is one of the most deadly viral infections of the CNS. Usually acquired through the bite of an infected dog, the virus travels up the peripheral nerves to the spinal cord and brain, causing an acute encephalomyelitis which is fatal if untreated or if clinical symptoms develop. Treatment is based on giving the bitten person antibodies in an attempt to prevent involvement of the nervous system.

Many mammals are capable of transmitting the disease, including bats that infect archeologists in Egyptian tombs, one possible source of the "mummy's curse." In Thailand up to 200 deaths per year are due to rabies, despite knowledge of the mechanism of the disease and rules pertaining to stray animals. It is contrary to Buddhist practice to destroy such strays and the deaths continue (Hopps, 1977).

Typhus is a rickettsial disease of worldwide distribution and great historical importance. The disease is louse-born and becomes epidemic in unsettled periods such as wars. The organism damages small blood vessels, and those lesions in the brain account for the clinical features of delirium, stupor or coma. Death may be due to neural or myocardial involvement, pneumonia, shock or renal failure. Incapacitation of whole armies by typhus has played a major role in European military history (Zinsser, 1963).

Bacterial infection of the brain is usually in the form of abscesses, areas of necrosis containing many bacteria and acute inflammatory cells. The pathways of infection are the same as those for meningitis, and the need to prevent a metastatic brain abscess is one of the reasons for vigorous treatment of abscesses elsewhere in the body. In addition to the localized destruction of neural tissue and the damage due to secondary brain swelling within the encasing skull, such abscesses are notoriously difficult to treat. They may progress despite medical therapy, and require surgical drainage.

Syphilis may involve all parts of the nervous system and its coverings, together or separately. It spreads to the NS during the secondary stage and follows an unpredictably variable course. Treatment with antibiotics is effective. If untreated, some patients develop **general paresis**, a progressive syphilitic meningoencephalitis. The brain becomes atrophic and there is severe loss of neurologic function. Transplacental infection can cause this picture at an early age. Many notorious cases have been seen in literature and history, including Oswald in Ibsen's *Ghosts* and Randolph Churchill, Winston Churchill's father.

Syphilitic infection of the spinal cord is known as **tabes dorsalis.** The dorsal, sensory roots of the spinal cord are affected, producing anesthesia in the areas supplied by these segments of the cord. Trauma to these now unprotected areas may be severe, as in the production of Charcot's joint, a totally and painlessly destroyed large joint, usually the knee.

Fungal infections are rare and usually secondary to infection elsewhere in the body, often in a compromised host. Parasitism is equally rare. Occasionally, cerebral **cysticercosis** is seen in pork tapeworm infestations (Chapter 6).

Vascular Disease

The brain, comprising 2 per cent of the body weight, uses 20 per cent of its oxygen. As the brain has no reserves of oxygen or carbohydrate, it is exquisitely dependent on an intact flow of blood. Vascular diseases of the brain are labeled **cerebrovascular accidents** (CVA) by the clinician and are of three main types: infarcts; hemorrhages; or aneurysms.

Infarcts. Interruption of blood flow may be on an atherosclerotic or embolic basis, and results in a large area of necrosis. Infarcts may be pale (anemic), red (hemorrhagic) or mixed, depending on whether or not blood flow is restored into the necrotic area. Hypertensive patients are more likely to suffer hemorrhagic infarcts, which tend to be larger and therefore more serious.

Hemorrhage. CNS hemorrhage may be due to damage to blood vessels or to a bleeding tendency. Massive hemorrhage is a common cause of death in hypertensives, the blood dissecting through and destroying the brain. Patients on anticoagulant therapy or with coagulopathies such as leukemia or thrombocytopenia are also liable to this mode of exodus. Occasionally hemorrhages develop in metastatic brain tumors.

Aneurysms. Most intracranial aneurysms are congenital and located in the circle of Willis, the confluence of blood vessels at the base of the brain. These small saccular arterial dilatations are found in 5 to 6 per cent of adults undergoing postmortem examination and are twice as common in women as in men. Many of these patients are hypertensive and this particular group is liable to bleeding or frank rupture. Although the anatomic lesion is congenital, the clinical disease is one of hypertensive adults, affecting 3 to 4 per cent of the total population. Death following rupture of an aneurysm is common and occurs shortly after rupture, owing to increased intracranial pressure or associated cerebral infarction. Surgical clipping of an aneurysm is possible and is sometimes a life-saving procedure.

Degenerative Diseases

Nerve cells are postmitotic and do not regenerate. Neurologic aging consists of a continuous loss of neurons and their processes. If severe, **dementia** may result. **Alzheimer's disease** is a premature and severe version of this aging process, occurring as early as the second decade of life.

Parkinson's disease is a degenerative disorder of the CNS with multiple recognized etiologies, as well as some idiopathic cases. Many cases follow viral encephalitis and have been linked to the influenza epidemic of 1918–1919. Clinical signs include tremulousness and psychiatric manifestations, and focal lesions are seen in the pigmented areas of the brain.

An interesting example of a culturally associated degenerative disorder is **kuru.** This was the first disease demonstrated to be due to a "slow" virus, one with a very long incubation period (Gajdusek, 1977). Beginning with tremors and progressing to neurologic incapacitation and death within a year, the disease was confined to the Fore people of the interior of New Guinea, and affected male and female children and female adults. It was found that these individuals were acquiring the disease by engaging in ritual cannibalism of the brain as a rite of mourning for deceased kinsmen. Male adults did not participate in this ceremony. With the cessation of the practice, the disease has greatly decreased in incidence.

Anthropologic studies were important in finding the cause of kuru. It was initially thought that the disease was hereditary, but Lindenbaum (1979) showed that Fore kinship was based as much on social interaction as on biologic heredity. The Fore themselves thought the disease was due to sorcery, and as the incidence increased accusations of sorcery in the community multiplied. This effect, and the fact that most of the impact of the disease was on the women, the childbearers and agriculturalists, threatened the very existence of Fore society.

Other degenerative diseases are **amyotrophic lateral sclerosis** (ALS, "Lou Gehrig disease") and **Huntington's chorea,** a genetic disorder which is manifested late in life after the patient has passed the disease on to offspring. The clinical characteristics of Huntington's chorea are a progressive chorea and dementia. This is the disease that afflicted the late folksinger, Woody Guthrie.

Epilepsy

Epilepsy is a CNS state of excess activity characterized clinically by convulsions. Many CNS diseases can provoke epileptic attacks, but most cases are idiopathic. Modern drug therapy is quite effective.

Tumors

Brain tumors, **gliomas,** arise from the supporting glial cells of the CNS, the postmitotic neuronal cells apparently not having a malignant potential. Brain tumors are strikingly different from the neoplasms of the other organs of the body in several important respects. These tumors are essentially all malignant, in that they cause the death of the patient. They invariably recur after excision and destroy the brain either by direct infiltration or by increasing the intracranial pressure. On the other hand, brain tumors remain restricted to the CNS and do not metastasize elsewhere.

There are several types of gliomas, depending on the specific origin of the tumor cells. **Astrocytomas, oligodendrogliomas** and **ependymomas** are the most common. Brain tumors usually present with headache, and there is progression to other evidences of increased intracranial pressure such as nausea and vomiting, coma, etc. Survival for more than four years after diagnosis is rare, and in the more malignant forms of astrocytoma death usually occurs in less than two years.

Approximately 15 per cent of intracranial tumors are **meningiomas,** arising from the meninges. These are benign tumors that may produce local bone erosion but only rarely recur after excision.

Neurofibromas are fibrous tumors of the peripheral nerves that also may involve the cranial nerves, particularly in **von Recklinghausen's disease,** consisting of multiple neurofibromas and *café-au-lait* pigmentation of the skin. These lesions have a low but definite malignant potential.

Metastatic tumors to the CNS spread from primary tumors of the lungs, breast, kidney, skin (melanoma), gastrointestinal tract and prostate. The pathway is arterial embolization following involvement of the lungs. Up to 30 per cent of intracranial neoplasms are metastatic. Occasionally, intracranial metastases are the first evidence of an occult visceral malignancy. Cerebral metastases are usually multiple, unresectable and quickly fatal.

PSYCHIATRIC DISORDERS

Psychiatric disorders can be broken down into a number of separate headings for study purposes, although such a classification scheme is an artificial division of many overlapping abnormalities. Despite these artificial separations, similar stresses seem to produce similar changes in different regions of the world. For example, the stresses of early industrialization have resulted in virtually identical patterns of psychiatric behavior in Yoruba tribesmen of western Nigeria and whites of northern Canada (Dubos, 1971).

McHugh (1975) has divided psychiatric disorders into three groups. In the first group pathologic changes can be demonstrated in the brain; a number of these conditions have been discussed above under neurologic disorders. The second and third groups consist of diseases lacking demonstrable pathologic changes. Whereas the normal person is capable of dealing with reality, in the **psychoses** the individual is divorced from reality, unable to distinguish a delusional state from the outside world and thus unable to function in society. Intermediate reactions are at worst partially disabling and comprise the third group, the **psychoneuroses.**

The Psychoses

Psychotic individuals are socially disabled by their delusional states. In some societies they are limited to a specific social niche. Murphy (1964) has noted this effect in Eskimo shamans of St. Lawrence Island, Alaska. The role of a shaman is well defined, and the psychiatrically impaired are able to operate within this role, without being expected to fit into the broader context of Eskimo society.

Two major types of psychosis are recognized: manic-depressive psychosis and schizophrenia.

MANIC-DEPRESSIVE PSYCHOSIS

This consists of episodic periods of mania, depression or both. The individual becomes extremely agitated, physically and mentally, acting in a very uninhibited fashion. The condition has degrees ranging from simply excessive talking through loss of coherence to an uncontrollable hyperacute manic state with hallucinations and delusions. Such manic episodes may last for weeks to months and gradually subside.

Depression is the opposite picture, with apathy ranging to a depressive stupor, in which the patient remains in a psychically contracted state in bed. This type of attitude is more common than mania, but both are subject to recurrences. The long-term prognosis is generally good, especially as drug therapy with a variety of agents has proved to be helpful.

SCHIZOPHRENIA

This is a chronic disease that affects adolescents and young adults and has no effect on the life span. The etiology is unknown, although twin studies (Kringer, 1969) have suggested a significant genetic factor. The disease is widespread, and is not limited to western society, having been recognized in the Yoruba of Nigeria (Prince, 1964), the Iban of Sarawak (Schmidt, 1964) and the Shona of Rhodesia (Gelfand, 1964).

The schizophrenic is characterized by a bland affect (lack of external reaction), irrelevant and illogical thought and statements, and lapses of attention. There is a gradual deterioration of the personality, with loss of intellectual capacity, including thinking, conduct and insight. Delusions and hallucinations are common. Delusions are frequently grandiose or persecutory (**paranoid**), and somatic or nihilistic. The hallucinations may involve any of the senses and are very real experiences for the sufferer.

A variety of subtypes are recognized. **Catatonic** schizophrenics show immobility and mutism of an often extraordinary duration and degree.

In most societies these disturbances in thought and behavior make normal function impossible. However, in western societies the recent development of effective psychotherapeutic drugs has allowed most psychiatric inpatients to return to their families. In 1955 there were 559,000 patients in public mental institutions in the United States. There has been a steady decrease since then, to less than 200,000 today. Although many of these individuals still have some symptomatology and require outpatient treatment, most have resumed their place in society. On the other hand, the remainder still will require lifelong hospitalization, at enormous cost to society.

The development of these psychotherapeutic agents has led to an interesting ethical question, that of involuntary treatment. Some argue that mentally disturbed patients have a right to refuse treatment (Szasz, 1963), but most feel that involuntary treatment is appropriate and humane for those with abnormal behavior patterns such as suicidal or delusional ideations. The potential abuse of such medications, as in control of dissenters by totalitarian states, must be kept in mind (Berger, 1978).

The Psychoneuroses

These disorders are qualitative abnormalities in thinking and behavior, particularly in regard to social interaction.

ANXIETY AND FATIGUE

Anxiety is often combined with **fatigue (neurasthenia)** in a chronic neurosis. Some individuals suffer only acute anxiety attacks, characterized by a sense of impending doom and a variety of physical symptoms such as difficulty in breathing and a smothering sensation. Hyperventilation may be so pronounced as to cause tingling sensations **(paresthesias)** of the lips and fingers, or even spasms of the hands and feet. This is the same mechanism operating in the Eskimo disease *piblokto* (Chapter 8). Anxiety attacks often occur in crowds and up to several times a day. In between times the patient is generally well.

In the chronic neurosis, periods of several weeks of fatigue, restlessness and nervousness, and pressure headaches are interrupted by acute attacks. Such patients may be incapacitated by these attacks. A variant, **neurocirculatory asthenia**, is characterized by excess fatigability on heavy exertion, and such patients usually adjust by limiting their activity. This course is acceptable in civilian life, but these individuals are unfit for military duty. As a result, most of the studies of this condition have been undertaken in wartime.

Hallowell (1941) has studied the role of anxiety in Ojibwa society. These Canadian Indians have evolved a vision of disease as punishment for certain acts. Anxiety about the disease consequences of forbidden behavior acts as a psychic mechanism enforcing the social code, maintaining standards for interpersonal behavior in the society.

Anxiety has also been postulated to play a role in the Melanesian phenomenon of Cargo cults (Burton-Bradley, 1973). The stress of adaptation to a western life style produces anxieties among the population that facilitate recruitment into these cults, which seek a millennium on earth by the attainment of European goods through various rituals. The name Cargo cult originated from the arrival of the goods as cargo on European vessels. Most of this behavior, particularly by the leaders, also falls into the realm of schizophrenia, as seen from a western perspective (Lidz et. al., 1973).

PHOBIC NEUROSIS

This is characterized by obsessive fears of high places, dirt, closed or open places, and so on, which may impair the sufferer's function to varying degrees.

OBSESSIVE-COMPULSIVE NEUROSIS

This presents in various forms. Obsessions are persistent thoughts that overwhelm the mind. Obsessions to commit objectionable acts are rarely realized, but can be disturbing to the point of temporary incapacitation.

Compulsions are acts that the patient carries out to relieve his nervousness. Like obsessions, the acts are repeated, and take the form of adjusting clothing, hand-washing, etc.

HYSTERIA

This is almost exclusively a female neurosis, although it is said to occur rarely in males when there is material compensation for the illness. The disorder simulates other diseases, evincing a wide spectrum of symptoms that often do not follow the distribution of known diseases. An example is hysterical loss of all sensation on one side of the body, an anatomic impossibility owing to the crossing over of sensory nerves from the trunk and extremities in the brain stem. In hysterical deafness, the individual may raise his voice in order to be heard over ambient noise. Other symptoms of hysteria may include vomiting, paralysis, amnesia, seizures or loss of consciousness, all without organic cause.

The types of psychosomatic symptoms seen provide interesting insight into the sufferer's concept of the interrelationship between mind and body and the functioning of the body. Thus, cultural and historical variations are seen in the symptomatology of the disease (Fabrega, 1974).

Malingering is a related process, being the deliberate simulation of an illness or disability to achieve a specific goal. This condition occurs in males and females, and shows many of the features of hysteria. Malingering is seen frequently in those with **psychopathic personalities,** who seem constitutionally incapable of interacting with society. Such individuals react only to immediate gratification, and our population of social misfits, such as drug addicts, habitual criminals and the chronically unemployed, includes many who suffer from this disorder.

HYPOCHONDRIASIS

This is defined as excessive preoccupation of the individual with his own bodily functions and state of health. As in hysteria, these patients exhibit bizarre symptom complexes and may also blend into depression.

DEPRESSION

This may be idiopathic or a reaction to illness, death of family members, financial problems or other stressful situations. Fabrega (1974) points out that its expression is culturally determined, and suggests that the investigator in cross-cultural psychiatric disturbances begin by constructing a model of the culture. Although the entity of depression is probably universal, a wide range of expression is observed, related to cultural determination of identity and habitual and deviant behavior.

Recovery from depression, particularly when an inciting cause is known, is the rule. However in some individuals the depression becomes disabling, sliding over into psychosis.

REFERENCES

Adams, R. D. (1970): Psychiatric disorders. *In* Harrison's Principles of Internal Medicine, 6th ed. M. M. Wintrobe, G. W. Thorn, R. D. Adams et al., eds. McGraw-Hill, New York, pp. 1859–1887.

Bennett, K. A. (1972): Lumbo-sacral malformations and spina bifida occulta in a group of proto-historic Modoc Indians. Am. J. Phys. Anthropol., *36*:435–440.

Berger, P. A. (1978): Medical treatment of mental illness. Science *200*:974–981.

Burton-Bradley, B. G. (1973): The psychiatry of cargo cult. Med. J. Aust. *2*:388–392.

Dubos, R. (1971): Man Adapting. Yale University Press, New Haven.

Epstein, H. T. (1973): Possible metabolic constraints on human brain weight at birth. Am. J. Phys. Anthropol. *39*:135–136.

Fabrega, H., Jr. (1974): Disease and Social Behavior: An Interdisciplinary Perspective. M. I. T. Press, Cambridge, Mass.

Gajdusek, D. C. (1977): Unconventional viruses and the origin and disappearance of kuru. Science *197*:943–960.

Gelfand, M. (1964): Psychiatric disorders as recognized by the Shona. *In* Magic, Faith and Healing. A. Kiev, ed. Macmillan, New York, pp. 156–173.

Hallowell, A. I. (1941): The social function of anxiety in a primitive society. Am. Sociol. Rev. *6*:869–881.

Hopps, H. C. (1977): Geographic pathology. *In* Pathology, 7th ed. W. A. D. Anderson and J. M. Kissane, eds. Mosby, St. Louis, pp. 692–736.

Kringler, E. (1969): Schizophrenia in twins: an epidemiological-clinical study. *In* Behavioral Genetics; Method and Research. M. Manosevitz, G. Lindzeg and D. D. Thiesson, eds. Appleton-Century-Crofts, New York, pp. 692–709.

Lidz, R. W., Lidz, T. and B. G. Burton-Bradley (1973): Culture, personality and social structure; cargo cultism: a psychosocial study of Melanesian millenarianism. J. Nerv. Ment. Dis. *157*:370–388.

Lindenbaum, S. (1979): Kuru Sorcery: Disease and Danger in the New Guinea Highlands. Mayfield, Palo Alto.

McHugh, P. R. (1975): Psychologic illness in medical practice. *In* Textbook of Medicine, 14th ed. P. B. Beeson and W. McDermott, eds. Saunders, Philadelphia, pp. 562–577.

Murphy, J. M. (1964): Psychotherapeutic aspects of shamanism on St. Lawrence Island, Alaska. *In* Magic, Faith, and Healing. A. Kiev, ed. Macmillan, New York, pp. 53–83.

Prince, R. (1964): Indigenous Yoruba psychiatry. *In* Magic, Faith and Healing. A. Kiev, ed. Macmillan, New York, pp. 84–120.

Risse, G. P. (1972): Rational Egyptian surgery: a cranial injury discussed in the Edwin Smith Papyrus. Bull. N. Y. Acad. Med. *48*:919–929.

Schmidt, K. E. (1964): Folk psychiatry in Sarawak: a tentative system of psychiatry of the Iban. *In* Magic, Faith and Healing. A. Kiev, ed. Macmillan, New York, pp. 139–155.

Szasz, T. (1963): Law, Liberty, Psychiatry. Macmillan, New York.

Van Valen, L. (1974): Brain size and intelligence in man. Am. J. Phys. Anthropol. *40*:417–424.

Zimmerman, M. R. (1976): A Paleopathologic Investigation of the Human Remains of the Dra Abu el-Naga Site, Egypt: Based on an Experimental Study of Mummification. Ph.D. Thesis, University of Pennsylvania, Philadelphia.

Zinsser, H. (1963): Rats, Lice and History. Little, Brown, Boston.

Appendix 1
Laboratory Aids to
Diagnosis

A wide range of laboratory techniques is available to the medically oriented social scientist (provided funding is available for these often expensive procedures). Laboratories offering these services come under the general heading of **clinical pathology** and include chemical, microbiologic, hematologic and serologic tests, as well as a variety of special studies.

Laboratory determinations are performed on blood, urine, feces, saliva, sputum, pus, semen and other bodily fluids and secretions. Procedures for obtaining these specimens are available in various standard texts. Studies involving the entire individual, including **radiology** and **histology (anatomic pathology),** will also be discussed below.

I. CARDIOVASCULAR SYSTEM

A. Electrocardiogram (ECG)

1. **Principle.** The contractions of the heart are associated with the generation of electric potentials which can be detected by placing electrodes in various positions on the body. The potentials measured are plotted on a moving strip of paper, thus providing a spatial and temporal representation of the heart's electrical activity (Fig. App. 1).

2. **Interpretation.** As normal cardiac activities follow a rhythmic sequence, irregularities in rhythm can easily be detected on the ECG. Areas of damaged myocardium, as in myocardial infarction, do not conduct electricity normally, causing changes in the pattern of the ECG complexes.

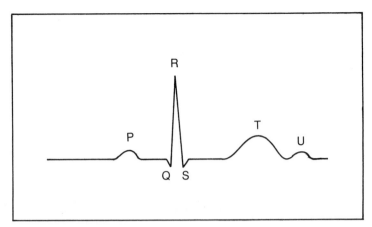

Figure App. 1   A normal electrocardiogram. The P wave corresponds to atrial contraction and the QRS complex to ventricular contraction. The T and U waves correspond to electrical repolarization of the myocardium.

B. Blood Enzyme Tests

1. **Principle.**   Damage to myocardial cells causes leakage of their enzymes into the serum. Detection of increased enzyme levels suggests myocardial infarction.
2. **Interpretation.**   These enzymes, including serum glutamic oxaloacetic transaminase (SGOT), lactic acid dehydrogenase (LDH) and others, are not specific to the myocardium, and elevations must be evaluated in the context of other clinical and laboratory evidence.

C. Blood Lipids

1. **Principle.**   Elevated blood lipids (**hyperlipidemia**) are at least correlated with, if not causative of, a high rate of coronary artery disease. Elevation of serum cholesterol, triglycerides and other lipids can be detected by biochemical studies.
2. **Interpretation.**   Early detection of hyperlipidemia may allow prevention of the subsequent development of anatomic lesions in the coronary arteries, by identification of the dietary and environmental factors implicated in the disorder.

D. Blood Cultures

1. **Principle.**   Infections, particularly on the heart valves (**endocarditis**), can shed bacteria into the blood stream.
2. **Interpretation.**   Other sources of infection must be considered, as well as the possibility of contamination of specimens. Antibiotic sensitivity studies determine the therapeutic approach.

E. **Histologic Studies**

1. **Principle.** Specimens of blood and bone marrow can be analyzed for the absolute and relative numbers of red and white blood cells and platelets, and their precursors, and abnormal cells.

2. **Interpretation.** Such studies are indispensable in the evaluation of anemias, leukemias and other hematologic disorders. A nonspecific elevation in the white cell count is seen in infectious diseases. Parasitism causes an eosinophilia.

II. RESPIRATORY SYSTEM

A. **Cultures for Microorganisms**

1. **Principle.** Pulmonary infections involve the lung primarily and may spread to the pleura or blood. Cultures of sputum, pleural effusion or blood may be diagnostic.

2. **Interpretation.** The organism cultured must be evaluated in the context of the clinical and radiologic picture. Special cultures are necessary for tuberculosis and fungal diseases.

B. **Skin Tests**

1. **Principle.** Patients with tuberculosis, sarcoidosis or fungal infections develop an immune reaction for which standard antigen preparations are available. Small amounts are injected into the skin.

2. **Interpretation.** If positive, the skin becomes reddened and firm at the injection site within 24 to 72 hours. Such a reaction indicates that the patient has been exposed to the antigen, but does not necessarily indicate acute infection.

C. **Cytologic Examination**

1. **Principle.** Lung tumors shed malignant cells into the sputum. These can be detected microscopically.

2. **Interpretation.** Malignant cells have diagnostic cytologic features, primarily nuclear abnormalities. Drawbacks are that cancer cells can be simulated by cells irritated by chronic infection, and peripheral lesions may not shed cells into the sputum.

D. **Pulmonary Function Studies**

1. **Principle.** Parameters for normal pulmonary function have been established and relatively simple tests are available for assessing various pulmonary capacities.

2. **Interpretation.**   Alterations in pulmonary function occur in patterns relatively specific for various diseases.

III. DIGESTIVE SYSTEM

A. Examination of the Feces

1. **Principle.** The feces can be examined chemically and microscopically for the presence of blood, fat and parasites.
2. **Interpretation.** Blood may indicate ulcer, tumor or hemorrhoids. Fat is seen in the stool in malabsorption. Most parasites and their ova are readily detected on stool examination.

B. Blood Studies

1. **Principle.** Damaged organs release specific and non-specific enzymes and products into the blood.
2. **Interpretation.** In pancreatic disease, an elevated serum lipase and amylase is seen. Liver damage is associated with elevated transaminase and bilirubin levels. The type of bilirubin found is indicative of the type of disease process. The finding of hepatitis B antigen is associated with clinical hepatitis and the carrier state.

IV. URINARY SYSTEM

A. Urinalysis

1. **Principle.**   The volume and contents of urine can be determined.
2. **Interpretation.**   Normal volume is 1,200 to 1,500 cc. per day. More indicates possible diabetes; less, renal failure. The presence of red or white blood cells or protein is abnormal and can indicate infection, inflammation or tumor.

B. Urine Culture

1. **Principle.**   Urinary tract infections are detected by the presence of bacteria in the urine.
2. **Interpretation.**   Infection may be in the kidney, bladder or both, and must be evaluated in the clinical context.

C. Blood Studies

1. **Principle.**   Failure of renal function causes the accumulation of waste products in the blood.

2. **Interpretation.** The serum concentration of urea, creatinine, phosphorus and various electrolytes is elevated in renal failure. The patterns of these abnormal levels may indicate specific diseases.

V. ENDOCRINE AND REPRODUCTIVE SYSTEMS

A. Hormone Analysis
1. **Principle.** Levels of hormones in the blood and urine (reflective of the blood levels) can be measured by chemical or biologic assays, or by the very sensitive radioimmune assay method.
2. **Interpretation.** Abnormal levels of the various hormones are correlated with the clinical state in arriving at the proper diagnosis.

B. Cytogenetics

1. **Principle.** The chromosomal make-up of cells can be determined microscopically, usually on blood cells or cells scraped from the oral mucosa.
2. **Interpretation.** Abnormalities of the number and quality of the sex and autosomal chromosomes can be detected.

C. Serum Calcium and Phosphorus

1. **Principle.** These levels are reflective of parathyroid function.
2. **Interpretation.** Many disease processes, especially renal disease, can alter serum calcium and phosphorus, and clinical correlation is essential. Hypercalcemia is a potentially dangerous condition, with the possibility of stone formation.

VI. NERVOUS SYSTEM

A. Analysis of the CSF

1. **Principle.** Normal CSF is virtually acellular, sterile and under low pressure. Almost all blood tests are applicable to the CSF, including microbiologic studies.
2. **Interpretation.** Increased pressure indicates a space-occupying lesion or cerebral edema. Red cells suggest hemorrhage; white cells, infection. Positive serologic tests for syphilis indicate neurosyphilis. Cultures of bacteria indicate specific infections.

B. Electroencephalography (EEG)

1. **Principle.** Brain activity generates electrical activity which is recorded in a fashion similar to the ECG.
2. **Interpretation.** A variety of normal and abnormal patterns are known and there is correlation with certain disease states, such as seizure disorders.

VII. RADIOLOGY

A. Principle. X-rays are high energy electromagnetic radiations able to penetrate organic matter and register an image on photographic film.

B. Interpretation. Materials vary in their degree of radiolucency, thus showing up as black, shades of gray, or white on the exposed film. Gas or air is radiolucent, fat moderately so, and most body tissues are intermediate in nature. Bone and calcium are moderately radiopaque and heavy metals are densely radiopaque. Parts of the body may be visualized radiologically by their naturally occurring surrounding fat or contained gas (as in the lungs) or minerals (such as bone salts), or by abnormal fat, gas or calcium.

1. For certain studies artificial contrast media, either radiolucent or radiopaque, can be placed into or around the area to be studied. Foreign objects can also be distinguished radiologically.
2. Radiologic examination is useful in the study of virtually all of the body and is indispensable in the diagnosis of skeletal lesions, in both modern and archeologic populations (Steinbock, 1976).

VIII. SEROLOGY

A. Principle. The presence of genetically determined blood group antigens on red cells has been known since the early 20th century. There are many blood group systems present in humans, but those of clinical significance, in relation to blood transfusion, are the ABO and Rh systems. Humans are of group A, B, AB or O and are independently assorted as Rh-positive or -negative.

1. Testing for these antigens by using sera containing specific antibodies allows for blood grouping.
2. The antigens are not confined to the red blood cells but also appear in bone and other tissues and in secretions. Techniques are available for their determination in such specimens, including archeologic material.

B. Interpretation. Anthropologists find blood groups useful in studies of population changes. For example, patterns of blood groups have helped clarify the descent of various tribes in Peru (Frisancho and Klayman, 1975).

1. Associations between blood groups and certain diseases have been demonstrated, although not consistently. For example, a recent study failed to show an association between blood group and viral diseases (Evans et al., 1972).
2. Paleoserologic studies have been done by multiple techniques, including simple absorption (Candela, 1939), the mixed cell agglutination reaction (Allison et al., 1976; Lippold, 1971), and fluorescent antibodies (Lengyl, 1975). Unfortunately, the results by different workers have often been contradictory, and these techniques at present are only of potential value.

IX. HISTOLOGY (ANATOMIC PATHOLOGY)

A. **Principle.** Tissue specimens removed under anesthesia from living individuals or at autopsy can be prepared in thin sections, stained, and examined under the microscope. These procedures require the services of physicians, including a pathologist.

B. **Interpretation.** The various diseases have specific patterns of microscopic anatomy, generally allowing for definitive diagnosis. This procedure is primarily of clinical medical value, but is of major importance in paleopathology.

REFERENCES

Allison, M. J., Hossaini, A. A., Castro, N. et al. (1976): ABO blood groups in Peruvian mummies. Am. J. Phys. Anthropol. 44:55–62.

Bauer, J. D., Ackermann, P. G. and G. Toro (1974): Clinical Laboratory Methods, 8th ed. Mosby, St. Louis.

Candela, P. B. (1939): Blood-group tests on stains, mummified tissues and cancellous bone. Am. J. Phys. Anthropol. 25:187–214.

Evans, A. S., Sheppard, K. A. and V. A. Richards (1972): ABO blood groups and viral diseases. Yale J. Biol. Med. 45:81–92.

Frisancho, A. R. and J. E. Klayman (1975): ABO and Rh affinities between Highland and Lowland Quechua-speaking Peruvian populations. Am. J. Phys. Anthropol. 43:285–290.

Halsted, S. A. (1976): The Laboratory in Clinical Medicine. Saunders, Philadelphia.

Lengyl, I. A. (1975): Paleoserology: Blood Typing with the Fluorescent Antibody Method. Akad. Kiado, Budapest.

Lippold, L. K. (1971): The mixed cell agglutination method for typing mummified human tissue. Am. J. Phys. Anthropol. 34:377–384.

Miller, S. E. and J. W. Weller (1971): Textbook of Clinical Pathology, 8th ed. Williams and Wilkins, Baltimore.

Steinbock, R. T. (1976): Paleopathological Diagnosis and Interpretation. Charles C Thomas, Springfield, Ill.

Appendix 2
Glossary

Abortion   Interruption of pregnancy, either spontaneous or induced, with delivery of an embryo or nonviable fetus.

Abrasion   A scraping injury, removing the surface epithelium.

Abscess   A collection of pus in solid tissue, usually due to bacterial infection.

Achondroplasia   Congenital dwarfism due to failure of enchondral bone formation, resulting in a normal-sized head, shortened trunk, and markedly shortened and bowed extremities.

Adenocarcinoma   A malignancy arising from glandular epithelium, as in the intestinal tract or lung.

Adenosis   The presence of glandular epithelium in the vagina. This condition is premalignant and has been associated with the administration of synthetic estrogen to pregnant women.

Affect   The emotional complex associated with a mental state.

Albinism   Generalized lack of pigment, due to congenital absence of melanin.

Allergy   A hypersensitive reactive state to a previously encountered allergen.

Alopecia   Baldness.

Alveoli   The air sacs of the lungs, the site of oxygen and carbon dioxide exchange.

Amenorrhea   Failure of menstruation. The condition may be primary (absence of menarche) or secondary (usually due to pregnancy).

Anabolism   The energy-requiring synthetic chemical processes of the body.

Anasarca   Generalized edema of the body cavities and subcutaneous tissues. In the older literature, dropsy.

Anemia   Deficiency of hemoglobin, due to either decreased concentration or decrease in total red cell mass.

Anencephaly   Congenital absence of the brain and cranial vault.

Aneurysm   A balloon-like dilatation of the heart or a blood vessel.

Anthracosis   The deposition of black carbon pigment in the lungs, usually due to exposure to open fires. The pigment is inert and does not harm the individual unless present in massive amounts.

Asbestosis   The deposition of asbestos particles in the lung, causing fibrosis and a predisposition to cancer, particularly of the membranes covering the lungs (mesothelioma).

Ascites   The accumulation of edema fluid in the peritoneal cavity.

Ascorbic acid   Vitamin C.

Atelectasis   Congenital or acquired failure of inflation of the lung.

Atherosclerosis   The accumulation of fatty material, including cholesterol, on the intimal surface and in the walls of arteries. Severe degrees impede blood flow.

Atrophy   A decrease in the size of cells, tissues or organs.

Axilla   The armpit.

Bilirubin   Bile pigment, produced in the liver from the hemoglobin of senescent red blood cells.

Bronchi   The larger air passages of the lung.

Calculus   An abnormal concretion of mineral salts occurring in the body. A "stone."

Callus   The reparative exudate formed around the fragments of a fractured bone, or hypertrophy of the skin due to irritation.

Cancer   *See Neoplasia.*

Carcinoma   A malignant tumor of epithelial origin.

Carcinoma in situ   Malignant change on a cytologic level, with no invasion of surrounding tissues.

Catabolism   The energy-producing destructive chemical processes of the body.

Cerebrospinal fluid   A clear, almost cell-free fluid that circulates in the four ventricles of the brain and over its outer surfaces.

Cestodes   Flatworms. The "tapeworms."

Chancre   An ulcer, usually applied to the painless lesion of primary syphilis.

Cholecystectomy   Surgical removal of the gallbladder.

Cholelithiasis   The presence of gallstones.

Citric acid cycle   An aerobic pathway for energy production by the oxidation of glucose. Also called the Krebs cycle or tricarboxylic acid (TCA) cycle.

Clavicles   The collarbones.

Clot   A coagulum of blood formed after death or outside blood vessels, differing grossly and microscopically from a thrombus.

Coagulopathy   Any disorder of the blood-clotting mechanism.

Concussion   Loss of neurologic function after blunt injury to the head. Pathologic change is seen only at the microscopic level.

Congenital   Present at birth, usually applied to deformities or infection.

Congestion   An acute or chronic increase in the volume of blood in an organ, in dilated vessels.

Contusion   Bruising due to direct trauma.

Coprolites   Fossilized fecal material.

Cor pulmonale   Cardiac disease secondary to pulmonary disease.

Coronary arteries   The branches of the aorta supplying oxygenated blood to the muscle of the heart.

Corpus luteum   The progesterone-producing yellow residual structure after the ovum is released from the ovarian follicle.

Curettage   Scraping, usually in reference to the lining of the uterus, the endometrium.

Cutis   The skin.

Cyanosis   A blue discoloration of the lips and extremities due to a high concentration of unoxygenated hemoglobin in the blood.

Decidua   The altered endometrial stroma seen in pregnancy.

Degenerative joint disease (DJD)   A chronic arthritis due to degeneration of the articular cartilage, primarily affecting the large weight-bearing joints. The condition may be secondary to stress, fracture, infection or rheumatoid arthritis. Formerly called osteoarthritis.

Delusion   A false belief that cannot be corrected by reason. Characteristic of psychosis.

Diabetes mellitus   A disorder of carbohydrate metabolism caused by insulin deficiency and characterized by hyperglycemia, glucosuria, and the clinical triad of polydipsia, polyuria and polyphagia.

Diaphysis   The shaft of a long bone.

Diastole   The relaxation and filling phase of the cardiac cycle.

Diuresis   An increased urine flow.

Dwarfism   Abnormal lack of height which may be proportionate, as in growth hormone deficiency, or disproportionate, as in achondroplasia.

Dysphagia   Difficulty in swallowing.

Dysplasia   Abnormality of development. Used by pathologists to indicate premalignant change.

Dyspnea   Difficulty in breathing.

-ectomy   Suffix used to indicate excision of an organ, as appendectomy, colectomy, etc.

Edema   The accumulation of an increased volume of fluid in the tissues, outside of the cells and vascular system.

Electrocardiogram   A recording of the electrical activity of the heart.

Electroencephalogram   A recording of the electrical activity of the brain.

Embolus   A mass carried in the blood stream. Embolization may involve thrombus, air, fat, bone marrow or foreign materials, and causes obstruction of flow.

Emphysema   Overexpansion of the lung, often accompanied by destructive and fibrotic changes. Air in the tissues is also referred to as emphysema.

Endometriosis   Ectopic islands of endometrium located in organs other than the uterus.

Epiphysis   The end of a long bone.

Epistaxis   Nosebleed.

Epithelioid cells   Enlarged histiocytes seen in granulomatous inflammation.

Epithelium The covering of the external surface of the body and of the internal surface of the hollow organs.

Erythrocytes Red blood cells, which carry oxygen to the tissues.

Erythropoiesis Production of erythrocytes.

Etiology The study of the causation of disease.

Exudate Material passed actively out of a tissue. Usually used in reference to pus.

Fertilization Union of germ cells.

Fetus The unborn offspring of any viviparous animal. In humans the fetus is called such at eight weeks after fertilization, being an embryo before then and an infant when outside the body.

Fibrin A serum protein active in thrombosis.

Frozen section A technique allowing for rapid preparation of a microscopic section, used for rapid diagnosis while a patient is under anesthesia and awaiting definitive surgery.

Gametes Germ cells, the spermatozoa and ova.

Germinal cells *See Gametes.*

Gingiva The gums.

Glia The supporting substance of the nervous system.

Glucosuria The presence of sugar in the urine.

Glycolysis An anaerobic pathway for energy production by the breakdown of glucose. Used primarily by red blood cells and muscle as a short-term energy source. Also called the Embden-Meyerhof pathway.

Goiter Enlargement of the thyroid gland, of any cause.

Gram stain A stain for the microscopic examination of bacteria. Bacteria are classified as gram-positive (blue) or gram-negative (red).

Granulation tissue A highly vascular reparative tissue.

Granulomatous inflammation A special type of chronic inflammation, seen in tuberculosis, fungal infections and foreign body reactions. The process is characterized by epithelioid and giant cells, and may or may not show necrosis.

Gumma The destructive lesion of tertiary syphilis.

Hallucination A sense perception not founded on objective reality.

Harris line A radiopaque density in a long bone, corresponding roughly to a period of growth arrest.

Helminths Worms.

Hematemesis Vomiting of blood.

Hematogenous Produced in or spread by the blood.

Hematoma A tumor-like collection of blood in the tissues.

Hematuria Blood in the urine.

Hemodialysis Clearing of wastes from the blood by an artificial kidney.

Hemoglobin The iron-containing, oxygen-carrying compound of red blood cells.

Hemopericardium Filling of the pericardial sac with blood, usually due to perforation of the heart, either spontaneous, as after an infarction, or traumatic.

Hemoptysis Coughing-up of blood.

Hemorrhage Loss of blood from the heart or blood vessels, usually due to rupture.

Hemosiderin The breakdown product of hemoglobin in tissues, responsible for the blue-green color seen in old bruises.

Hepatization Consolidation of the lung, producing a liver-like appearance, as seen in pneumonia.

Hernia A weakness in the wall of the peritoneal cavity, usually containing a portion of the small intestine.

Histiocyte A type of phagocytic cell seen in chronic inflammation.

Hormone A chemical secreted by an endocrine gland or tissue into the blood, which carries it to other sites where its effects occur.

Hydronephrosis Dilatation of the urinary collecting system, due to obstruction.

Hydropericardium The accumulation of edema fluid in the pericardial sac.

Hydroperitoneum *See Ascites.*

Hydrothorax The accumulation of edema fluid in the pleural cavities.

Hypercalcemia An excess of calcium in the blood.

Hyperglycemia Elevated blood sugar.

Hyperplasia Enlargement of organs due to excessive division of the constituent cells.

Hyperthermia Abnormally high body temperature; fever.

Hypertrophy An increase in size of cells, tissues or organs.

Hyperuricemia An excess of uric acid in the blood, seen in gout.

Hyperventilation Rapid and deep breathing, which can cause the blood to become alkaline and hypocalcemic.

Hypocalcemia Low blood calcium.

Hypoglycemia Low blood sugar.

Hypothermia An abnormally low body temperature.

Hysterectomy Surgical removal of the uterus.

Iatrogenic Resulting from the activity of a physician.

Impotence Failure of erection.

Incision A cut, made with a knife.

Infarction Necrosis of tissue due to interruption of the blood supply.

Infection Invasion of tissues or organs by microorganisms.

Infestation Invasion of tissues or organs by macroorganisms (visible to the unaided eye).

Inflammation The response of the body to tissue injury involving neurologic, vascular, humoral and cellular reactions within the site of injury.

Insulin The endocrine hormone produced by the pancreas which facilitates the entry of glucose into cells. Deficiency of insulin is seen in diabetes mellitus. Insulin-producing tumors cause hypoglycemia.

Intermitotics Cells that retain the potential of mitotic division and are therefore between mitoses.

Intussusception Telescoping of the bowel upon itself.

Ischemia Decrease in blood supply.

Jaundice Yellow discoloration of the skin and eyes due to excessive circulating bilirubin.

Kyphosis Hunchback.

Laceration A tearing injury.

Lactation The production of milk.

Leukemia A malignant proliferation of white blood cells.

Libido The sexual drive.

Lipping Proliferation of bone at the margins of a joint, seen in degenerative joint disease.

Lumbar puncture Insertion of a sterile needle through the lumbar intervertebral spaces into the spinal canal to procure a small sample of cerebrospinal fluid for examination.

Lumen The cavity of a hollow organ or vessel.

Lymphadenopathy Enlargement of lymph nodes.

Lymphocyte A type of white blood cell seen in large numbers in chronic inflammation.

Mandible The lower jaw.

Mastectomy Surgical removal of the breast. Simple mastectomy removes the breast alone. Radical mastectomy includes removal of the adjacent axillary lymph nodes and the underlying pectoral muscle. Modified radical mastectomy leaves the muscle.

Maxilla The upper jaw.

Meiosis The splitting of primordial germ cells to form sperm and ova with half the normal complement of chromosomes.

Melanin The brown pigment that gives skin, hair and eyes their characteristic colors.

Menarche Initiation of menses in the pubescent female.

Meningitis Inflammation of the meninges, the membranes covering the brain.

Metaphysis The growth zone of a long bone, at the junction of the diaphysis and epiphysis.

Metaplasia The replacement of one cell type by another that is not normal for the tissue and usually more resistant to stress.

Metastasis The spread of a pathologic process to distant sites. Usually used in reference to the spread of malignant tumors, and occasionally in reference to abscesses.

Mitosis The process of cell reproduction.

Mixed tumor A tumor arising from two germ cell layers, either benign or malignant.

Myelin The fatty substance ensheathing certain nerve fibers.

Necrosis Death of tissues or cells.

Nematodes Roundworms.

Neoplasia The formation of a new and abnormal growth, a cancer.

Neurons Cells specialized for the transmission of messages along processes by electrochemical impulses.

Niacin One of the B vitamins.

Oligohydramnios A decreased amount of amniotic fluid in a pregnancy, usually due to fetal renal hypoplasia or aplasia.

Osteoblast The bone-producing cell.

Osteoblastic A process causing proliferation of bone.

Osteoclast The cell that breaks down bone.

Osteocyte The mature phase of the bone cell, entrapped in an osteoid matrix.

Osteoid The organic matrix of bone, composed primarily of collagen.

Osteolytic A process destructive of bone.

Osteomalacia Deficient mineralization and softening of osteoid, usually due to vitamin D deficiency. In children, the condition is called rickets.

Osteomyelitis   Infection of bone involving both the cortical bone and the marrow cavity.

Osteoporosis   A decreased amount of bone, seen in elderly or immobilized individuals. Such bones are liable to fracture.

Ovulation   The discharge of an ovum from the ovary.

Paget's disease   Focal hypertrophy of bone, usually in the skull, pelvis, femur or tibia of the elderly. Predisposes to fracture and osteosarcoma.

Pap smear   Cytologic examination of superficial cells for premalignant and malignant changes, generally used in reference to the uterine cervix. Developed by and named for Dr. George Papanicolaou.

Parenchyma   The functional element of an organ.

Parity   Number of children. Nulliparous women have had no children and multiparous women many.

Parturition   The birth of a living child.

Pathogen   A disease-causing organism or material.

Pathogenesis   The development of disease.

Pathogenicity   Ability to cause disease.

Pathologic fracture   A fracture due to some defect in the bone, such as osteoporosis or a lytic tumor.

Pelvic inflammatory disease (PID)   Chronic inflammation of the fallopian tubes, usually beginning as a venereal gonococcal infection.

Placenta   The cake-like organ within the uterus that connects the mother and child by the umbilical cord.

Plasma cells   Antibody-producing cells seen in the tissue infiltrate of chronic inflammation.

Platelets   Thrombocytes, subcellular circulating cell fragments necessary for blood coagulation.

Pneumoconiosis   The abnormal deposition of exogenous pigments or minerals in the lung.

Pneumothorax   Air in the pleural cavity, potentially causing collapse of the lung.

Polycythemia   An increased number of erythrocytes in the blood, either in response to anoxia, as at high altitude, or due to an abnormal proliferation of erythrocytes, polycythemia vera.

Polydipsia   Excessive drinking of water or other fluids.

Polymorphonuclear leukocyte (PMN)   The white blood cell involved in inflammation. Neutrophilic PMNs (neutrophils, "polys") are involved in acute inflammation and form pus. Eosinophilic PMNs (eosinophils) are seen in allergic inflammation, as in asthma or parasitism.

Polyphagia   Excessive eating.

Polyuria   Diuresis, the passage of abnormally large amounts of normal urine.

Postmitotic   Cells which have become highly specialized and have lost the power of division.

Proteinuria   Protein in the urine, seen in glomerular disease.

Psychoneurosis   A partially disabling psychiatric disorder.

Psychosis   A state of being divorced from reality, rendering the individual incapable of functioning in society.

Pus   The product of inflammation, made up of white blood cells and thin fluid.

Pyogenic   Inflammation or infection producing pus.

Pyuria   Pus in the urine, seen as cloudiness and due to infection.

Radiolucent   Transparent to x-rays.

Radiopaque   Not permitting the passage of x-rays.

Releasing factors   Hormones produced by the hypothalamus that control the activity of the pituitary gland.

Remodeling   The process of bone resorption and reformation in response to various stresses.

Rheumatoid arthritis   A painful chronic arthritis involving peripheral joints. Destruction of the joints is disabling.

Rickets   *See Osteomalacia.*

Sarcoma   A malignant tumor of mesenchymal or mesodermal (soft tissue) origin.

Scapulae   The shoulder blades.

Sclerosis   Hardening, as in inflammation or fibrosis. A variety of special forms are described, particularly in the nervous system.

Scoliosis   Lateral curvature of the spine.

Shock   A clinical state characterized by loss of consciousness, pallor, a weak and rapid pulse, and decreased blood pressure. Inciting causes are hemorrhage, trauma, infections, perforated organs, and others.

Silicosis The deposition of silicone dioxide particles in the lung, usually provoking a fibrous reaction.

Somatic cells The cells making up the nongerminal tissues and organs of the body.

Spina bifida Incomplete closure of the posterior sacrum which may involve only the bone (spina bifida occulta) or the spinal cord and overlying tissues. Paralysis may result if the defect is extensive.

Spirochetes A group of spiral bacteria, the most prominent member of which is *Treponema pallidum,* the causative agent of syphilis.

Squamous carcinoma A malignant tumor arising from squamous epithelium, as the skin or uterine cervix.

Sternum The breast bone.

Striae Streaks or lines seen in the skin as a result of abnormal stretching.

Stroma The supportive element of an organ.

Systole The contraction or emptying phase of the cardiac cycle.

Tamponade Compression of an organ, as in cardiac tamponade in hemopericardium.

Teratoma A tumor arising from all three germ cell layers, either benign or malignant.

Tetany Irregular muscular twitching, weakness and convulsions, associated with a low serum calcium level.

Thiamine One of the B vitamins.

Thrombosis Coagulation of blood within the vascular system in life, forming a thrombus.

Thrombus An *in vivo,* intravascular coagulum of blood cells, platelets and fibrin.

Tinea A fungus infection of the skin.

Transudate Fluid passed passively through a membrane. Seen in heart failure.

Trematodes Flukes, parasitic worms that infest the vascular system of various organs.

Trepanation Surgical removal of a piece of the skull, without damaging the underlying blood vessels, meninges or brain.

Trephination *See Trepanation.*

Trophoblast The tissue that attaches the ovum to the uterine wall and supplies nutrition to the embryo.

Tumor Any mass lesion, used in modern medical practice synonymously with cancer.

Varicose veins Elongation and dilatation of veins, with decreased flow.

Vesicle A fluid-filled area of cleavage in the skin.

Virulence *See Pathogenicity.*

Viscera The internal organs of the body.

Vitamins Organic catalysts needed for maintenance of normal cell structure and function.

Vitiligo Localized depigmentation due to lack of melanin.

Volvulus Twisting of the bowel on its mesentery.

Zygote The fertilized ovum.

Index

Page numbers in *italics* indicate illustrations.